The Mexico City Reader

The Mexico City Reader

Edited by
Rubén Gallo

Translated by
Lorna Scott Fox and Rubén Gallo

THE UNIVERSITY OF WISCONSIN PRESS

The University of Wisconsin Press
1930 Monroe Street, 3rd Floor
Madison, Wisconsin 53711-2059
uwpress.wisc.edu

3 Henrietta Street
London WC2E 8LU, England
eurospanbookstore.com

Printed in the United States of America

Library of Congress Cataloging-in-Publication Data
The Mexico City reader / edited by Rubén Gallo;
translated by Lorna Scott Fox and Rubén Gallo.
p.   cm. – (The Americas)
Includes bibliographical references and indexes.
ISBN 0-299-19710-7 (hardcover: alk. paper)
ISBN 0-299-19714-X (pbk.: alk. paper)
1. Mexico City (Mexico) — Description and travel.
2. Mexico City (Mexico) — Social life and customs — 20th century.
I. Gallo, Rubén.   II. Fox, Lorna Scott.   III. Title.   IV. Series.
F1386 .M654   2004
917.2′530482 – dc22   2004016474

ISBN 978-0-299-19714-8 (pbk.: alk. paper)

In memory of

TITO MONTERROSO

(1921–2003)

Contents

Illustrations

Acknowledgments

First and foremost, I would like to express my gratitude to Princeton University's Committee on Research in the Humanities and Social Sciences and the Office of the Dean of the Faculty for funding the translation of many of the essays included in *The Mexico City Reader*. I thank Professor Angel Loureiro, chair of the Department of Spanish and Portuguese Languages and Cultures at Princeton, for his support of the project and his suggestions of external funding sources. The Mex-Am Foundation in New York City provided generous support for including works by young Mexican artists.

I first thought of assembling an anthology about modern-day Mexico City in 1998, during a conversation with Juan García de Oteyza, then the executive director of the Mexican Cultural Institute in New York City. I am indebted to Mr. García de Oteyza for his enthusiastic support of the book, as well as for recommending several writers and texts for the anthology. Some of the texts included in this book were first published in the Mexican Cultural Institute's web journal, *La Vitrina*, then edited by Mónica de la Torre, who provided excellent suggestions for revising the translations.

In Mexico City, many writers and critics were kind enough to discuss the project and recommend additional texts. Christopher Domínguez Michael, Juan Villoro, Rafael Pérez Gay, José Emilio Pacheco, Carlos Monsiváis, and José de la Colina shared their encyclopedic knowledge of contemporary Mexican literature.

I thank Professor Ilán Stavans and Irene Vilar for selecting *The Mexico City Reader* for publication in the Americas series and for sharing his insights on the Mexico City literary world. I am also indebted to Robert Mandel, director of the University of Wisconsin Press, for his support, and to Tricia Brock for her help with permissions and other administrative matters.

Jean Franco and Maarten van Delden read an early version of the manuscript and offered numerous suggestions for revision. I am grateful for their expert advice.

I wish to thank Marcelo Uribe, director of Ediciones Era, for granting permission to translate and reprint the texts by José Joaquín Blanco, Elena Poniatowska, and Carlos Monsiváis. Rafael Pérez Gay granted permission to use texts by several authors represented by Cal y Arena, including Guadalupe Loaeza. Ray Gude Mertin and Nicole Witt facilitated the inclusion of Gonzalo Celorio's "Mexico, City of Paper" in this volume.

I am grateful to Lorna Scott Fox for masterfully translating the texts included in the anthology and offering helpful suggestions. Elyse Kovalsky proofread the manuscript and helped with countless clerical tasks.

As I worked to put together an anthology to convey the chaotic, unpredictable nature of Mexico City, I often thought of Tito Monterroso and his gift for balancing insight and wit, intelligence and humor. When I told Tito about the project, he said he "craved" reading it ("se me antojo") thus suggesting that the book could be as appetizing as a delicious meal—a staple of life in Mexico City. As I was finishing the manuscript and getting ready to send it off, I received extremely sad news: Tito passed away at age eighty-two on February 7, 2003. *The Mexico City Reader* is dedicated to him and to his life-affirming wit.

Permissions

"Insurgentes" was originally published as "Insurgentes en días lluviosos" in *Pequeños actos de desobediencia civil* by Fabrizio Mejía Madrid (Mexico City: Cal y arena, 1996), 63–140.

"Zona Rosa, 1965" was originally published in *Talacha periodística* by Vicente Leñero (Mexico City: Editorial Diana, 1983), 147–54.

"San Rafael" was originally published as "Prólogo a un San Rafael" in *Anticuerpos* by Gerardo Deniz (Mexico City: Ediciones sin nombre, 1998), 29–36.

Guillermo Sheridan's "Coyoacán I" was originally published as "Yes, in Coyoacán you can" in *Vuelta* 261 (August 1998): 91–92.

"Coyoacán II" was originally published as "Los misterios del Distrito Federal (II)" in *¿Olvida usted su equipaje?* by Jorge Ibargüengoitia (Mexico City: Joaquín Mortiz, 1997), 40–42.

"Plaza Satélite" was originally published in *Función de medianoche* by José Joaquín Blanco (Mexico City: Ediciones Era, 1981), 84–87.

"Las Lomas I" was originally published as two stories, "Hacia las Lomas voy, dulce retiro" and "La realidad donde menos se la espera," in *Función de medianoche* by José Joaquín Blanco (Mexico City: Ediciones Era, 1981), 99–104.

Juan Villoro's "The Metro" was originally published as "La ciudad es el cielo del metro" in *Número* 10 (June–August 1996): 43–46.

"Voyage to the Center of the City" was originally published as "Viaje al centro de la ciudad, 1975" in *¡Lo que ve el que vive!* by Ricardo Garibay (Mexico City: Excélsior, 1976), 311–18.

"Metro Insurgentes" was originally published as "La plaza del metro" in *Función de medianoche* by José Joaquín Blanco (Mexico City: Ediciones Era, 1981), 68–71.

"The Metro: A Voyage to the End of the Squeeze" was originally published as "La hora del transporte. El metro: viaje hacia el fin del apretujón" in *Los rituales del caos* by Carlos Monsiváis (Mexico City: Ediciones Era, 1995), 111–13.

"La Diana" was originally published as "Una Diana para la Diana" in *Talacha periodística* by Vicente Leñero (Mexico City: Editorial Diana, 1983), 167–76.

José de la Colina's "The Chinese Café" was originally published as the pamphlet *La princesa del café de chinos* (Mexico City: Ediciones Bonetería Rosita, 1996).

"Armando's Tortas" was originally published as "Tacos y tortas compuestas" in *Sálvese quien pueda* by Jorge Ibargüengoitia (Mexico City: Editorial Novaro, 1975), 192–96.

"Vips in the Early Morning" was originally published as "Frío del martes por la madrugada" in *Función de medianoche* by José Joaquín Blanco (Mexico City: Ediciones Era, 1981), 73–76.

"Call the Doctor" was originally published as "Esta Ciudad (I)" in *La casa de usted y otros viajes* by Jorge Ibargüengoitia (Mexico City: Joaquín Mortiz, 1991), 96–98.

"Tacubaya, 1978" was originally published as "Panorama bajo el puente" in *Función de medianoche* by José Joaquín Blanco (Mexico City: Ediciones Era, 1981), 62–65.

"Avenida Álvaro Obregón, 1979" was originally published as "Avenida Álvaro Obregón" in *Función de medianoche* by José Joaquín Blanco (Mexico City: Ediciones Era, 1981), 90–93.

"San Juan de Letrán" was originally published as "Calle San Juan de Letrán" in *Función de medianoche* by José Joaquín Blanco (Mexico City: Ediciones Era, 1981), 93–96.

"Cuauhtémoc" was originally published as "Una limosna para la Diana" in *Álbum de pesadillas mexicanas* by José Joaquín Blanco (Mexico City: Ediciones Era, 2002), 9–14.

"'Who's There?' The Art of Opening and Closing the Door" was originally published as "¿Quién es?: Arte de abrir y cerrar la puerta" in *Instrucciones para vivir en México* by Jorge Ibargüengoitia (Mexico City: Joaquín Mortiz, 1990), 74–75.

"Klaxons and the Man" was originally published as two stories, "El claxon y el hombre" and "El arauca vibrador," in *Instrucciones para vivir en México* by Jorge Ibargüengoitia (Mexico City: Joaquín Mortiz, 1990), 85–87, 88–90.

"The Earthquake" was originally published as "'Está temblando', dije en voz alta: Beatriz Graf" in *Nada, nadie: las voces del temblor* by Elena Poniatowska (Mexico City: Ediciones Era, 1988), 71–79.

"Maids I" was originally published as "Las criadas" in *Movimiento perpetuo* by Augusto Monterroso (Mexico City: Ediciones Era, 1991), 95–97.

"Maids II" was originally published as two stories, "Lucha en las Lomas" and "Upstairs," in *Las reinas de Polanco* by Guadalupe Loaeza (Mexico City: Cal y arena, 1988), 71–73; 73–75.

"Chapultepec and the Maids" was originally published as "Chapultepec y las criadas" in *Álbum de pesadillas mexicanas* by José Joaquín Blanco (Mexico City: Ediciones Era, 2002), 56–59.

"Trimmins for the Comanche" was originally published as "Mochada pal Comanche" in *Obras reunidas: crónica uno* by Ricardo Garibay (Mexico City: Editorial Océano, 2001), 115–16.

"In the Same Boat" was originally published as "En el mismo barco" in *Obras reunidas: crónica uno* by Ricardo Garibay (Mexico City: Editorial Océano, 2001), 155–57.

"Garbage" was originally published as "Mexico City 1990" in *The Heart that Bleeds* by Alma Guillermoprieto (New York: Vintage Books, 1995), 47–67.

"SEMEFO: The Morgue" was originally published in English and in French as "Zones de Tolérance: Teresa Margolles, SEMEFO et (l')au-delà/Zones of Tolerance: Teresa Margolles, SEMEFO and Beyond," *Parachute* 104 (October–December 2001): 31–52. Reprinted in *Entre líneas*, edited by Santiago B. Olmo et al. (Madrid: La Casa Encendida, 2002), 103–17, 167–72.

The Mexico City Reader

Introduction

Delirious Mexico City

RUBÉN GALLO

The Mexico City Reader is an anthology of literary texts about life in Mexico City over the past thirty years, a period in which the capital has grown at a precipitous rate to become a megalopolis of over twenty million and one of the largest—and most delirious—cities in the world. The writers included in this selection not only live in Mexico City but have made it one of the most prominent themes in their work. They are avid *flâneurs,* persistent explorers of the most recondite corners of the capital, even at a time when highways, expressways, and *periféricos* have left many parts of the city inaccessible to pedestrians. This collection of varied texts about life on the city's streets aims to replicate the experience of walking through the streets of Mexico City, where one's five senses are constantly bombarded by the cultural contradictions that make life in the capital unpredictable.

Strolling through the streets remains the best strategy for understanding the cultural complexities of Mexico City: its delirious nature, its endless contradictions (it is a place of extreme poverty and extreme wealth), its surreal images (André Breton famously called it the most surreal place on earth), and its jumbling of historical periods (modernist

3

high-rises next to eighteenth-century palaces are a common sight). Like
the visitor wandering through city streets, the reader should expect to be
constantly surprised. The book contains stories of palaces demolished to
build parking lots, anecdotes of a subway system that transports almost
six million people a day (and which bored teenagers have turned into an
underground cruising area), an account of a mafioso who has made millions by trading garbage, an essay about an artist who finds her materials in the city morgue, a text on a city park that is taken over by thousands of maids every Sunday, an analysis of a street that claims to be the
longest in the world, the history of a monument containing an ex-
president's severed hand, and the recollection of a night out at a seedy
bar where soldiers arrive with a girlfriend and go home with a boyfriend.

The essays collected in *The Mexico City Reader* are among the most recent
manifestations of a literary tradition that is as old as the city itself: accounts of life in Mexico's capital. The history of these texts stretches
back to pre-Columbian times, when the poet-king Nezahualcóyotl devoted dozens of poems to celebrating the natural beauties of the valley
of Mexico. As the conquest unfolded, Spanish conquistadors often di-
gressed from their bureaucratic dispatches to the king of Spain to extol
the marvels of the Aztec city, which Cortés compared to Venice. Once
Mexico City had become the capital of New Spain, Bernardo de Balbuena composed *Grandeza mexicana* (1627), the continent's first epic
poem, hailing the grandness of the Spanish city that had risen over the
ruins of the Aztec capital. And throughout the nineteenth century, illus-
trious travelers from Fanny Calderón de la Barca to Alexander von
Humboldt chronicled the splendors and incipient urban problems of a
city that had become the capital of independent Mexico. The literary
corpus about the city grew steadily in the twentieth century, as figures
like Artemio de Valle-Arizpe and Salvador Novo became official
"chroniclers of Mexico City," and wrote thousands of pages depicting
the colorful streets of a sleepy town that had not yet awakened to the
crude reality of life in the twentieth century. In the 1950s modernity
struck the city like a speeding train, a collision Carlos Fuentes narrated
in his 1958 novel, *Where the Air Is Clear*. Since the 1950s, Carlos Monsiváis
has emerged as the undisputed chronicler of the city, and his texts examine an aspect of the city that had been ignored by his predecessors:
the popular culture—from songs to sayings to the texts on T-shirts—
flourishing on city streets.[1]

Readers familiar with today's Mexico City cannot peruse the literary canon devoted to the capital without feeling perplexed, since the city described by Humboldt or Novo has very little in common with the megalopolis of today. Aside from a few buildings in the Centro, there is almost nothing left of the wonders described by generations of awe-struck writers: gone are the Aztec water canals that Spanish conquistadors described as a "Venice of the new world"; gone are the majestic baroque buildings that graced the eighteenth-century capital; gone are the unobstructed views, the fresh mountain air celebrated by Humboldt; gone are the tranquil streets and the small-town atmosphere chronicled by Valle Arizpe; and gone is the orderly, modernist city of the 1940s that made Salvador Novo proud of living in one of the world's metropolises.

Today, Mexico City is a very different place. It is a megalopolis of over twenty million people, spread over an area of 579 square miles, riddled by violent crime that has turned it into one of the most dangerous places on the continent (only Bogotá, Colombia, has a higher rate of murders and kidnappings);[2] it suffers from the world's most serious pollution problems (on certain days the smog is so thick that one cannot see across the street, and radio broadcasts advise parents against letting their children play outside); its millions of cars and over one hundred thousand taxis cause endless traffic jams (over the years, the city government has unsuccessfully attempted to ease the problem by demolishing entire streets to make room for six-lane expressways); it must pump in water from hundreds of miles away, draining the country's rivers, and is always in peril of drying up; its dangerous and corrupt police officers are in league with organized crime. The city has become a monster, an urban disaster, a planner's nightmare. For those living in an increasingly blighted urban space, some of Mexico City's most celebrated literary portraits—like Humboldt's description of the crisp mountain air and clear blue skies—now read like sarcastic jokes meant to rub salt on the city's wounds.

And yet not everything in Mexico City is all that bad. "Why don't all inhabitants of this urban disaster flee at once?" is a question often posed by Juan Villoro, Carlos Monsiváis, and other writers included in this anthology. Villoro suggests one answer: like Stravinsky's Don Juan, we have fallen in love with the circus's bearded lady. Another answer is that Mexico City is one of Latin America's cultural capitals, home to one of the most influential publishing houses in the Spanish speaking world (Fondo de Cultura Económica), a booming film industry, a lively music

scene, an irreverent political cabaret (El Hábito, run by Jesusa Rodríguez and Liliana Felipe, which routinely stages Brechtian political satires
against the president, the mayor of Mexico City, the pope, and anyone
else who incurs their activist ire), spectacular museums displaying a cultural heritage ranging from pre-Columbian sculpture to revolutionary
murals, and the world's largest university, the Autonomous National
University of Mexico (UNAM), with a student enrollment of over two
hundred fifty thousand taught by almost thirty thousand faculty members. And above all, the city is one of the most vibrant urban spaces in the
world. One has only to walk through the Centro Histórico to find streets
brimming with life and crowded with flâneurs, flirtatious students, Indian dancers, food vendors, fortune tellers, political activists, and peasant
protesters. Together they form an unlikely cast of characters that turn
the city into a vast stage for unpredictable everyday dramas: a chaotic,
vibrant, delirious city.

A project like *The Mexico City Reader*—like all previous attempts to write
Mexico's capital—confronts us with the thorny question of how to theorize the city. What intellectual framework can help us make sense of a
place long associated with disorder and chaos? Or, put in simpler terms:
What kind of questions should we ask to try to understand Mexico City?
What can be our frame of reference, our point of comparison? Should
we discuss the problems facing Mexico City in the year 2000 by con-
trasting it to the city of 1950 or 1900? Or is it more productive to compare today's city with other megalopolises around the world?
  One of the most popular models for theorizing Mexico City posits the capital as a place that has evolved gradually but consistently
through the centuries, where cultural traditions dating from the Aztec
city survive in the megalopolis of the twenty-first century. Examples of
this model can be found in recent cultural histories of the city, including
Jonathan Kandell's *La Capital: The Biography of Mexico City* (1988), Serge
Gruzinski's *Histoire de Mexico* (1996), and Emmanuel Carballo and José
Luis Martínez's *Páginas sobre la Ciudad de México* (1988). These works
present the history of Mexico City as an unbroken continuum from pre-
Columbian times to the age of NAFTA, and insist on the city's historical continuity throughout time. Kandell's five-hundred-page study sets
out to prove that "Mexico City can trace its existence continuously from
Paleolithic site to cradle of ancient civilizations, and from colonial
stronghold to contemporary megalopolis."[3] In a similar vein, Gruzinski

describes the city as a magical space where the Aztec past coexists harmoniously with a postmodern present, where Western culture lives side by side with Indian traditions, and pre-Columbian culture thrives amid the chaos of the modern city.[4] Following a similar assumption, Carballo and Martínez, the editors of *Páginas sobre la Ciudad de México*, published an anthology of texts about the city written between the fifteenth and the twentieth centuries.

There are several problems with insisting on the city's historical continuity through the centuries, as these approaches do. First of all, they tend to present today's Mexico City as an appendix—a tragic coda—to a grand narrative spanning over five hundred years of historical continuity. For obvious reasons, a study discussing the evolution of Tenochtitlán into the current megalopolis cannot devote more than a few pages to the present-day reality of Mexico City. Kandell's five-hundred-page book, for example, devotes merely one chapter out of eighteen to the modern city. Second, since these cultural histories focus on the past, their understanding of the current city's problems tends to be limited and superficial: if one's frame of reference is the baroque splendor of eighteenth-century Mexico, one can say very little about today's pollution and overpopulation aside from lamenting the loss of a glorious past with cleaner air.

There is another variation on the "five-centuries" model for theorizing Mexico City: cultural histories that focus on present-day Mexico City but take the city's past as the sole frame of reference, like Guillermo Tovar de Teresa's *The City of Palaces: Chronicle of a Lost Heritage* (1990). Although the book is ostensibly about present-day Mexico, Tovar de Teresa's perspective remains fixed in the past—a past that is seen as wholesome, glorious, and trouble free. His extreme cultural nostalgia (he cherishes the splendor of baroque Mexico and his purist outlook considers even the nineteenth century as a period of cultural decline) hinders his ability to make sense of the present, and his observations on the modern city are reduced to a litany of lamentations about a vanished heritage: "We Mexicans suffer from an illness, a rage, a desire for self-destruction, to cancel and erase ourselves, to leave no trace of our past. . . . We Mexicans still believe that it is necessary to destroy the past to make way for the present. More than just a bad habit, this is a serious problem of national identity."[5]

Tovar believes Mexico City reached its golden age in the eighteenth century. He posits the baroque city of the 1700s as the "heritage" that has been unrelentingly destroyed for almost three hundred years. In his view, the first wave of destruction came in the nineteenth century—when baroque aesthetics fell from grace and most of the city's façades were redone in the neoclassical style that had become fashionable—a misstep that was followed by a more vicious rash of twentieth-century demolitions in the name of modernization. What Tovar does not realize is that his reasoning could well be invoked to attack the baroque city of the eighteenth century: following his logic, colonial Mexico City could be denounced for leveling the Aztec capital, Mexico's true heritage, unless of course we decided that the building of Tenochtitlán was itself a barbaric act responsible for the destruction of the pristine lagoons that filled the valley of Mexico—our original natural heritage. Tovar cannot grasp that every act of creation is also an act of destruction, and that the notion of a wholesome, innocent past can only exist in nostalgic minds.

Aside from its idealization of the past, Tovar's study fails to take into account the most important element of Mexico City: its inhabitants. In his obsession with buildings (or "monuments," as he calls them), Tovar loses sight of the human beings who built and inhabit the city. In all his passionate diatribes against the destruction of the Centro, which was once graced by majestic palaces, he never takes notice that even though some of its buildings were demolished, today this neighborhood is one of the most vibrant and lively areas of Mexico City: streets teem with vendors, students, shopkeepers, parking attendants, tourists, beggars, protesters, and proselytizers. At a time when urbanists around the world lament the loss of public space—and the transformation of downtown districts in cities from Dallas to Sydney into architectural shells devoid of life—Tovar's obsession with monuments keeps him from recognizing the value of a human "heritage" that has not yet been lost.

Tovar's nostalgia for baroque Mexico blinds him to the presence of human life that is the most crucial element in any theorization of cities. His book leaves no doubt that, if given the choice, Tovar would gladly replace today's pockmarked but vibrant metropolis with an architecturally intact but dead city—a baroque Mexico City with no life on its streets. Ultimately, Tovar longs for a baroque, open-air museum: a city of buildings, not of people.

As Salvador Novo shrewdly pointed out in his *Nueva grandeza mexicana* (1946), cities and their inhabitants must choose one of two possible destinies: they can either die and keep their architecture intact (like the Mayan city of Chichén Itzá), or they can remain alive by constantly transforming and renewing themselves. Novo believed that all cities faced a choice between "either solemn grave or unpredictable life; either mummification or life; either museum or city." Since Aztec times, Mexico City has survived—and preserved its street life—at the expense of constant transformations, constructions, and destructions.[6]

In the end, though Tovar takes the opposite approach from Gruzinski (and other proponents of Mexico City's historical continuity), the two critics end up in a similar quagmire: the French writer idealizes present-day Mexico City to the point where he cannot see the city's problems, while Tovar demonizes the modern metropolis to the point where he cannot recognize its virtues. If Gruzinski is blinded by his insistence on historical continuity, Tovar is blinded by his obsession with historical discontinuity (the "destruction" which separates the modern city from its glorious past). Both perspectives are similarly reductive, since their black-and-white approach fails to account for the complexities and contradictions that characterize city life today. Given the shortcomings of their approaches, we might now wonder about an alternative model for theorizing Mexico City that avoids these extremes—the overly pessimistic and the overly optimistic—and allows us to reach a more balanced view of the capital in the twenty-first century.

Aside from positing the past as a golden age, cultural studies of Mexico City from Kandell to Gruzinski suffer from one obvious shortcoming: they never compare the capital to anything but its former self. Mexico City's cultural critics often suffer from a form of urban solipsism, comparing the modern city only to its past incarnations, as if it floated in a vacuum, isolated from other cities around the world. Even Néstor García Canclini's sociological and urban studies of Mexico City in the 1990s fail to consider other cities around the world as possible points of reference.

Why didn't Tovar de Teresa, for example, contrast Mexico City's demolition of historical monuments in favor of modernization to the experience of other cities with comparable histories—like Lima or New Delhi? Wouldn't it have been more productive to compare Mexico City's twentieth-century expansion to Moscow or Bogotá than to simply lament the destruction of a "lost heritage"? In the twenty-first century, Mexico City has undoubtedly more in common (in terms of urban culture, social problems, and planning issues) with other developing cities around the world—from Buenos Aires to Karachi—than with the bygone City of Palaces extolled by Humboldt. In his essay entitled "The

Metro" (included in this anthology), for example, Juan Villoro has shown how the Mexico City subway was created to serve urban and ideological needs similar to those of the Moscow underground.

Mexico City should be theorized from a comparative perspective, abandoning the traditional solipsism of cultural critics and acknowledging that it now faces the same challenge as dozens of other cities around the globe: balancing the preservation of a rich cultural heritage with the inescapable requirement of modernization. Such a comparative perspective would allow us to develop a deeper understanding of the city as it exists today, and it would certainly be a more productive endeavor than merely demonizing modern Mexico City as a devalued, mutilated version of a lost original projected into the distant past. But how can one think comparatively about Mexico?

One of the most useful models for theorizing modern cities from a comparative perspective can be found in Rem Koolhaas's writings. This Dutch architect's numerous essays about urban matters—most of which have been collected in his *S, M, L, XL* (1995)—provide a framework for thinking comparatively about megalopolises. One of his boldest assertions is that large cities around the world—from Tokyo to Atlanta, from Singapore to Barcelona—are destined to become "generic cities," indistinguishable urban spaces where the forces of modernization will erase all cultural differences to produce an architectural and cultural homogeneity. In Koolhaas's view, the model for the generic city is the modern airport. Airports are spaces that look the same, regardless of geographic location, and have the same shops, layout, and the same lack of distinguishing features. But what does the generic city have to do with Mexico?

Writing in 1967, Carlos Monsiváis observed that Mexico City was on its way to becoming a generic city. In the prologue to a revised edition of Novo's *Nueva grandeza mexicana*, he argued that in the twenty years that had elapsed since the original publication of the book in 1946, Mexico City had undergone tremendous changes: the capital was now full of highways, skyscrapers, and work was about to begin on an ambitious subway system. "The reigning tendency is towards uniformity," Monsiváis concluded. And by uniformity he meant not only that these urban projects were making Mexico City's various neighborhoods—from working-class Colonia Guerrero to ritzy Coyoacán—look the same, but that the city itself was beginning to look increasingly like other cities around the world, from Los Angeles to São Paolo, metropolises which were also busy widening roads, building highways, and digging subway tunnels. Monsiváis expressed mixed feelings about this tendency toward urban uniformity: he foresaw urban problems to come, but at the same time he was seduced—like Novo—by the city's newly found modernity. He wrote, "El México de hoy [es] la ciudad ambiciosa, que crece sin recato, violenta, tímida, colonial, llena de sojuzgamiento y altiveces, libérrima, horrenda, indescriptible, magnífica, ávida, voluntariosa" ("Today Mexico City is an ambitious city growing shamelessly: violent, shy, full of prejudices and snobbery, free, horrendous, indescribable, magnificent, eager, ready").[7] Uniformity was a sign of modernity, and Monsiváis celebrated the "avid, eager" energy that was making Mexico City more generic day by day.

But what are the cultural implications of a modernizing force that transforms all cities into generic spaces? What happens to a city's cultural life as its architecture and urban design approach the generic? The generic city lacks character, identity, and, above all, history. Koolhaas describes it as a "city without history" and he writes: "It is easy. It does not need maintenance. If it gets too small it just expands. If it gets old it just self-destructs and renews. It is equally exciting—or unexciting—everywhere. It is 'superficial'—like a Hollywood studio lot, it can produce a new identity every Monday morning."[8] The generic city not only lacks history; it contains a mechanism preventing it from ever developing a historical identity, since it self-destructs whenever it begins to get old. The generic city must eternally be a blank slate, an ahistorical space eternally condemned to periodic erasures and renewals.

Contrary to what the reader might expect, Koolhaas does not lament the generic city's ahistoricity. He actually celebrates its rejection of history as liberating: he believes that cities with strong cultural identities are doomed to degenerate into motionless monoliths, paralyzed by the weight of their own tradition. "The stronger the identity," Koolhaas writes, "the more it imprisons, the more it resists expansion, interpretation, renewal, contradiction."[9] He points to Paris as an example of a city that has been immobilized by the weight of its history (and by the preservationist prohibition against demolishing old buildings), and laments that "Paris can only become more Parisian—it is already on its way to becoming hyper-Paris, a polished caricature."[10]

To make his case against the tyranny of historical identity—and to enhance his reputation as architecture's *enfant terrible*—Koolhaas

submitted a proposal in 1991 for redeveloping the area behind La Dé-
fense in Paris (the most ungeneric of cities), freeing it from the chains of
tradition (and bringing it closer to the generic city) by demolishing its
buildings. "What would happen," Koolhaas asked, maliciously, "if,
even in Europe—especially in Europe—we declare every building in
the entire zone that is older than 25 years worthless—null and void—or
at least potentially removable? . . . We analyzed this question in numerical terms and discovered that if we laundered the site in five-year incre-
ments by simply erasing all buildings over the age of 25, vast areas would
gradually be liberated."[11]

Koolhaas's irreverent project was never realized, though it probably
sent shivers up the spine of more than one French preservationist. But
ironically, this project—included in *S, M, L, XL* under the rubric "Tabula Rasa Revisited"—describes the transformations undergone by Mexico City during much of the twentieth century. Entire sections of the city
were razed to make room for new neighborhoods and new buildings,
which in turn have been demolished after a few decades. The same
transformations that Tovar de Teresa lamented as barbarian destructions of the city's heritage are celebrated by Koolhaas as a "laundering"
of the urban fabric and a "liberation" from the chains of history. If
Tovar de Teresa's ideal city is one that remains immutable through the
centuries, Koolhaas imagines a space that can be "renewed" and wiped
clean every twenty-five years, much as Mexico City has been since
Aztec times. And it is precisely this type of obsessive, *historiophobic* renewal that makes a generic city generic: "All generic cities issue from
the tabula rasa: if there was nothing, now they are there; if there was
something, they have replaced it. They must, otherwise they would be
historic."[12]

So is Mexico City a generic city? It certainly seems to fit Koolhaas's
definition in terms of architecture and urban planning. Most of the
great urban projects of the twentieth century—from expressways to the
metro—have contributed to create a metropolis that is increasingly de-
tached from its historical identity. And as Monsiváis noted, expressways, subways, and other modernizing projects make Mexico City like
every other city in the world. Some recent urban projects—the development of Santa Fé, for example—are textbook cases in the creation of
generic cities. A former slum on the outskirts of Mexico City that was
home to one of the largest garbage dumps in the metropolitan area,
Santa Fé was redeveloped into a sparkling suburban city in the early

1990s. Its high-rises, condominiums, and gated streets now rise as monuments to Mexico's new identity in the age of NAFTA.

Santa Fé was developed using the same tabula rasa strategy that Koolhaas attributes to the birth of modern Singapore—the archetypal generic city—and which consists of wiping out insalubrious slums to make room for a brand new, orderly, and hygienic planned capital. Koolhaas's description of Singapore could have easily been written about Santa Fé: "It is managed by a regime that has excluded accident and randomness: even its nature is entirely readymade. It is pure intention: if there is chaos, it is authored chaos; if it is ugly, it is designed ugliness."[13] Today, Santa Fé is a wealthy residential and business district featuring dozens of high-rise condominiums, one of the country's largest malls, a prestigious private university—Universidad Iberoamericana—and eight-lane highways linking it to downtown Mexico City. Driving though Santa Fé—one can get there only by car—is an eerie experience: the streets are deserted, and nothing at all distinguishes this suburb from its counterparts in Atlanta, Caracas, or San José. Santa Fé has no history and no identity; it is a typical generic city. And the same could be said about many other faraway districts in Mexico City built to shelter their residents from the chaos and pollution of downtown life: Satélite, Interlomas, Herradura, the sprawl that has spread to the Cuernavaca highway . . .

And yet not everything in Mexico City corresponds to Koolhaas's model. One of the main traits of the generic city is its lifelessness. There are no public spaces and, as Koolhaas writes, "the street is dead."[14] Generic cities are dominated by vast stretches of empty space: "The serenity of the Generic City is achieved by the evacuation of the public realm, as in an emergency fire drill."[15] The "dead streets" described by Koolhaas characterize all generic cities, which have been designed for buildings and cars and not for pedestrians. And while this description fits a few of the city's quasi-suburban neighborhoods—from Santa Fé to Satélite—it certainly does not apply to downtown Mexico City, where the Centro—with its street vendors, open-air markets, and endless crowds of shoppers—is one of the liveliest, most crowded places on the planet. If the generic city's streets are dead, the Centro's avenues and alleys teem with life; if the generic city lacks public spaces, the Centro is one giant public square; if the generic city "is a place of weak and distended sensations, few and far between emotions, discreet and mysterious, like a large space lit by a bed lamp," the Centro is just the opposite:

a place where strollers are constantly—and relentlessly—bombarded with unexpected sights and overwhelming emotions.[16]

In *All That Is Solid Melts into Air*, Marshall Berman offers a perspective on generic cities that is more sobering than Koolhaas's bad-boy enthusiasm. Writing about his visit to Brasilia, an archetypal generic city that was built from scratch in the 1950s, Berman deplores it as a cold, inhuman space. "From the air," he writes, "Brasilia looked dynamic and exciting: in fact, it was built to resemble the jet plane from which I (and virtually all other visitors) first observed it. From the ground level, however, where people actually live and work, it is one of the most dismal cities in the world . . . One's overall feeling—confirmed by every Brazilian I met—is one of immense empty spaces in which the individual feels lost, as alone as a man on the moon. There is a deliberate absence of public space in which people can meet and talk, or simply look at each other and hang around. The great tradition of Latin urbanism, in which city life is organized around a *plaza mayor*, is explicitly rejected."[17]

Berman mourns the death of street life in Brasilia, and he finds its vast, generic spaces tragically depressing. He considers street life one of the most important aspects of the modern city—and of modernity itself—and his book can be read as an homage to public space. His chapters on urban poets from Baudelaire to Pushkin celebrate the explosive character of city streets, with their amalgamation of people of different ages, genders, professions, and social classes. Streets are impure spaces where everything necessarily gets mixed, and Berman credits them with the birth of revolutions—boulevards "bring explosive material and human forces together"[18]—political activism, love, and even avant-garde literature, since modernist experiments sought a form of writing that recreated the intense, fragmentary, and heterogeneous character of city streets.

Berman would have loved downtown Mexico City, an urban space that is the exact opposite of Brasilia: unplanned, chaotic, crowded, and as heterogeneous as it gets. The entire Centro is a "space where people can meet and talk, or simply look at each other and hang around" and even, for those who so decide, a place to set up temporary residence: Irate protesters from the countryside routinely set up tents on the Zócalo, the central square, where they camp day and night for the duration of their stay. Berman would probably find that the streets of Mexico City—like Baudelaire's Paris or Pushkin's Saint Petersburg—are full of revolutionary potential. The crowds choking the streets provide an end-less source of "anarchic, explosive forces," ready to be channeled into creative texts, street demonstrations, or even revolutionary movements.

Berman's theory of the explosive character of street life casts the proliferation of public works—especially the obsession with building expressways—inflicted on Mexico City residents since the 1960s in a new light. A government that in 1968 panicked upon realizing the rev-olutionary potential of the streets—three hundred thousand people marched down the city streets on August 27, 1968, to protest the govern-ment's handling of the university crisis[19]—has been gradually chipping away at public space, demolishing streets to make room for expressways and replacing potential places of assembly and protest with routes re-served for motorists. In contrast to the street, expressways do not breed revolutions. If, as Berman notes, "the boulevard, [was] a medium for bringing explosive material and human forces together", then "the hall-mark of twentieth-century urbanism has been the highway, a means for putting them asunder."[20] As cities become more generic, they also be-come fortified against revolutions: their architecture and master plans are designed to keep their inhabitants isolated and away from the streets.[21]

Berman's theory also explains why Mexico City is not a generic city—at least not yet—and also why poets and writers continue to be drawn to the city's streets. Like Baudelaire in Paris, they wander the streets to experience the chaotic, heterogeneous energy of a damned city. The vast body of literature written about Mexico City by authors like Carlos Monsiváis, Juan Villoro and Elena Poniatowska focuses al-most exclusively on the life of its streets, and not—as Tovar de Teresa seems to suggest—on the magnificence of its buildings. Like Baudelaire, the writers included in *The Mexico City Reader* are flâneurs intent on ex-ploring the metropolis's darkest recesses and most recondite corners.

Aside from lively downtown streets, relentless crowds, and anarchic en-ergy, there is one aspect of life in Mexico City that sets it apart from generic cities: the strange penchant its inhabitants show for weaving elaborate narratives out of everything that happens to them, from natu-ral disasters to political scandals. Although these narratives can take various forms—ranging in complexity from lighthearted jokes about the latest corruption scandal to impromptu dramatizations of an ex-president's gaffes performed by a troupe of street kids at a traffic light—they have one thing in common: they all emerge from the lively popular culture that thrives on the streets of Mexico City.

Here is one compelling example of how the city's denizens turn tragedy into narrative. In the 1980s—as AIDS was taking its death toll in large American cities and making inroads into Mexico—New York, and Mexico City responded to the epidemic in radically different ways. New Yorkers, pragmatic as always, focused on ways to stop the epidemic: they formed ACT UP, organized marches on the streets, launched safe-sex campaigns, and lobbied the city government to close down bath-houses. In contrast, there were no activist groups or marches to be seen in Mexico City. But there was a proliferation of symbolic actions against the disease, including the emergence of a new player in the city's ani-mated wrestling scene: a heavyweight who dressed in black, wore a mask adorned by a white skull, and called himself El Sida, the Spanish acro-nym for AIDS. The first time he climbed into the wrestling ring, the crowd booed, heckled, and bombarded him with chewing gum, candy wrappers, crunched up cigarette boxes, and whatever else happened to be in their pockets. After several quick victories against other lesser known figures, El Sida fought against a formidable enemy: Superbarrio, a superhero wrestler who had become a social activist after the 1985 earthquake and gained a reputation as a crusader for the poor, a de-fender of tenants facing eviction, and a man who always wore the same outfit: red mask, spandex tights, and yellow cape.

When Superbarrio wrestled against El Sida (the match was captured by Yolanda Andrade in her photograph *Superbarrio contra el Sida*)—the arena was packed to the limits. Crowds sweated nervously and held their breath as they watched the grim reaper trapping Superbarrio in an arm lock, pinning him against the ground, crushing him with his body. One second, two seconds, three seconds went by, and suddenly Super-barrio rebounded, jumped up. Now it was he who was on top, sitting on El Sida, crushing him, and threatening to break his bones to the wild cries of the audience ("*dale, dale*, get him, get him"). The referee came on stage and after a swift countdown declared Superbarrio the victor. The crowd cheered. AIDS had been defeated.

Pragmatic-minded readers might object that Superbarrio's ritual defeat of AIDS could have detrimental side effects: the quick victory might lead the audience to underestimate the gravity of the epidemic and to think that nothing—not even disease—threatens those defended by Superbarrio. And in contrast to ACT UP activism, these imaginative wrestling matches produce no tangible results: no drug trials, no discounted medicine programs, no health code changes. Wouldn't Mexico City be better off in the long run if its inhabitants spent less time staging metaphorical acts and devoted their energies to political activism?

In the symbolic logic of Mexico City, however, Superbarrio's fight against AIDS is a form of political activism: in addition to providing entertainment, the wrestling match had the virtue of educating vast numbers of people who otherwise might never have thought or talked about the epidemic. The famous fight also sparked a lively debate about AIDS that spilled into the pages of Mexico City's newspapers. And if we look closely, we discover that Superbarrio has scored as many political victories as any ACT UP activist: the wrestler-activist often meets with city officials—always clad in his red-and-yellow superhero outfit—to lobby in favor of poor tenants and social outcasts, and his proposals are taken seriously, precisely because of his enormous popularity as a local star.[22]

Superbarrio's ritual defeat of AIDS is not an isolated event but a representative instance of how Mexico City's inhabitants often deal with traumatic events by transforming them into elaborate narratives. There seems to be a correlation between the intensity of the trauma and the complexity of the narrative it generates: the more traumatic an event, the more elaborate the narratives it will inspire. Think, for example, of the cultural response to the 1995 economic crisis and the popular reactions it sparked.

After President Carlos Salinas de Gortari left office in December 1994, the country experienced one of the most severe financial crises in its recent history. The peso lost over 50 percent of its value against the dollar, inflation soared, the banking system nearly collapsed, and unemployment and violent crime in Mexico City spiraled out of control. Although the causes were manifold and complex—including the social panic and flight of foreign investment that followed the 1994 Zapatista uprising in Chiapas—it was generally acknowledged that that crisis was precipitated by Salinas's administrative missteps during his last year in office. During the first months of the crisis, Salinas was reviled as the epitome of bad government, mismanagement, corruption, personal ambition, and hypocrisy.

The first months of the 1995 economic crisis coincided with another calamity: dozens of goats and other farm animals in northern Mexico were found dead, some with suspicious tooth marks around their necks. Somehow, word got out that the animals had been attacked by a goat sucker, and the myth of the *chupacabras*—a wild, blood-drinking beast that was roaming the Mexican countryside and threatening to make its way to the cities—was born. Stories of encounters with the chupacabras became increasingly baroque and farfetched. During a televised interview, a young peasant girl in tears claimed she had been attacked by the bloodthirsty beast, who climbed into her bed in the middle of the night and left her with a mark resembling a hickey (her husband was unconvinced and filed for divorce).[23]

On the streets of Mexico City, imaginative citizens collapsed the two crises—Salinas and the chupacabras—into a fantastic narrative. Someone, somewhere concluded that the chupacabras existed, and the dangerous beast was none other than Carlos Salinas de Gortari. The news spread like fire throughout Mexico City. Street vendors began peddling masks and T-shirts depicting Salinas as a devilish beast with sharp, bloodied fangs; overnight, buildings were spray-painted with graffiti announcing that Salinas was the chupacabras (or the *chupadólares*, "dollar-sucker," as vandals with a keener understanding of international finance called him); at busy intersections, street kids abandoned their juggling and fire-throwing acts to perform a sixty-second dramatization of "Salinas the chupacabras" as they danced to the recently released chupacabras cumbia. Impressed by the symbolic power of Salinas-inspired tchotchkes, the artist Vicente Razo began collecting them and later placed them in a "Museo Salinas" located in the bathroom of his apartment.[24]

Though readers might be tempted to dismiss it as a baroque flight of fancy, the myth of Salinas as chupacabras deploys extremely complex symbolic strategies, including the processes of condensation and displacement that Freud attributed to the workings of the unconscious. Like dream images, the bizarre creature invented by the popular imagination condensed two different elements: Salinas and the chupacabras. Like dream images, this postmodern monster was a shorthand notation of the manifold fears and anxieties experienced by those wrecked by the economic crisis; like dreams, Salinas the chupacabras could be analyzed to reveal a complex representation of reality, since the features that the popular imagination attributed to the chupacabras—its surreptitious, nighttime blood-sucking excursions—were eloquent metaphors for the ex-president's handling of the country's economy: Salinas had quite literally sucked the life-blood out of Mexico. And like dreams and other activities that deploy the unconscious processes of condensation and displacement—jokes, parapraxes, slips of the tongue—the construction of a mythological blood-sucking president was an efficient antidote to the generalized gloom and despair caused by the 1995 crisis: if a dream, as Freud argued, is always the fulfillment of a wish, the masks, T-shirts, and performances of "Salinas the chupacabras" transform fantasy into reality and mete out poetic justice to the ex-president.

As in the case of Superbarrio's defeat of AIDS, the identification of Salinas as the chupacabras is not only a fascinating symbolic strategy but also a form of political activism. The campaigns to ridicule Salinas by exposing him as a blood-sucking beast—as well as other ingenious performances staged on Mexico City streets during 1995, including countless parades of Salinas look-alikes in chains or behind bars[25]— were so effective that the ex-president was literally laughed out of the country. He eventually left for Ireland (a country chosen, perhaps, because its people have a more benign sense of humor than the Mexicans), where he remained in self-imposed exile for several years. In the end, the symbolic strategies deployed against Salinas on the streets of Mexico City sentenced him to a more painful punishment—by making him into an object of ridicule and preventing him from holding a position of power ever again (his prospects as head of the World Trade Organization, for example, were cut short by the generalized outage voiced by Mexicans in the early months of 1995)—than any Mexican court could have imposed, since an unspoken rule guarantees ex-presidents immunity from prosecution.

In addition to providing a means for citizens to vent their emotions, imaginative narratives like "Salinas the chupacabras" keep life in Mexico City interesting, unpredictable, and fun. The abundance of these symbolic elaborations has saved the capital from the sterility and stagnation that characterize generic cities. Despite the relentless public works that make Mexico City look like other nondescript cities, the vibrant, chaotic street life of its downtown districts—the birthplace of Superbarrios and chupacabras—continue to set it apart from other cities around the world.

The Mexico City Reader is a literary portrait of Mexico City as it stands today. These pages document not the City of Palaces mourned by Tovar de Teresa, but the vibrant, chaotic, anarchic, and nongeneric city of the 1980s and 1990s—the city of Superbarrio and Salinas-as-chupacabras. Although there is no great work of literature about the Mexico City of today (a modern-day version of Carlos Fuentes's *La región más transparente,* the great novel about 1950s Mexico City, has yet to be written), I discovered that there were hundreds of short texts, scattered throughout various newspapers, literary journals, and popular magazines that could be brought together to assemble a many-faceted portrait of the city as it exists today.

I decided to make an anthology of these texts, focusing on pieces written after 1968, the date of the student massacre at Tlatelolco and a symbolic turning point for Mexico and its capital. It was on this year that the PRI, the Institutional Revolutionary Party, which had ruled the country since 1929 and was perceived by most Mexicans as a benign—if intransigent—institution, showed a totalitarian, repressive, and murderous side that few had imagined. On October 2, 1968, Mexico City became the stage of a bloodbath that brought back memories of atrocities not seen since the Revolution: hundreds of students were killed by the army, and hundreds more were wounded, imprisoned, or "disappeared."[26] For Mexico City's residents, 1968 marks not only the time when the government devolved into a totalitarian ogre but also the point at which Mexico City degenerated into an urban disaster plagued by smog, traffic, crime, hopelessness, and became unlivable. During the 1950s and 1960s, the city grew exponentially (from about 1.5 million inhabitants in 1940 to nearly 5 million in 1960),[27] but most residents interpreted the population explosion as an auspicious sign of modernity.[28] And around 1968, the dream of modernity devolved into an urban nightmare, and a panicked city government launched an offensive of public works—highways, bridges, collectors, and overpasses—that radically changed the city forever.

In "Call the Doctor," a text included in this anthology, Jorge Ibargüengoitia compares Mexico City to a baby boy who grew taller every day. The more he grew, the prouder his mother felt, until one day he reached the height of ten feet, could no longer fit in the house, needed three beds to sleep, and devoured the maid. Only then did his mother decide to call the doctor, but it was too late. The point at which the boy's growth ceased to be a sign of pride and became pathological occurred around 1968.

In order to make *The Mexico City Reader* as cohesive as possible, I decided to select only nonfiction essays and to focus on *crónicas*—short texts that are a cross between literary essay and urban *reportage*, and usually read like journal entries about a writer's experience of the city. Although there are many novels—like Luis Zapata's *El vampiro de la colonia Roma*—and poems—like Efraín Huerta's *Circuito interior*—about life in post-1968 Mexico City, I focused on crónicas to make the book more original for North American readers: most Mexican poems and works of fiction are eventually translated into English, but crónicas rarely make it across the border, apparently because they constitute a hybrid genre which most publishers are afraid to touch.[29] And it is precisely this hybrid quality that makes crónicas a perfect genre for writing about a city where everything—from architectural styles to social classes—is jumbled, chaotic, and falls in between traditional categories.

This volume includes texts by writers who have chronicled life in Mexico City since the 1960s. They range from well-known figures like Carlos Monsiváis to younger writers whose work has not been translated into English before, like Fabrizio Mejía Madrid or Julieta García González. My search for post-1968 crónicas yielded over three dozen texts dealing with a wide range of topics: from monuments along Reforma, the city's main avenue, to garbage dumps on the edge of town; from life in the ritzy neighborhood of Lomas to corruption in the city morgue; from the devastation caused by the 1985 earthquake to police raids launched against prostitutes in Zona Rosa. Taken together, these texts form a mosaic of life in Mexico City, and their variety replicates on paper one of the most striking characteristics of the city: its heterogeneity.

Urban theorists have argued that one of the key aspects of the modern city is that it cannot be represented in its totality: the modern city is so spread out that it can never be seen all at once by a single person, and thus it can never be given form—in literature, photography, or film—as a coherent whole. Its citizens can only experience their city in fragments, in momentary and broken glimpses.[30] Given the impossibility of creating an anthology to represent Mexico City in its entirety, I aimed for a book that would take the reader though a series of fragments, creating a reading experience that would approximate the feeling of walking down the streets of the capital and being relentlessly bombarded by heterogeneous impressions and sensations. The book's textual itinerary is organized as follows:

The Mexico City Reader opens with Gonzalo Celorio's "Mexico, City of Paper," an encyclopedic overview of the literature devoted to Mexico City from pre-Columbian times to the twentieth century. Celorio highlights the abyss that now separates the two cities: on one end of the abyss lies a "city of paper," built by admiring writers through the centuries, while on the other rises the urban nightmare that is Mexico City today, "a runaway stain spreading up the mountainsides."

The rest of the book takes us on a tour of this "runaway stain." The section devoted to "Places," opens with Fabrizio Mejía Madrid's "Insurgentes," an ode to an avenue that traverses Mexico City from north to south and has been proclaimed the longest street in the Americas. Mejía Madrid reads Insurgentes as a microcosm of Mexico City: not only does this avenue contain some of the most significant national monuments—including one to the Mexican Revolution—but it leads from the affluent southern district of San Ángel to the urban slums of the north. Traversing Insurgentes as a postmodern flâneur, the author describes the jumble of images he finds along the way, including the mummified hand of a revolutionary hero, police raids against transvestites, and a violent strike in a soda factory.

"Insurgentes" is followed by Vicente Leñero's legendary text on the Zona Rosa, a district familiar to contemporary visitors as the main tourist and entertainment district. Leñero immortalized the Zona Rosa in its heyday during the 1960s, when it was a very different place. Filled with the city's best restaurants, art galleries, and designer shops, it was "chic," "arrogant," "pretentious," and crowded with aspiring artists and poets. In contrast to the Zona Rosa's long-lost haughtiness, San Rafael—the subject of Gerardo Deniz's text—is a down-to-earth, middle-class neighborhood, filled with sounds. Deniz focuses on the sounds of the street—the cries of street vendors, the discordant notes played by traveling musicians, the whistle of the sweet-potato cart.

Coyoacán, once a peaceful village where Hernán Cortés built his country house, has been swallowed by the megalopolis and is now a southern neighborhood within the city. In "Coyoacán I," Guillermo Sheridan describes the central plaza as a site of cultural contradictions where trashy tourists rub elbows with new-age dancers and bureaucrats walk past pious church ladies. Writing about the same neighborhood, Jorge Ibargüengoitia ridicules the city government's efforts to artificially transform Coyoacán into an open-air museum of colonial architecture—a campaign that yielded countless eyesores of unclassifiable style.

No anthology about life in Mexico City would be complete without an essay on the absurd, an aspect of life in the capital that residents experience whenever they visit government offices or deal with corrupt traffic police. Julieta García González located a paradigmatic manifestation of the Mexico City absurd along División del Norte, where several shops specializing in bathroom and kitchen supplies began displaying stuffed animals—from polar bears to African lions—in front of their shops. We find a different kind of absurd in the flamboyant depictions of the city's wealthy districts in Blanco's texts and Rossell's photo series.

The third section of *The Mexico City Reader* is devoted to the metro, a subway system used by over six million people daily and laden with symbolic imagery. In "The Metro," Juan Villoro explores the mythology and political symbolism of the Mexican subway, analyzing the nationalist imagery in the design of its station names and revealing the system's bizarre obsession with mythologizing the past. In the 1970s, when the subway was still a novelty, Ricardo Garibay rode the subway every day for a week and wrote a journal of his "Voyage to the Center of the City," narrating his encounters with desperate mothers unable to get past the throngs of people and with teenagers who ride the cars not to get across the city but to grope as many women as they can. Unlike Garibay, José Joaquín Blanco felt no need to ride the metro: his "Metro Insurgentes" recounts how the exterior of a futuristic metro station became a set for an American science-fiction film, which Hollywood aficionados might recognize as *Total Recall*. And in "The Metro: A Voyage to the End of the Squeeze," Carlos Monsiváis sketches a theory of the metro that posits the Mexico City subway as a metaphor for the city's greatest problem: overpopulation.

Section 4 includes two texts on monuments: Guillermo Sheridan's "Monuments," which ponders the city's most bizarre memorials—including a famous tower that housed General Álvaro Obregón's severed hand—and Vicente Leñero's "La Diana," a humorous account of how a prudish city official draped a loincloth on one of the capital's landmarks, prompting the outraged sculptor to fight a decades-long battle for the right to monumental nudism.

In section 5, "Eating and Drinking," four writers pay tribute to their favorite gastronomic locales. José de la Colina writes about the Centro's Chinese-owned coffeehouses. Jorge Ibargüengoitia reminisces about a legendary eatery, Armando's Tortas, and categorizes the various types of sandwiches (and their political symbolism) once served at the famous dive. In "Vips in the Early Morning," a generic, twenty-four-hour chain restaurant becomes the setting for José Joaquín Blanco's tale of an anonymous drunk. Long known as Mexico City's *antrólogo* (a connoisseur of *antros*, or nocturnal dives), Carlos Monsiváis, in "Nightlife," portrays a night out at El Catorce, a soldier's bar in the Centro frequented by transvestites and featuring a live-sex show.

Section 6, "Urban Renewal/Urban Disasters," focuses on the radical transformations undergone by the city in the 1970s, when the city government unleashed a master plan of expressways, overpasses, and other public works designed to modernize the transportation network. In "Call the Doctor," Jorge Ibargüengoitia compares Mexico City to a child afflicted with a severe case of gigantism. José Joaquín Blanco discusses the impact of public works on some of the city's most traditional streets and neighborhoods: Tacubaya, Avenida Álvaro Obregón, San Juan de Letrán, and Cuauhtémoc. In "Ambulantes," a photographic series, Francis Alÿs documents one aspect of city life that has remained impervious to modernization: the hundreds of street vendors who choke the sidewalks with their carts, cloths, and makeshift stands—a resistant bunch that Marshall Berman would have celebrated as a triumph of anarchic street life over urban planning. Alÿs's photographs capture the vendors as they push and pull carts loaded with the most unlikely objects: plants, mattresses, fluorescent tubes, eggs, and even a bouquet of balloons. In "Who's There?" and "Klaxons and the Man," two pieces filled with his traditional black humor, Jorge Ibargüengoitia itemizes the nuisances—including traffic jams, noise pollution, and the proliferation of solicitors—that plagued residents as their city was modernized.

But not all disasters afflicting Mexico City have been man-made. The city was built on some of the most unstable subsoil in the world—the Spaniards filled the Aztec city's water canals and built their colonial capital over muddy terrain—and over the centuries it has been prone to floods, sinking and earthquakes. Out of all the earthquakes in recent history, the one that hit Mexico City in 1985 was the most devastating: dozens of high-rise buildings plummeted, crushing thousands and trapping hundreds inside the ruins. Elena Poniatowska's "The Earthquake" contains the first-person testimonial of Elia Palacios, a woman who spent several days buried under the rubble and lived to tell her story.

Section 8 is devoted to domestic servants, who play an important but often unacknowledged role in city life. Augusto Monterroso's "Maids I" is a literary homage to servants: he praises them as keepers of the city's unconscious—they know all the secrets—and hails their freedom to wander from one primal scene to another as they move from job to job. In "Maids II," Guadalupe Loaeza parodies a typical exchange between a maid and her employer, where anxiety and repressed social resentment underlie what appears as a casual conversation. In "Chapultepec and the Maids," José Joaquín Blanco describes how thousands of maids—and their admirers—pour into Mexico City's largest park every Sunday.

"Corruption and Bureaucracy," two staples of city life, are examined in section 9. This section opens with "Trimmins for the Comanche," one of Ricardo Garibay's "Mexican Dialogues," devoted to the bizarre and unlikely situations that the city's inhabitants routinely face. In this dialogue, an unsuspecting citizen arrives at a police station, hoping to visit a detained relative, but is met by a policeman asking for some monetary "trimmins for the Comanche." Garibay's "In the Same Boat" relates a visit to a state-owned business, an adventure that reads like a trip to the belly of a bureaucratic beast. Continuing with the theme of nightmares, "The University," a photo-conceptual project by Jonathan Hernández, documents every step needed to replace a UNAM student ID card and chronicles a labyrinthine process that would have confounded Kafka.

"The Margins," the final section in *The Mexico City Reader*, deals with two of the darkest institutions in Mexico City: garbage dumps and the city morgue. In "Garbage," Alma Guillermoprieto narrates a journey into the underground world of refuse, garbage pickers, and mafia bosses that reads like a descent into a tropical version of Dante's *Inferno*. And, to close with a bizarre tale of necrophilia, the art critic Cuauhtémoc Medina's "SEMEFO: The Morgue" analyzes the work of Teresa Margolles, a conceptual artist who assembles provocative installations and other conceptual pieces out of human remains filched from the city morgue.

After such a dizzying textual itinerary, the reader might conclude that none of the theories surveyed in this introduction do justice to the complex reality of Mexico City. The city does not live in the past—as Gruzinski, Kandell, and Tovar de Teresa suggest—but very much in the present, and although parts of the capital, like Santa Fé, correspond to the model of "generic cities" developed by Koolhaas, many others do not; the streets are alive, especially in downtown neighborhoods, and their energy approximates the "modernism on the streets" which Berman located in Baudelaire's Paris and Pushkin's Petersburg. But Mexico City's streets inspire something which not even Berman's essay considered: a penchant for transforming traumatic events like AIDS and political corruption into complex symbolic narratives.

How, then, should we theorize Mexico City? Jorge Ibargüengoitia suggested an ingenious solution in a book titled *Theory and Practice of Mexico City:* the only way to theorize Mexico City is to *practice* it by exploring its streets and neighborhoods. (Salvador Novo reached the same conclusion: in *Nueva grandeza mexicana* he refers to his *flâneries* as a "practice" of the city.) And the best way to explore the city is to write about it, as Ibargüengoitia and many other writers did regularly for newspapers and magazines. Following Ibargüengoitia's model, the writers included in *The Mexico City Reader* are expert theorists precisely because they are seasoned practitioners of the city. The texts collected in this anthology are among the most striking examples of this concomitant "theory and practice" of Mexico City, that most delirious of megalopolises.

Notes

1. The most complete anthology of texts—including poems, novels, and essays—devoted to Mexico City from pre-Columbian times to the 1970s is *Páginas sobre la Ciudad de México,* edited by Emmanuel Carballo and José Luis Martínez.

2. Néstor García Canclini, who has written extensively about the population statistics of Mexico City, has discussed its growth in population from about 1.65 million in 1940 to over 18 million in 1997 and in area from 3.5 square miles to 1900 to over 579 square miles today. García Canclini, *Cultura y comunicación,* 1:15. His sobering statistics on crime include "cada día 10 manifestaciones y 2 asaltos bancarios; por sus calles, 25,000 mendigos y 15,000 prostitutas" ["every day 10 street protests and 2 bank robberies; 25,000 beggars and 15,000 on the street."] (2:20).

3. Kandell, *La capital,* 8.

4. Gruzinski writes: "Depuis près de cinq siècles, Mexico décline une histoire qui, pour le meilleur et pour le pire, associe l'Occident et l'Amérique indienne, l'Étranger et l'Autochtone, le Soi avec l'Autre. Voilà pourquoi Mexico métis—où résonnent les tambours teponaztl, les opéras baroques et les orchestres de rock—est l'antidote de notre fin de siècle. Au moins, mon antidote." ["For almost five centuries, Mexico City has lived a history that, for better and for worse, brings together Western and indigenous cultures, foreigners and natives, self and other. This is why mixed-blood Mexico—where *teponaztl* drums sound alongside baroque operas and rock bands—is the antidote to this *fin de siècle.* At least my antidote."] *Histoire de Mexico,* 408.

5. Tovar de Teresa, *City of Palaces,* 14.

6. Novo writes: "las ciudades, como los hombres que las forman y habitan, se enfrentan por escapable determinismo a un incómodo dilema: o la cripta honorable o la vida imprevisible: o la momia o el hombre: o el museo o la urbe: razones que se van ejerciendo en el curso del tiempo y del espacio para alejar al hombre y a las ciudades de la muerte, a costa de irlas despojando de cuanto pueda congelarlas con su hálito y al precio de irles imprimiendo los moldes de una adaptación imprescindible a su supervivencia, y por ella condicionada. Desde Tenochtitlán . . . y a diferencia de Teotihuacan . . . ha sido el destino de México sobrevivir a costa de transformarse. El empeño, por los visto, vale la pena." ["Cities and their inhabitants are faced with an uncomfortable dilemma: either honorable tomb or unpredictable life; either mummies or people; either museum or metropolis. Throughout history and around the world, these reasons have saved men and their cities from death by freeing them from whatever might congeal them in time, at the price of stamping them with the traces of the adaptations necessary for their survival. Since Tenochtitlan—and unlike Teotihuacan—this has been the destiny of Mexico City: to survive by transforming itself. The effort, it seems, is worth while."] *Nueva grandeza mexicana*, 121.

7. Ibid., 17.

8. Koolhaas, *S, M, L, XL*, 1249–50.

9. Ibid., 1248.

10. Ibid., 1248.

11. Ibid., 1105.

12. Ibid., 1253.

13. Ibid., 1011.

14. Ibid., 1253.

15. Ibid., 1251.

16. Ibid., 1250.

17. Berman, *All That Is Solid*, 6–7.

18. Ibid., 165.

19. Poniatowska, *La noche de Tlatelolco*, 279.

20. Berman, *All That Is Solid*, 165.

21. The 1968 student massacre at Tlatelolco was made possible to a great extent by Corbusier-inspired urban planning. The Nonoalco-Tlatelolco housing complex surrounding the square was built by Mario Pani, an admiring disciple of Le Corbusier, as a collection of modernist apartment blocks. Modernist architecture is designed to control people, their movements, and their living quarters—a fact that was made abundantly clear when the army closed all access points to the Tlatelolco complex, leaving the student demonstrators trapped in the plaza and facilitating their massacre.

22. In real life, Superbarrio showed a penchant for transforming traumatic events into narratives. When asked about the origins of his social activism, he offered the following account: "Un día, el 12 de junio de 1987, como a las siete

y media de la mañana cuando abrí la puerta de la casa para salir a trabajar, entró a mi cuarto una luz roja y amarilla muy intensa que no me permitía ver, y un viento que revolvió todo lo que tengo en la vivienda. Cuando esto se calmó, cuando la luz desapareció y el viento dejó de soplar, yo estaba con la máscara y con la ropa de Superbarrio y una voz me dijo: Tú eres Superbarrio, defensor de los inquilinos pobres y azote de los caseros voraces." ["One day, on June 12, 1987, around 7:30 A.M., when I opened the door to leave for work, there came into the room a bright, red and yellow light that blinded me, and a gust of wind that scattered all my things. When the wind stopped and the light dimmed, I found myself wearing Superbarrio's mask and outfit, and a voice said to me: 'You are Superbarrio, defender of poor tenants and nemesis of greedy landlords.'"] Cuéllar Vázquez, *La noche es de ustedes*, 77.

23. On the history of chupacabras sightings, see Julia Preston, "In the Tradition of Bigfoot and Elvis, the Goatsucker," *New York Times*, Sunday, June 2, 1996, sec. 4.

24. Even Carlos Monsiváis took part in the debate about Salinas and the *chupacabras*. In an interview, he told Elena Poniatowska that "the *chupacabras* . . . vanished as soon as they associated it with Salinas. It couldn't stand the comparison." Elena Poniatowska, "Los pecados de Carlos Monsiváis," *La jornada semanal*, Feb. 23, 1997. See also Vicente Razo's *The Official Mujeo Salinas Guide*.

25. See, for example, the photographs of political protests during the 1990s included in Francisco Cruces' "El ritual de la protesta." The photos show political activists dressed up as Salinas, enchained or riding in a makeshift cage through the streets of Mexico City. Cruces comments: "Carlos Salinas encadenado. Carlos Salinas entre rejas. Juicio popular contra el ex presidente. Latigazos a Carlos Salinas. Carlos Salinas con la horca al cuello . . . La imagen es recurrente y forma parte del folclor de la protesta. ¿Revancha simbólica o chivo expiatorio?" ["Carlos Salinas in chains. Carlos Salinas behind bars. A people's trial of Carlos Salinas. Carlos Salinas whipped to death. Carlos Salinas with a noose around his neck . . . The image recurs and forms part of protest folklore. Is this a symbolic revenge or has the ex-president become a scapegoat?"] García Canclini, *Cultura y comunicación*, 2:64.

26. None of the texts included in this anthology deal expressly with the Tlatelolco massacre, but its violent aura hangs over many of them. For the most comprehensive journalistic account of the student massacre, see Poniatowska, *La noche de Tlatelolco*.

27. García Canclini, *Cultura y comunicación*, 2:15.

28. Salvador Novo, for example, celebrated the Mexico City of 1947 with a mixture of pride and wonder, proclaiming that "it has come of age as a city." . . . "México ha alcanzado ya una mayoría de edad urbana que le depara sitio honorable entre las capitales cosmopolitas . . . del sueño y del trabajo de todos esos hombres, ejercidos en el valle más hermoso del mundo, está labrada la

grandeza de la Ciudad de México." ["Mexico City has reached the urban legal age that guarantees it a place among the world's cosmopolitan capitals . . . the greatness of Mexico City is made of the dreams and the labor of all these men, in the most beautiful valley in the world."] Novo, *Nueva grandeza mexicana*, 127.

29. I can think of only one book of crónicas that has been translated into English: Carlos Monsiváis's *Mexican Postcards* (New York: Verso, 1997). Ignacio Corona and Beth E. Jörgensen recently published a study of the "crónica" as a genre, *The Contemporary Mexican Chronicle*.

30. García Canclini, for example, has written, "De la ciudad histórica de tantos siglos hemos pasado en los últimos cincuenta años a vivir en una metrópoli policéntrica, desarticulada, en la que resulta impensable alcanzar una visión de conjunto." ["In the last fifty years we have gone from a centuries-old historical city to a polymorphous and disarticulated metropolis, which can never be seen as a coherent whole."] García Canclini, *La ciudad de los viajeros*, 22. And in his essay on the Mexico City subway (included in the "Metro" section in this anthology), Juan Villoro writes that Tokyo and Mexico City are "cities so ungraspable that their writers must renounce the project of painting an all-encompassing fresco. Since critics cannot treat the city as an external landscape, they must operate from within its boundaries."

1

Mexico City on Paper

Mexico, City of Paper

GONZALO CELORIO

The blank page, peopled little by little with buildings, windows, corridors.

Vicente Quirarte

My house—or your house, as Mexican politeness calls it, to the bewilderment of foreign visitors—is tucked into one of the starched crinoline folds of the Ajusco hills, in a village graced by the name of San Nicolás and surnamed Totolapan in deference to turkeys. To reach this village, which is lodged high up, you set off along Avenida del Hospital Ángeles; then go through the Fuentes del Pedregal development, and follow Matamoros Street until you reach a cemetery beside the railway track. Then it's Calzada de la Soledad as far as a second graveyard, whose headstones, always garlanded with flowers, stick up over the wall. Take a right there, pass an altar devoted to the Virgin of Guadalupe perched in the branches of a mesquite tree, and, just before reaching the bend where a battered cross for Indian prayer meetings still stands, turn left and mount a steep, pot-holed little lane that rejoices in the daunting name of Progreso. This is what it takes to get to my house in San Nicolás Totolapan.

The village, belonging of course to the Federal District and more particularly to the Magdalena Contreras jurisdiction, marks the southeastern limit of Mexico City. There are two windows in my bedroom:

one looks out, though not for much longer I suspect, over a mountain-side combed with magueys and backed by a blue sky that still dresses in stars to come out at night; the other looks northwest, as my big study window also does, and through it I can see the whole of Mexico City, buried under a lather of miasmas. Between here and the few mangy hills—spiked with telecommunications antennae—which have not yet been overrun by housing, the city's tallest buildings stand out against the gray cyclorama of a landscape dulled by the black smoke of factories drifting evilly into the sky.

At night, the view is different. The city seems to have recovered its ancient wateriness: the whole valley of Mexico has become a lake of rippling lights. I don't know why, but the lights twinkle ceaselessly, as though they were breathing, or shifting, like countless tiny skiffs on an inland sea.

It was from equally high up, from the dip between the volcanoes—now obliterated—that the Spaniards first laid eyes on the then-bright valley of Anahuac and the prodigy of an amphibian city, built on the lake and around its shores. The arrow-straight causeways; the "water streets," as Bartolomé de Las Casas called them in hallucinatory comparison with Venice, the supremely fantastical city; the masonried strongholds; the towering temples; the ornate palaces; the plain stone houses; a constellation of forty settlements, which thus contemplated from the heights led the Dominican to wonder if there could exist any "sight gayer and more gracious in all the world."

This peerless vision, as it was afforded to the first Spaniards to reach these lands, was wiped out by the Spaniards themselves. In order to break the Aztecs, Hernán Cortés besieged and destroyed the great Tenochtitlán. From that time on, the city of Mexico became the unwitting embodiment of the myth of Coyolxauqui, she who paints her cheeks with bells, and was hurled from the top of the temple by her brother Huitzilopochtli, the boy warrior, he who acts on high, and lay broken and dismembered at the foot of the temple battens. It is grimly significant that the giant monolith of the Templo Mayor, such part of it as survived the devastation of Cortés's troops, should be precisely and paradoxically the image of destruction, as though our sole permanence lay in the constancy of our annihilation.

More than time, which has altered and corrupted it; more than nature, which has swamped, flooded, and shaken it; more than any other cause, it is the negligence of men that has ruthlessly wrecked the city of their forbears.

The history of Mexico City is the story of its successive destructions. Just as the colonial city overlaid the pre-Columbian city, so did the edifications of Mexican independence supplant those of the viceroyalty, and so did the postrevolutionary capital, which continues to mushroom today, erase the nineteenth- and early twentieth-century city—as though culture were not a business of accumulation so much as of displacement.

Like the invisible cities of Italo Calvino, Mexico is an imaginary place whose history must be divined rather than observed: "The city . . . does not tell its past, but contains it like the lines of a hand, written in the corners of streets, the gratings of windows, the banisters of the steps, the antennae of the lightning rods, the poles of the flags, every segment marked in turn with scratches, indentations, scrolls."[1]

On the site of so many cities revoked: a crumbling pyramid with nothing to show but its own excavated nakedness, the lopsided columns of an early church, a cloister held up by a pastry shop, a monastery doubling as a self-service store, a Churrigueresque arcade with no pilgrims to protect, a neoclassical façade that moved house, a church half-buried by an expressway and another actually bent sideways by Avenida 20 de Noviembre, a slender Porfirian residence crushed between two skyscrapers of blinding glass.

And yet the bygone glories of the city of Mexico live on, in the voices of those who sang them with delicate lyricism when here was "the most transparent region of the air"; those who described the city with all the amazement of recent arrivals from across the sea, or found the Latin words that might give it a place among the wonders of the world; those who magnified it with artful hyperbole and those who scientifically broke it down; those who set it free in civic oratory and fearless journalism, and those who immortalized its ways and tales; those who even now are busy recording, defining, inventing, and otherwise saving it from destruction by the offices of the written word. In short, the voices that raised it up, letter by letter, in the enduring reality of literature. Ours is a city of paper.

The great Tenochtitlán survives in the accounts of many friars who applied themselves, with scientific meticulousness, to consigning the history and culture of indigenous societies; it can also be glimpsed through the writings of the soldier-chroniclers who wielded (as Alonso de Ercilla says in his epic poem *La araucana*) now the sword, now the pen, and laced the reality they were experiencing with all the feverish imaginings that colored European notions of the unknown West. Providing a bridge between the literature of chivalry and the chronicles of conquest, Bernal Díaz del Castillo recalls his first sight of the Anahuac valley:

> Y desde que vimos tantas ciudades y villas pobladas en el agua, y en tierra firme otras grandes poblazones, y aquella calzada tan derecha y por nivel como iba a México, nos quedamos admirados y decíamos que parecía a las cosas de encantamiento que se cuentan en el libro de Amadís, por las grandes torres y cúes y edificios que tenían dentro el agua, y todos de calicanto, y aun algunos de nuestros soldados decían que si aquello que veían, si era entre sueños, y no es de maravillar que yo escriba aquí de esta manera, porque hay mucho de ponderar en ello que no sé cómo lo cuente: ver cosas nunca oídas, ni aun soñadas como veíamos.[2]

> [And when we saw so many cities and villages built in the water and other great towns on dry land and that straight and level causeway going toward Mexico, we were amazed and said that it was like the enchantments they tell of in the legend of Amadís, on account of the great towers and cués [temples] and buildings rising from the water, and all built of masonry. And some of our soldiers even asked whether the things that we saw were not a dream. It is not to be wondered at that I here write it down in this manner, for there is so much to think over that I do not know how to describe it, seeing things as we did that had never been heard of or seen before, nor even dreamed about.][3]

And even Cortés, normally sparing of admiration toward anything other than the glories of his own enterprise, is unable to contain his astonishment at the Indian metropolis, whose beauty he compares to that of Granada, whilst only Córdoba and Seville can rival it for size. Lost for words, he throws his hands up: "The city is so vast and so full of wonders, that though much indeed could truthfully be said about it, I reckon that even what little I say will beggar belief."[4]

Sure enough, Tenochtitlán was a most improbable city, one that seemed to spring from poetic imagination rather than from reality. A settlement founded by men but governed and sustained by the god Huitzilopochtli, as the poet-king Nezahualcóyotl reminds us, with a rare mixture of pride and humility:

> Flores de luz erguidas abren sus corolas
> donde se tiende el musgo acuático, aquí en México
> plácidamente están ensanchándose,
> y en medio del musgo y de los matices
> está tendida la ciudad de Tenochtitlán:

la extiende y la hace florecer el dios:
tiene sus ojos fijos en sitios como éste,
los tiene fijos en medio del lago.

. . . .

A ti, Nezahualcóyotl, y a ti, Moteuczomatzin,
os ha creado el que da la vida,
os ha creado el dios en medio de la laguna.

[Tall flowers of light open their buds
here, where the water-moss spreads, in Mexico,
quietly they unfold,
and amid the moss and the colors
it unfolds, the city of Tenochtitlán:
The god spreads it forth, he makes it blossom:
His eyes are steady on this place,
He looks steadily at the middle of the lake.

. . . .

You, Nezahualcóyotl, and you, Moteuczomatzin,
you were created by the one who gives life,
you were created by the god in the middle of the lake.][5]

This is the only explanation for the way the great city was founded in the center of a briny lagoon, on a site of expulsion and persecution. When the Mexicans arrived at the Valley of Mexico, after centuries of wandering, they were not exactly welcome. The established residents rose against them, and if they were able to maintain a presence at all in such conditions, it was by dint of making war and developing a contempt for death, as the *Annals of Tlatelolco* record. From Chapultepec they were pushed out to Tizapán, where they fed on serpents until they were once more dislodged and beaten back into the water, among marshes, forced to lie low in the bulrushes. This is the point at which Huitzolopochtli formulates his transcendental design, preserved in *La crónica mexicáyotl* as the stunning moment of turnaround in the Aztec epic: he determines to build a city on an island in the middle of the lake, the position from which his people are destined to subjugate their enemies. "With arrow and shield we shall confront the foes surrounding us, and all of them shall be conquered and captured, because there shall our city be, Mexico, at the place where the eagle cries, deploys himself and eats, the place where the fish swims and the serpent is torn."[6] Only because of their fanaticism and indifference to suffering did the Aztecs succeed in implanting and expanding a great center that grew, over the years, into the Mexico-Tenochtitlán encountered by the conquistadors. A center crisscrossed by canals and tethered to the shore by long, broad causeways, enlarged by the use of canoes—a device that postponed the use of the wheel—and sustained by the agricultural marvels known as *chinampas*, floating gardens, like their hanging counterparts in Babylon. Earth and water: it was a city that harbored nature, rather than exclude it. It ranged from an imposing ceremonial complex, where the great *teocalli* towered above palaces and lesser temples to host the ritual sacrifices to Huitzilopochtli and Tláloc, to the orchards and gardens that cultivated an abundance of flowers and vegetables. A city encapsulated in the line by Carlos Pellicer, which so tersely portrays the ancient Mexican soul: "a taste for death and a love of flowers."

Prompted by the learned imagination of Alfonso Reyes, I see an essentially diurnal city, all order, space, and light between crystal-clear of water and air; a peaceful city, notwithstanding the bloodthirsty rituals performed by its inhabitants, whose culture wedded war with flowers for the sake of the sustenance of the gods and the perpetuation of the world.

> Allí, donde se tiñen los dardos, donde se tiñen los escudos,
> están las blancas flores perfumadas, las flores del corazón:
> abren sus corolas las flores del que da la vida,
> cuyo perfume aspiran en el mundo los príncipes de Tenochtitlán.[7]

> [There, where arrows are stained red, where shields are stained,
> stand the white scented flowers, the heart's blossoms;
> the flowers of the life-giver open out,
> their scent to be inhaled by princes in the world: it is Tenochtitlán.]

Cortés justified his razing of the Aztec capital as an unavoidable military strategy to ensure victory:

> Y yo, viendo que . . . había ya más de cuarenta y cinco días que estábamos en el cerco, acordé de tomar un medio para nuestra seguridad y para poder estrechar más a los enemigos, y fue que como fuésemos ganando por las calles de la ciudad, que fuesen derrocando todas las casas de ellas del un cabo y del otro, por manera que no fuésemos un paso adelante sin lo dejar todo asolado.[8]

> [Seeing that the affair was continuing in this way, and that we had been besieging the city for more than forty-five days, I decided to take steps to ensure our greater safety and to place the enemy in further difficulties; my plan was to raze to the ground all the houses on both sides of

the street along which we advanced, so that we should move not a step without leaving everything behind us in ruins.][9]

And yet, beneath the writer's intentions, the detailed, lengthy account of the siege of Tenochtitlán provided by Cortés conveys a passion of outrage, rising not only against the violence of the historical events but also, and more damningly, against the man responsible both for the account and for the thing it tells. We do not need to read the precious testimonies of Sahagún's informants or of the authors of the *Annals of Tlatelolco* in order to sense the anguish, the utter extremity, of the conquest; it is enough to see Cortés's "Third Letter" to Charles V. No words can mend the "net of holes" through which the pride of a trampled people bled away, a people which at that precise moment (if I may be allowed a detour of connotation) ceased to be Aztec and became Nahuatl only. After the conquest, these terms expressing a specific difference and a broader genus, *azteca* and *náhuatl*, began to split apart to the point of antinomy: the first evokes death and the empire that ruthlessly reduced neighboring groups to vassalage; the second is redolent of life and culture, philosophy and lyric verse. The word "Aztec" designates the victors of insatiable sacrificial wars; the word "Nahuatl" belongs to the vanquished. One is the sound of battle, the other of song. One is an obsidian dagger, the other a flower.

The coarse thunder of conquest—the yells of the soldiers calling on their patron Santiago, a Saint James who had traded his apostolic pilgrim's robes for breastplate and sword during the Spanish campaigns of reconquest and was now upgrading his nickname of Santiago Matamoros, the Moor Slayer, to that of Santiago Mataindios, the Indian Slayer; the exploding powder of muskets and cannons, the clangor of armor, the neighing of horses—silenced the indigenous voice, that slight, musical, twittering tongue, strung between a hum and a whisper; a speech that, in Alfonso Reyes's words, "runs from the lips of the Indian soft and sweet as maguey juice."

As the earliest token of their subjection to Spanish rule, the Mexicans were forced to carry out the agonizing destruction of their own city—first, under pressure from the blockade within which they were confined by their attackers, and later urged on by the lashes of foremen and the blandishments of pioneer friars. And once the old town had been demolished, it was they who had to construct the new one upon the rubble of Mexico-Tenochtitlán.

In the same way that the Castilian language ultimately asserted itself over the Nahuatl, so too the Spanish city overlaid the indigenous one, and while the Spaniards *castilianized* the Indians they did the same to their physical environment. But just as many Nahuatl terms crept across into Spanish and enriched it (even if these were mostly nouns, referring to external reality without transmitting the complexities of culture), it also happened that many blocks from the torn-down temples and palaces came to be recycled, in a similarly substantive mode, into the structures of a new city tuned to a different worldview and expressive of a different syntax. There is no better image of this phenomenon than the main church, a prefiguration of the cathedral, erected over the foundations of the Temple of the Sun with the same stones that had gone to build the great teocalli of Tenochtitlán—hewn down to the octagonal shape of medieval bases, but still incised with the striations of plumed serpents.

The first colonial city was half medieval, in the image and likeness of the towns preserved in the emigrants' memory, and half Renaissance, in keeping with the modernity triggered by the irruption of the New World into European culture—Renaissance in the reticular layout that was wonderfully compatible with the pre-Columbian grid; medieval in its earliest buildings, heavily fortified and studded with battlements, turrets, and moats.

In his "Third Letter," dated 1522, Cortés informed the emperor:

> De cuatro o cinco meses acá, que la dicha ciudad de Temixtian se va reparando, está muy hermosa y crea vuestra majestad que cada día se irá ennobleciendo en tal manera, que como antes fue principal y señora de todas esas provincias, que lo será también de aquí en adelante; y se hace y se hará de tal manera que los españoles estén muy fuertes y seguros y muy señores de los naturales, de manera que de ellos en ninguna forma puedan ser ofendidos.[10]

> [In the four or five months we have been rebuilding the city it is already most beautiful, and I assure you Your Majesty that each day it grows more noble, so that just as before it was the capital and center of all these provinces so shall it be henceforth. And it is being built so that the Spaniards will be strong and secure and well in charge of the natives, who will be unable to harm them in any way.][11]

Soon after, we find the following stipulation in the section of the *Laws of the Indies* devoted to colonial buildings: "When these are seen by the

Indians, they should move them to awe, and make them understand that the Spaniards have come here to stay, and incite fear and respect toward them, courting their amity and shrinking from offence." As though the builders had not been the Indians themselves.

The Spaniards, then, grounded their impunity and impregnability upon the consolidation of the city. Needless to say, this was not only a question of their physical safety as military conquerors; it also bore on their moral legitimacy as spiritual conquerors. The city built by Cortés was an allegory of the stability that was ardently desired, once the phase of adventure had served its purpose. It was a stratified, hierarchical, compartmented place. The center. The viceroy's palace. The high church. The archbishopric. The chapter houses. The four districts assigned to the natives, piously sanctified: San Pablo Teopan, San Sebastián Atzacualco, San Juan Moyotla, Santa María Cuepopan. Indians from here to there, Spaniards from there to here. The monasteries of the different orders: Franciscans, Augustinians, Mercedarians, Jesuits. Separate schools for Indians, half-breeds, and *criollos*. The two universities, one royal, the other pontifical. The jail. The market.

In his "Latin dialogues," intended less as an exercise in the language of Virgil than one to preserve, albeit in words alone, the sixteenth-century city, Francisco Cervantes de Salazar evokes the splendor of the buildings safeguarding colonial institutions. His well-drawn characters—a pair of criollos and a recent arrival from the peninsula— tour the city and its environs, an experience that sends the visitor into ecstasies at the beauty and grandeur of the capital of New Spain, which invariably comes out on top in the comparisons he makes with Spanish towns. Possibly owing to the Toledan origins of the celebrated humanist, he evinces a pride in the viceroyal city that was not always shared by the criollos. Human nature being what it is, the Spaniards born here nursed a certain nostalgia for the metropolitan delights they knew of only through the yarns of their elders, whereas newcomers from Spain had no hesitation in recognizing the majestic beauties of this town.

Many and proficient were the Spanish poets who came to seek their fortunes here. Dazzled by the reputation of the viceroyal city, they made sure to build it up further with panegyrics of their own invention. Such was Eugenio de Salazar, from Madrid, who regales us among other things with a vivid description of the woods of Chapultepec and of the lagoon; one memorable passage has no less a personage than Neptune surfacing there, on the back of a prodigious whale.

Half a century after Cervantes de Salazar paid tribute to the capital of New Spain, the great verbal architect from La Mancha, Bernardo de Balbuena, sang its praises in *Grandeza mexicana*. The poet moved to Mexico in time to witness the transformation of the city of conquistadors into a city of settlers:

> Toda ella en llamas de belleza se arde,
> y se va como fénix renovando;

> [All here in flames of beauty is consumed
> and, phoenix-like, renews itself afresh]

This place is no longer reminiscent of the "enchantments we have read of in the book of Amadís," as it was for Bernal Díaz; now it is "the seat of famed Mexico."

> Oh ciudad bella, pueblo cortesano,
> primor del mundo, traza peregrina,
> grandeza ilustre, lustre soberano;

> fénix de galas, de riquezas mina,
> museo de ciencias y de ingenios fuente,
> jardín de Venus, dulce golosina;

> del placer madre, piélago de gente,
> de joyas cofre, erario de tesoro,
> flor de ciudades, Gloria del Poniente[12]

> [O handsome city, courtly abode,
> world's gem, of rarest design,
> illustrious grandeur, sovereign beacon,

> phoenix in finery, of riches a mine;
> cradle of sciences, fount of invention,
> garden of Venus, morsel of sweetness,

> mother of pleasures and ocean of souls,
> bed of bright jewels, of treasures exchequer,
> fair flower of cities, the West's glory bold]

Although the chroniclers express a more genuine feeling for the New World than the poets do, none can match Balbuena's passion for the colonial center, or his extravagant, raving grandiloquence. That said, the heightened pitch of *Grandeza mexicana* may not be wholly unwarranted if we consider that it concerned an equally hyperbolic city, just beginning to be remade and enriched by the art of the baroque. Here

was an environment of fabulous architectural opulence, its grand plazas
and streets teeming with luxurious carriages—"altars on wheels," Fernando Benítez termed them—and prancing horses; lavish with religious
and civil ceremonies, outstanding in the arts and complex in its crafts
and trades, expressing its festive spirit through processions, indigenous
mitotes and countless other "opportunities for good cheer." The city was
also dramatically baroque in its contrasts, an aspect which Balbuena's
eulogies preferred to overlook: at once magnificent and miserable, radi-
ant and obscure, sonorous and silent. Insulated by the color of their
skins and the eloquent terminology of their clothing, the colonial lords
passed one another in the everyday bustle of the main square, the market, or the crowded canals, as well as in the pomp of viceroyal or ecclesiastical celebrations. But if criollos, mestizos, Indians, blacks, and mu-
lattos kept a seemly distance from one another by day, they were liable
to make up for it by night when they mingled with the wildest abandon.

A late seventeenth-century painting by Cristóbal de Villalpando, or
a painting by Rodríguez Juárez from the second half of the eighteenth
century, provides a meticulous record of the seething human throng
that was Mexico City during the baroque period—similar to the witty
and erudite recreations that Artemio de Valle Arizpe or Luis González
Obregón made years later. Through a kind of miraculous synesthesia,
these paintings convey the sonority of the main square. The polyphonic
voice of a city in which Nahuatl and Spanish still prospered side by side:
one subordinate, speaking softly, and the other dominant, speaking
loudly, yet becoming ever more restrained, courtly, and refined, as Balbuena himself noted when he wrote that it is in criollo society

> donde se habla el español lenguaje
> más puro y con mayor cortesanía,
> vestido en un bellísimo ropaje
> que le da propiedad, gracia, agudeza,
> en casto, limpio, liso y grave traje.
>
> [that our Spanish tongue is spoken
> most purely and with the most grace,
> in a wondrous robe that betokens
> felicity, pleasantry and jest
> in a dress yet so sober, smooth, grave and chaste.]

The clatter of horse-drawn coaches; the hubbub of the market trading
in vegetables, fruit, fish, textiles, household goods, tools of all kinds; the

curses of the mule drivers. The wordy scholastic disputes of university students; the supplicant orations of blind beggars; the viceroyal edicts proclaimed through the streets; the preachers; the chorus of cattle, pigs, and sheep; the hawkers; the street brawls; the murmur of prayers; the braying of mules; the tolling, the ringing, the pealing, the clangor of bells. A cacophony barely interrupted by the passage of the viaticum or the curfew, which plunged the city into a night traversed by legends of apparitions and vanishings: the Weeping Woman, don Juan Manuel, the Mulatta of Cordoba.

Through the fiesta, the capital of New Spain exorcised the tedium imposed by its colonial status and its remoteness from the metropolis. There were endless jamborees, held to celebrate the high points of the liturgical calendar—which were legion—or civil and political occasions such as the arrival of a new viceroy or archbishop. Bullfights, re-enactments of naval battles—for the battles that wore down the great Tenochtitlán had also been naval, though no one would guess it today—cockfights, masques, banquets, fireworks. In the midst of these or as part of them, poetry contests took place in circumstances of great pomp and fanfare, although, unfortunately for poets, with strict rules prescribing the subjects, allegorical associations, and metric forms to which candidates were expected to restrict themselves, as if the poetic imagination were on the side of the judges and not of the poets. Thus hobbled, these found themselves either with nothing to say or helpless to say it.

Perhaps nothing reflects baroque Mexico in all its bombastic ephemerality better than the triumphal arches that sprang up to welcome viceroys and archbishops. In the design of these structures, likewise thrown open to competition, poetic conceit took precedence over architectural issues, and painters, sculptors, and craftsmen were in thrall to the writer's intentions. For the reception of the Marquis of La Laguna, Sor Juana Inés de la Cruz wrote her *Neptuno alegórico,* and an arch was put up over one of the cathedral doors. True to the text, the arch linked the viceroy's surname to the lake in which the city was founded, and depicted the classical god of the waters as its governing symbol. Carlos de Sigüenza y Góngora, for his part, who counted among his many skills a familiarity with pre-Columbian culture and the genealogy of its kings, exalted the god Huitzilopochtli along with eleven Aztec emperors in the arch that accompanied his *Teatro de virtudes políticas* on the occasion of the viceroy's entrance into Santo Domingo Square. He could hardly know that with the daring tenor of such a welcome, he was prefiguring the political and cultural emancipation of Mexico from the rule of the Spanish metropolis.

The baroque, as an early sign of our complicated national identity, altered the nature of Cortés's city by adding a decorative profusion which cannot be dismissed as a mere variation on classical paradigms; rather, it sums up the essence of the city's aesthetic, since for baroque art, the mask is a more telling countenance than the face. Such ornamentation coated the severity imposed by Philip II and designed by Juan de Herrera with a frosting of composites, excesses, and trifles. Aware of the transitory nature of life and work, it altered, if not destroyed, the preexistent spaces over which it brushed its artifice, and rendered them equally transitory. The few remaining traces of the sixteenth-century city are so tattered and mutilated as to speak of a past that is hopelessly lost. And neoclassicism, which had taken hold in Spain following the accession of the Bourbon dynasty, finally asserted itself here as well, though it did so in alternation—or rather, in conflict—with the baroque, which continued to thrive in Spanish America until well into the eighteenth century; and though transplanted to these shores as an art of the counter-reformation, it rapidly turned into an art of counter-conquest, as José Lezama Lima recognized:

> El barroco como estilo ha logrado ya en la América del siglo XVIII, el pacto de la familia del indio Kondori y el triunfo prodigioso del Aleijandinho, que prepara ya la rebelión del próximo siglo, es la prueba de que se está maduro ya para una ruptura. He ahí la prueba más decisiva, cuando un esforzado de la forma recibe un estilo de una gran tradición, y lejos de amenguarlo, lo devuelve acrecido, es un símbolo de que ese país ha alcanzado su forma en el arte de la ciudad.[13]

> [In eighteenth-century America, the baroque style achieved the family pact of the Kondori Indian, while the prodigious triumph of the Aleijandinho—preparing the ground for the following century's rebellion—was evidence that times were ripe for a break. And the most decisive proof is this: when a champion of form receives a style from a great tradition, and far from diluting it, returns it enhanced, it is a symbol of how that country has attained its form in the art of the city.]

Neoclassicism tamed baroque ostentation by liquidating, wherever possible, the features which its aseptic eye deemed most tasteless and, in the name of allegedly universal models, quashing the liveliest élans of an art that was exuberant to the point of insanity and quirky to the point of independence. Except for the ceaselessly overhauled National Palace, with its "child's or thimble stature," in one poet's description, nothing remains of seventeenth century lay architecture. The entire population relocated during the eighteenth century, parishes were rebuilt, and no more than a sigh remains of many cloisters, churches, and convents.

Nevertheless, it was during that century, as José Luis Martínez observes, that the colonial city reached the peak of its splendor, thanks to the impetus given by the Bourbons to public works. Under viceroys Bucareli and Revillagigedo, the baroque city—which had tried to sweep its dirt away behind the pageantry, the parades, and the masques, but was horribly plagued by foul gutters, flooding, quagmires, and excrement-clogged streets that served not only for human transit but also as cow pens and pig sties—was transformed into a civilized place, gleaming with cultural institutions, public services (including lighting, post offices, communal water fountains, sewage systems, and baths), broad avenues, decorative monuments, and plaques bearing street names and house numbers.

This version of the city, as ostentatious as its predecessors but more coherent and modern, was relatively neglected by the neoclassical literature of the eighteenth century, which preferred to marshal its impeccable hexameters for singing the praises of the Mexican countryside, where Greco-Roman goddesses strolled among prickly pears and magueys like characters in the books of the enlightened travelers of the early nineteenth century, who called the capital "the city of palaces." Its imposing size, the efficiency of its layout, the magnificence of its buildings, and the wealth of nature surrounding it charmed Baron Alexander von Humboldt into thinking that "this must surely be counted among the loveliest cities founded by the Europeans in either hemisphere."

In the wake of independence, the viceroyal period was regarded as an obscurantist dark age. Nationalism looked back to the pre-Columbian era, attributing classical status to it—much as the Renaissance had disowned its medieval past to invoke the values of Greek and Roman antiquity. Thus many eighteenth-century buildings began to exhibit a republican appearance, whilst the pre-Colombian ruins that were so much to the taste of the Romantic spirit were rehabilitated in the impregnable realm of lithography.

Like its predecessors, the nineteenth-century city was first and foremost a moral space, desired to be as well kept and dignified as a personal home. *The Itching Parrot,* by Joaquín Fernández de Lizardi, was the inaugural novel of our continent and, as such, constituted an unmistakable sign of independence. It is a high-minded, sermonizing portrait of Mexico City that attempts to draw in all of its inhabitants, from the loftiest to the humblest, as their age-old vices were condemned by virtues destined to prevail in the new homeland.

With the advent of ecclesiastical reform, the city was cleft by a profound dilemma: to preserve the past or to build the future; to maintain the old monasteries that stood for the fanaticism of colonial times or to demolish them, however regretfully, in order to prevent them from being reoccupied by religious groups. The rallying cries of liberal poets such as Guillermo Prieto and Ignacio Ramírez were as effective as the picks that brought churches and convents tumbling down, as hard as the cornerstones of the buildings raised to accommodate civilian institutions. Where there was prayer, now there is thought, said Ramírez. And the aisle of the former church of San Agustín, converted into a library at the instigation of Benito Juárez to store the books expropriated from the religious orders, was now lined, in place of the Christian saints, with statues of Confucius, Aristotle, Origen, and Descartes, worshipping in secular devotion the eagle of the national shield, poised beneath the apse.

Once the republic had been restored after Maximilian's imperial adventure, the city advanced in the direction of science and progress. This was the city of Vicente Riva Palacio, who studied the archives of the Inquisition in order to write novels narrating the colonial era's dark days; of Guillermo Prieto, whose rough and ready muse rejoiced at the departure of the French; of José Tomás de Cuéllar, who described urban mores with exemplary critical acumen. It is the city of the telegraph and the daguerreotype, under dim turpentine lights that begged assistance from the radiance of the mind, as Ignacio Manuel Altamirano had demanded in his anticlerical verses:

> Ilumínate más, ciudad maldita,
> ilumina tus puertas y ventanas;
> ilumínate más, luz necesita
> el partido sin luz de las sotanas.

> [More light, more light, accursed town,
> to brighten your windows and doors;
> more light, for light is needed to pour
> over the dark factions of the soutane.]

Embracing Ruben Darío's dictum that "art is blue and comes from France," the Porfiriato introduced French models into Mexico City which supplanted the architectural tradition of the colonial period. In many cases marble replaced the *chiluca* stone that had itself, under neo-classicism, displaced the older *tezontle*—a spongy, purplish material, like volcanic foam, that had lent such character to Mexican architecture that it had been described as "stone steeped in blood," by the poet Solís Aguirre. Porfirio Díaz presided over the construction of proud palaces to house the arts, legislature, and communications, brought entire residential districts under the sway of his aesthetic, and erected monuments that were national in purpose but French in character along Maximilian's former Imperial Drive, to complete its recasting as the boulevard now known as Paseo de la Reforma.

This is the smart, urbane, fastidious city of Manuel Gutiérrez Nájera, which he serenades in the same breath as his beloved:

> Desde las puertas de la Sorpresa
> hasta la esquina del Jockey Club,
> no hay española, *yanquee* o francesa,
> ni más bonita, ni más traviesa
> que la duquesa del duque Job.[14]

> [From the doors of the Surprise
> To the corner of the Jockey Club
> No Spanish, Yank or Paris prize
> Has prettier or more teasing eyes
> Than the Duchess of Duke Job.]

It is the city kept awake by electric light, the city with bags under its eyes depicted by Ramón López Velarde. (The city is barely present in his poem *La suave patria*, a composition of abrasive and quickened rhythms, but it resurfaces, morally enshrined with all its sins and atonements, in "Zozobra" and "El son del corazón.")

The nineteenth-century city expressed itself as demurely as its salons and hot chocolate. Madame Calderón de la Barca observed that even in the cockfight arenas no one "talked roughly," and the well-traveled Ludovic Chambon reported that "the very courtesans, in the exercise of their useful public duties, shrink from removing their veils and other accessories of love."

In a century that witnessed one war of independence, two foreign invasions, and a bout of civil strife, not a single memorable epic poem was produced; on the other hand, there was an outpouring of finely honed lyrical poetry and popular verse, the continuation of the criollo tradition—rooted in Francisco de Terrazas and Juana Inés de la Cruz—which Xavier Villaurutia saw as extending into the twentieth century. It is a meditative kind of poetry that keeps its head, deep yet diffident, almost murmuring, because, as the poet who was nostalgic for death once said, "the Mexican is silent by nature . . . though he may be awkward with words, he is a master at holding his peace." Can we fail to be amazed by the way our greatest lay poem is profoundly lyrical and finds utterance through a muted sense of epic?

Upon reaching the capital in 1914, Zapata's troops wrecked the little Japanese garden nurtured by José Juan Tablada, like an ecological haiku, at his home in Coyoacán. The revolution put an end to the modernist exoticism of the Porfirian city, in the same way that city had earlier abolished the Hispanic tradition.

Once in place, the Revolution plastered the entire history of Mexico over the walls of public buildings; many of these were originally religious in nature and had survived the reform only thanks to a change of function. It commissioned new structures on the site of nineteenth-century mansions and put up skyscrapers that represented the victory of North American modernity over the Frenchified shell of the past; an Americanization presciently detected by López Velarde, who recalled an importunate madman waking him up at all hours to complain that "Plateros used to be a *calle*, then it became a *rue*, and now it's a *street!*" The revolution built mass housing for the people, paved over the rivers to build highways, and slashed through the city with expressways, with sidewalks like straitjackets, that gave a free rein to speed.

This is the city of Salvador Novo, "our city of mine," falling over itself to be modern whatever the cost in terms of destruction:

> [Q]ue la ciudad se hubiera conservado . . . colonial (o porfiriana; para el caso es lo mismo), habría seguramente colmado el sueño engreído y neurótico de muchos arcaizantes, o de quienes profesan que la nacionalidad, la autenticidad de un país o de una ciudad, estriba de que no se altere la residencia de su espíritu que ellos decretan por legítima; habría halagado y satisfecho a quienes claman contra la "obra demoledora de la piqueta" y se lamentan y añoran a la Ciudad de los Palacios, ciegos y renuentes a advertir, a examinar lo que pueda ofrecer de bueno, de normal, de evidencia de que sigue su vida, la ciudad sin palacios.

[For the city to have been preserved . . . in its colonial form (or Porfirian form, which amounts to the same) would doubtless have fulfilled the conceited, neurotic dreams of many backward-yearning fogies, and of those who claim that the nationhood, the authenticity of a country or a town, stems from a refusal to tamper with whatever residence of its spirit they have decreed legitimate; it would have flattered and molli-fied those who moan about "the devastations of the pickaxe," and in their blindness regret the long-lost City of Palaces, unable to perceive or sound out the good that may come of a city without palaces—the normality of it, the sign that its life courses on.][15]

A believer in the kind of renovation that can map out the future while preserving the past, and one who opposes pointless extermina-tion, I listen to the aching voices of poets stranded in this "dispalaced" city. The yellowing city like "a prematurely withered leaf" evoked by Alfonso Reyes in "Palinodia del polvo"; the city of "one-eyed lights," "broken statues," "humbled palaces, / waterless fountains, / affronted façades" that haunts the dreams of Octavio Paz in his "Nocturno de San Ildefonso"; the city "with an outer rind, some woods and / one hundred and fifty cemeteries / for some ten million half-lives" that one of its harrowed lovers, Efraín Huerta, suffers in his *Circuito interior*.

This outsize, hectic city is the one that stamps its monstrosity onto *Where the Air Is Clear* by Carlos Fuentes, the first novel in our literature to treat the city not only as a setting or a moral environment but as a main character endowed with a riotous multiplicity of voices. Perhaps this was the last work of literature that aspired to represent the city as a to-tality. For since then the capital has reproduced itself uncontrollably, breaking into separate, distant pockets that might as well be partitioned off from one another, though they cannot even be guessed at from the aerie in San Nicolás Totolapan where my house, which is your house, stands. A city whose edges are on the move, tending to brutal demo-graphic accidents; a city that has tripled a hundred times the space it oc-cupied under the conquistadors, and multiplied by god knows how many the number of its inhabitants until becoming the largest human hive in the history of the world.

Who would have thought of it? With a private, reactionary sadness I realize that the city that in Fuentes's novel wallows in the magnitude of its own freakishness is also the homely, tranquil world of my childhood. The house of ritual high teas and ready-blessed bread rolls, of doctors' home visits and inherited books, effects a transposition whereby the whole city slides into the metonymy of my street; the kiosk, the chimes of the ice-cream sellers, the vague, sporadic car interrupting our game but dodging the goalposts, the bicycle summoning up friendships as fortuitous as they are enduring, the neighborhood cop, the bogeyman, the hollers of the gas man, the rag-and-bone man, the honeycomb man, the grille of unripe love. And the street, the elemental city, equally transposed: around the block, down the road, the church, the park, the pharmacy, the bakery, the avenue, the bus with its crew of seated women and standing men, the expressway named after Miguel Alemán, the Chilpancingo circus, the monument to Cuauhtémoc, the statue nicknamed "caballito," or little horse, Juárez Avenue, the Alameda, the Palace of Fine Arts, and the center, its ancient blood dripping through the window displays of Tacuba, Madero, and Cinco de Mayo.

The teenage city. Equivocal and elusive.

The city regained, along with its arteries and its heart—where the earth shakes. The city of profane bells and reckless flags, of slaughtered plazas. Silent, shunned, and banished.

The self-made city, plunged night after night into a sleepless underworld.

The city shaken by earthquakes.

The city in pieces.

What is Mexico City today? A runaway stain spreading up the mountainsides. An enormous dried-up lake gnawing at the foundations of buildings, in revenge for its destruction, until it has swallowed them all up. A crowd of jerry-built houses bristling with the hopeful rods of a second floor that never happens. A sampler of abject styles. A vast warehouse of showy advertisements parading their barbarisms. An uproar drowned out by car horns, the omnipresence of television sets and the government loudspeakers against the background roar of the ring road, beneath planes close enough to touch. A traveling and sedentary market of smugglers' junk and pornography. An outdoor circus where acrobats, fire-eaters, and children dressed as clowns offer their pitiful clumsiness for sale. A baroque revelry full of contrasts, daily matching misery with ostentation, like a sacramental play by Calderón de la Barca turned slice-of-life. A beckoning stepmother for migrants from the provinces. A den of thieves and muggers whose feats we now relate, all of us, in the first person. It is a city that we barely recognize from one day to the next, one night to the next, as though between last night and this, yesterday and today, years, decades, centuries had passed. It is a city where memory cannot be recharged, a place its own residents do not know. A tower of Babel that, rather than grow upward, ramifies outward into sibling tongues impossible to comprehend. It is the city of protective anonymity, secret smiles, hopeful fiestas, forgiving weather, watchful eyes. Terrible and beloved, alluring and dismaying, unlivable and inevitable. The lost city above all others; retrieved by the literature that builds it day by day, restores it, reveals it, ministers to it, and defies it.

Notes

1. Calvino, *Invisible Cities*, 11.
2. Díaz del Castillo, *Historia verdadera*, 147.
3. Díaz del Castillo, *Discovery and Conquest of Mexico*, 190–91.
4. The quote is from Cortés's "Second Letter" (1520), where he writes: "La cual ciudad es tan grande y de tanta admiración que aunque mucho de lo que de ella podría decir dejé, lo poco que diré creo que es casi increíble." Cortés, *Cartas de relación*, 98. Translated in *Letters from Mexico*, 67. Translation modified.
5. Martínez, *Nezahualcóyotl*, 220–21.
6. Alvarado Tezozómoc, *Crónica mexicáyotl* 3–4.
7. From the Nahuatl poem "Grandeza de Tenochtitlán," in Garibay K., *Poesía indígena de la Altiplanicie*, 74–75.
8. Cortés, *Cartas de relación*, 257.
9. Cortés, *Letters from Mexico*, 248.
10. Cortés, *Cartas de relación*, 277.
11. Cortés, *Letters from Mexico*, 270.
12. Balbuena, *Grandeza mexicana*, 71–73.
13. Lezama Lima, "La curiosidad barroca," 398.
14. Gutiérrez Nájera, *Poesías*, 20.
15. Novo, *Nueva grandeza mexicana*, 120–21.

2

Places

Insurgentes

FABRIZIO MEJÍA MADRID

An Aerial View

From above, Insurgentes is just a broad thoroughfare cutting vertically through Mexico City, jammed with little cars. They say it's the longest road in the world because it goes from Acapulco all the way to Nuevo Laredo, but in fact, if we could join together all the streets in Mexico called Insurgentes, the resulting highway would stretch all the way to Hawaii. Insurgentes spirals through the entire country like a labyrinth. Every year, someone tries to be original by choosing this name for a street in a newly built town. Not even Mexico City has avoided this repetition: between 1985 and 1995, twenty-three streets, boulevards, alleys, drives, courts, and avenues were given the name Insurgentes.

In the future, all the roads in Mexico will be called Insurgentes. We'll wander aimlessly, turning left and right along Insurgentes, wondering "Where am I?" only to hear the same word repeated over and over again, among people circling helplessly around the maze and staring blankly into the rain. There are as many streets called Insurgentes as there are lost souls: men whom no Minotaur awaits at home, women whose lives will be written by no one.

It is almost impossible to tell the story of this road. Its existence is a tale of rapid and ephemeral change, of compulsory modernization imposed from above and the reckless destruction it engenders. Insurgentes was not designed to blend in with the buildings it contains; on the contrary, it merely contributed to the turmoil and chaos. The development of Insurgentes marked the shift from carriages to cars: the road slashed through the old mule-drawn tramway terminal that stood on Artes Street since 1868. That first Insurgentes ran from Gómez Farías to San Cosme and was irrevocably associated with San Ángel. Later, when the railroad linking Mexico City to Nuevo Laredo was completed in 1877, Insurgentes was extended to James Sullivan, a street named after the developer of the railway line. (Estación Colonia, the terminal station, was erected on the grounds of Hacienda de Teja, a former plantation owned by Rafael Martínez de la Torre. The plantation—along with the neighboring Hacienda del Cebollón—was eventually paved over to develop Colonia Cuauhtémoc, which was eventually demolished to make room for . . . et cetera). Modernization always tells its own story as a chain of events leading to a single goal, like a ship that can stay afloat only by sacrificing the crew.

In the journey along Insurgentes (a neologism—*insurgentear*—defined the point when the city ceased to be walkable and became drivable; the term was made obsolete by traffic jams), every landmark is threatened by demolition. No one can tell the story of this avenue without being attentive to arbitrariness, destruction, and oblivion. Insurgentes's tracks have been effaced by the rain. David Huerta wrote: "Avenida Insurgentes is the pretext for remembrance and forgetting and knowing how we forget those alterations/those spells and destructions of which we are made."

The Center: Substitutions

A mythic origin: grandfather was fixated on a photograph portraying a bald man standing on a giant map of Mexico City and pointing down to an avenue. Grandfather had a good memory for powerful men.

"It's Emilio Peralta Uruchurtu, Mexico City's 'mayor of iron,'" he told me late one night in 1983. When Emilio was six years old, his uncle perished aboard the *Titanic*. It thus makes sense that Uruchurtu's public works in Mexico City were always designed to exorcise the risk of drowning (by paving over rivers, as he did with Churubusco) or asphyxia (by widening roads). The mayor's only enemies were crowds and traffic jams.

"He should try living here now," I said. Grandfather didn't hear me.

"It happened down there," he said pointing out the window. "It was April fifteenth, at two twenty in the morning, exactly forty years after the *Titanic*'s sinking, when Emilio Uruchurtu arrived on Ramón Guzmán Street, accompanied by a pack of city workers and a squadron of PRI bodyguards. He stepped out of his truck, followed by a demolition crew. He raised a hand and in one fell swoop the workers bulldozed the Pasquel family's import business headquarters. Uruchurtu wasn't an enemy of the Pasquels, who were a very influential family. Imagine, my son, Jorge Pasquel was a son-in-law of former president Plutarco Elías Calles! The mayor often ran into the Pasquels at PRI functions, and he always said hello. But the headquarters of their import business stood in the way of Insurgentes, a road that had just been widened to the north. Anticipating Uruchurtu's plans, the Pasquel brothers had gotten a court order protecting their building from demolition. When they arrived later that night, their building had been half torn down.

"'You broke the law, Uruchurtu. We'll get you thrown in jail,' the Pasquel brothers screamed at him.

"'I didn't break the law,' said the mayor, laconically."

Grandfather said "laconically," which at the time sounded like a word describing something dark and metallic, like the inside of a pipe.

"'Here's the court order protecting our building from demolition,' retorted Gerardo Pasquel.

"Uruchurtu took the paper in his hands and smirked: 'This paper is worthless. This street isn't called "Insurgentes Norte." It has a new name since this morning,' and he pointed to the sign on the corner.

"The Pasquel brothers looked up at the street sign, shimmering in the early morning light. Uruchurtu was right. The new street sign read 'Insurgentes Centro.'"

Grandfather concluded his story and fell silent. In his old age, he liked remembering abuses as if they signaled happier days.

He asked me to help him get up from his armchair. I held my breath. I wanted to run away. He reached for his yellow cane, missed, and fell on the floor. Only then I ran to help him. When he got up, he had already wet himself.

The Monument to the Revolution

The middle stretch, Insurgentes Centro, is seriously damp. In 1983, the structures surrounding the Monument to the Revolution were in danger of collapse. From Plaza de la República to Reforma, from Ignacio Ramírez to Insurgentes, people braced themselves for catastrophe: all cars and nearby buildings—including the Central Workers' Union along with Fidel Velázquez, its leader-for-life—could crumble into a bottomless well. The monument's foundations were not threatened: they had been planned by Adamo Boari in 1897 to withstand a capitol ten times the weight, but they ended up supporting only a hollow dome. But the underground retaining walls were rotten from the rain, and the city government decided to reinforce the monument and prevent its collapse in order to forestall metaphorical allusions to the Mexican Revolution.

The monument's dirty bronze cupola was anything but revolutionary. Boari (who did not win the competition launched by Leandro Fernández, Porfirio Díaz's minister of communications and public works, due to the government's unwillingness to "incline publicly for any of the fifty projects") left the design and the supervision of the building to Emilio Bernard, a fan of Roman and North American imperial architecture. Surrounded by statues representing Virility, Labor, Eloquence, Peace, Truth, Strength, Law, Science, and so on, the legislative palace of the Porfirian regime would be crowned by "imposing capitals in the Corinthian style; above them, towering over the entire façade, the Aztec Eagle shall spread its mighty wings." But only the dome was built. The rest—three great halls, one for each chamber and one for joint sessions, a room of "lost steps," for relaxation, a reception room, a great library, individual cubicles for every congressman and senator, an archive, and a printing press—remained on paper, as did the project for the legislative palace. In Mexico, when something doesn't exist, one devotes a monument to it.

On the morning of September 23, 1910, less than two months before revolution broke out, General Porfirio Díaz dropped a paper certifying the laying of the first stone into a crystal bottle that was then set into a block of Ferrara marble "at the spot designated for the plinth for the great lamp, to the left of the portico, precisely below the intended site for the lovely statue symbolizing Youth." Díaz, who had just celebrated his eightieth birthday, sprinkled the marble with a mixture of cement, lime, and sand, scooping it with a silver spoon from the bucket proffered by a member of his cabinet. Along with the palace, he inaugurated his virile power anew. José R. Aspe was the speaker for the dictator's congress: "As the building progresses, so will democracy be consolidated." Prophetic words.

The shell of the legislative cupola was plundered by the revolutionary mob for the next ten years. From 1903 to 1911, the government spent 6,428,584 pesos and 67 cents on the job. In 1912, the contract with Bernard was revoked. In March 1928, Alfonso Rodríguez del Campo, the man in charge of public works in the districts of Coyoacán and Tlalpan, suggested that the dome be used to build a palace for the supreme court. Twenty-two years and ten million deaths after the first stone was laid, Abelardo L. Rodríguez turned that Porfirian cupola into a Monument to the Revolution and a burial site. The eagle meant to crown the legislative palace was diverted to La Raza, a monument to the Mexican race on Insurgentes Norte, and the lions flanking the steps wound up at the entrance to Chapultepec Park.

Neither revolutionary nor a monument, the Monument to the Revolution became a grave. Here were buried Madero, the headless Villa, Carranza, Calles, and Cárdenas (who unveiled his own sepulchre on November 20, 1938). Ever since the presidency of Adolfo López Mateos, the dome has been the setting for all acts of revolutionary pomp. Speeches are made about the heroes who slaughtered one another in glorious treachery; buried shoulder to shoulder, they now exorcise the rhetorical fear of "foreign powers."

In 1929 Ernesto Portes Gil and Dwight W. Morrow looked down from the National Palace onto a parade of peroxide-blonde girls in swimsuits, trundling past under cardboard palm trees. They were part of the procession of floats designed by Juan F. Azcárate, chief of the Aeronautics Department, to celebrate the anniversary of the Revolution. In 1982, the floats—and the chicks—were replaced by ordinary athletes and cart-wheeling policemen. Despite all attempts to smooth it over, the Mexican Revolution continues to be that space of the eternally unaccomplished, the promise of better days that never dawned, and the shell of a Porfirian palace turned stage for the Single Party and its canned applause. Only the tombs remain: the threat of massacre as the true face of our national history.

During the 1980s, fear of collapse—and of jokes cracked by the "reactionary Left," as President Miguel de la Madrid was fond of saying—moved the authorities to repair the underground walls of the Monument to the Revolution. The PRI's all-encompassing power reached everything, including the cold war. In 1984, Ronald Reagan proposed a limited nuclear war to defeat communism. It was assumed that Mexican oil-drilling zones would be one of the targets of Soviet reprisals. Watching *The Day After* on cable television chilled us almost as much as Reagan's little jest, broadcast on August 14 on Mexican channels: "I am pleased to inform you that I have signed a bill to wipe the Soviet Union off the map. Bombing will start in five minutes." That's why, when the sky turned fiery at 5:30 A.M. on November 19, the traffic on Insurgentes came to a halt. Drivers saw the mushroom cloud and waited hopelessly for the wind that would carbonize them. Nothing happened. Or not much, anyway. A Pemex refinery had just blown up, along with the entire working-class suburb of San Juanico.

One day later, under the cupola of the Monument to the Revolution: Humberto Lugo Gil, leader of Congress, speaks of the struggle against "foreign powers" in the time-hallowed manner: "How dearly have they paid, those who tried to act outside or against the revolutionary history of the Mexican people, and even worse: how limited and pitiful is the political fate that awaits those who try, today, to disparage the Revolution." There was no music during the revolutionary parade that year. Two hundred eighty charred corpses were being dumped into a mass grave in the Caracoles cemetery.

On the Southern end of Insurgentes, near the Cuernavaca highway, another capitol—this one *was* completed—offered a more compelling symbol of the Mexican Revolution: at kilometer mark 23.5 stood one of the mansions owned by Arturo Durazo Moreno, known as El Negro, Mexico City's former chief of police. Arturo Durazo's uncle, Francisco Durazo Ruiz, was the man who had ordered the dead Villa's decapitation on February 6, 1926. His nephew made history on Friday, June 29, 1984, when FBI agents arrested him in San Juan, Puerto Rico. Charged in Mexico with evading taxes, extorting 124 million pesos from police officers under his command, and controlling Mexico City's black market for drugs, prostitution, alcohol, and even abortions, Durazo came up with a remark worthy of our most revolutionary heroes: "Fucking wonderful country that can take a sonofabitch like me!"

Niza

On the night of March 4, 1984, Juan Carlos made his move: he went to wait for María Clara to finish her shift. He ordered a beer while Clara smiled at him from the back, her apron white against her dress. They chatted.

"Juan! What are you doing here?"

"I came to keep you company. I'll walk you home after work. Pretty full tonight, eh?"

"Sure. It's the heat. More people go out."

At two in the morning, they were walking up Niza toward Insurgentes. Juan Carlos put his arms around Clara. They kissed. A taxi drove by. It was about seventy degrees and windless. They walked along Insurgentes talking, though they could hardly hear each other over the shouts of the prostitutes screaming at cars parked along the avenue. No one bothered them at first. Juan Carlos stroked his girlfriend's hair and talked about their future.

The last thing he remembered that night was that he'd been clubbed behind the left ear. He fell onto the sidewalk and smashed his face. He woke up inside a van full of menacing, drunken bureaucrats brandishing government IDs. As Juan Carlos went crashing down, a cop grabbed Clara by the waist and dragged her toward a long line of bruised, disheveled women who were hurling shoes at the hundred or so policemen who had stormed the Zona Rosa. The line seemed endless. Days later, the press reported that more than a thousand had been rounded up. A cop was marching up and down, pointing his gun at the women, while three officers poked the women's breasts with their clubs. When one of the women collapsed, the others would help her to her feet. Meanwhile the police cars switched on their sirens and the cops raided restaurants and bars in pursuit of any man accompanied by a woman. A boy in a denim jacket was pleading, as they dragged him halfway down the block, that he'd only been talking on a public phone.

With the women watching, a cop seized the boy by the hair and another started kicking. The first blow got him in the mouth. Blood spurted. The second, on the right cheekbone, knocked him out cold. They loaded him into a van that was nearly full.

The line of women was getting longer. Clara saw everything in slow motion, as if it wasn't happening to her. She wasn't thinking about Juan Carlos; she was watching the people scatter, chased by teams of cops with drawn guns. Everything seemed very quiet. The woman next to her spat on Insurgentes: her saliva landed on an officer's pants. Three of them started kicking. Her blood sprinkled Clara's dress.

"Hey sir, this one's a guy," yelled one of the cops, his hand on the groin of the woman who had spat.

"OK, skirts up all of you!"

The cops stopped chasing the Zona Rosa crowd and gathered on the east side of Insurgentes. They inspected lingerie of all shapes and colors. A row of more than one hundred officers lined up facing the women. They forced them to drop their pants or lift their skirts. The show stopped every time they caught a transvestite. They tore off her wig and smeared her lipstick with the heel of a hand. Then the kicking began, always with the same slur: "It don't hurt there!" The transvestites would fall, then they were dragged to the vans, where they were stripped of stockings and shoes and their hands were tied. In the hubbub of clapping, whistling, and lewd jokes, it was Clara's turn.

"She's got her period, sir," shouted one of the cops. They all booed. Some forty minutes later, the line of women, purged of transvestites, exposed legs and underwear to the gray Insurgentes dawn. One policeman broke out laughing, looking at the sky, and some others clapped. A shivery wind brought them down to earth.

"Cover up, whores. We're going to the station," said the sergeant.

The convoy of detainees took five hundred people to the police station on Aldama and Mina, in the Guerrero neighborhood. Many were released on the way in exchange for a handful of bills. Clara didn't pay, hoping to find Juan Carlos at the station. By the time they arrived, only around two hundred women remained. Clara knew the process would take all morning when a fat matron handed her a token with a three-figure number on it. She looked around for Juan Carlos but he wasn't there. The boy in the denim jacket was, leaning with other men against a wall. His mouth was bleeding and one eye was shut. Less than one hour later, the women started sinking down and falling asleep on the floor. No sign of the transvestites. Around six thirty Clara was woken.

"Your turn."

Clara was not surprised to find herself paying a fine for a minor offense: urinating in public. She said nothing and paid up before they could accuse her of being a prostitute.

When she came out, her eyes hurt from the sun. She decided to walk to Insurgentes and call Juan Carlos from the restaurant. Niza was still strewn with shoes, stockings, and panties. A street-sweeper held up a pair of tights to the light. Clara sat waiting on the steps of the restaurant until eleven in the morning. She dozed until someone came to open up. Brushing away his questions, she ran to the telephone. Juan Carlos never came home. It was seventy-five degrees and windless.

The South: Farewells

La Paz

"The arm lost by General Obregón, while fighting against the Northern Division in the 1910 battle of Celaya, will be cremated on July 16, 1989." In this fashion, and giving the wrong date for the battle of Santa Ana del Conde, the press office of the Defense Ministry announced the end of the famous hand, the solitary limb that had been preserved inside the world's tallest mausoleum. But save for a bunch of bookish guerrillas who thought of outdoing the theft of Bolívar's sword in Colombia by making off with the general's hand, no one cared that the venerable pickle was to be cremated at last. Had they made their attempt, the guerrillas would have had to bring a handsaw: after Ignacio Asúnsolo completed the Monument to Álvaro Obregón in 1935, the key to the formaldehyde container got lost and was never to be found again, much like the key to the conspiracy that assassinated Obregón in 1928.

But who cares? When the monument was built, Insurgentes was widened and San Ángel was renamed Villa Álvaro Obregón. Most of the public works along the southern stretch of Insurgentes were the work of greedy bureaucrats eager for profitable conflicts of interest. The avenue was extended, for example, to link Casas Alemán's land in Chimalistac to the rest of the city: Caudillos, Cadillacs, and Revolution.

I imagine that the condition of the hand in 1989, seventy-four years after it was amputated, would inspire disgust or bewilderment rather than piety. I never bothered to see it, so I can't say for sure. Fifty years after its erection, the huge Stalinist chimney commissioned by Aarón Sáenz to protect the limb-suspended-in-formaldehyde had become a trysting place for maids and taxi drivers. Whether it symbolizes the one-term-limit-for-Mexican-presidents, the end of savage *caciquismo,* or the erection of the Single Party over the corpse of the last victorious land-owner, the Sunday-lacquered maids couldn't care less. Their offspring slide gaily down the ramps and treat the fountain like a public swimming pool, while they lie frolicking on the grass with slick-haired construction workers.

More important for city life is what stands opposite the Monument to the Hand: the San Angel branch of Sanborns, the chain restaurant-cum-mall, occupying the land of Abelardo L. Rodríguez's former casino. Sanborns is the place for waiting. There is no place in town more poignant than those steps leading up to the entrance, where so many are waiting for something or someone. *Desperado*, the 1995 film about drug lords, inspired a neologism to describe the Friday-night spectacle on the steps: *esperados*, the "waitees." There are impatient ones, irritably tapping the handrail; discreet ones who loll casually, whistling a popular tune; others who scan each passing car for a buddy, and yet others who focus on picking specks of dust off their clothes with thumb and forefinger. After all, it's embarrassing to be seen waiting endlessly for a person who never shows up.

Time in this city is so elastic, it's hard to determine at what point a delay can fairly be considered a stand-up. The impulse is always to wait just a little longer, imagining plausible excuses: heavy traffic, an accident—from some minor fender bender to a heart attack. Then you wonder if it's not your own fault. Did we plan to meet here or somewhere else? Is my watch fast? Is his slow? Well, I made him wait last time.

One of the *esperadas* has a raincoat slung over her arm (was she expecting rain at some point during her wait?) and fiddles obsessively with her hair. She powders her nose only once. Others near her have been chain-smoking, checking their watches, and wandering in and out of Sanborns (to search under the tables? use the phone?) before finally giving up. An hour goes by and the same woman is still there. She won't admit defeat, and there is dignity in her obstinacy. She seems serene, perhaps because she still hopes to see him again.

An hour and a half goes by, and still the raincoat woman waits. Perhaps she's a hooker? Or supervising something on the street? But on Insurgentes everything moves in irresolute ways, from cars to pedestrians who take nearly four minutes to cross the road. Could it be her idea of a Friday night out, to come and stand on these steps?

No one notices her; she's like an ugly duckling. If there were a man spying on her from the bar terrace, he might pay the bill, prepare to rise, see the girl is about to move; he would freeze, like a hunter before his prey; she would adjust her raincoat, toss her hair, and turn to face the man. He might wonder if she is missing her left hand, the one covered by the raincoat, but before he can be sure, everything turns to fog.

Barranca del Muerto

Being happy and thinking one is happy amount to the same thing. The corner of Insurgentes and Barranca del Muerto reminds me of Paulina. I walked by a few days ago, but La Cochera del Bentley, the café where we parted in 1988, no longer exists. The last morning I saw her, she had called me in tears. The dread of seeing her father, after ten years of thinking him dead, had driven her nearly crazy. She was afraid she would no longer recognize him. Father and daughter were due to meet for lunch at Ágora, a cafeteria that has also closed down. Between tear-sodden napkins, I worked out that Paulina's father lived in California and that he expected her to move there with him.

But I never understood exactly what made her cry so much. Resentment, unhappiness, fear, I guess. Nor could I understand my own passionate wish to console her. I came to say good-bye partly out of pity, partly because we had developed a fictitious routine in which we prepared to leave Mexico City and move to the small town of Mexico, Missouri. We laughed at that. We even dug up some tourist information about that home away from home. As I recall, it was called Mexico because the first establishment there, at the end of the nineteenth century, was named "Mexico that-a-ways." It was a saloon. A town that grew out of a saloon had to be nobler than one centered on a blood-soaked pyramid. At least, that's what we thought in 1988.

I recall very little of our last conversation. The image is of Paulina weeping over cold coffee spills on a tabletop. During the 1980s, no one could afford anything but coffee. It was barely ten thirty in the morning. We were the only patrons. The waiters were staring accusingly, and I remember the uncanny feeling of being unable to explain that no one was to blame for all those tears. Almost five hours later, we got the bill. I embraced Paulina and told her something that I later realized was pretty stupid: "This town's too small for you." Then something unexpected happened: she stopped crying.

It was early afternoon when we came out to Insurgentes. Paulina was wiping her eyes on the corner. I was heading south, she was going one block north. I never saw her again, and I never figured out why.

That afternoon, I hadn't realized that life feeds parasitically on memories. Paulina was leaving town that night and I was staying. We would never again be together in "Mexico City." Yet we couldn't budge from that corner. Our dilemma was simple: she would move away, bearing the full brunt of the separation, and I would stay, forever fossilized by her departure. Every time I was to walk past that intersection, I would remember that episode and feel a bit of joy.

But it didn't turn out that way. We said good-bye unsentimentally. Much later, through a mutual friend, I discovered that Paulina never met up with her father. Fear buckled her a few steps away from the meeting place, at a spot on Insurgentes that is no longer what it was, its past faded forever or living on in the ramblings of an elderly waiter. Now I realize that over the years, Paulina and I have often crossed paths but have never recognized each other in the crowd. I lost. He who tries to freeze-frame an afternoon in order to write his farewells will be condemned to an eternity of late arrivals.

Teatro de los Insurgentes

Saying farewell was a preoccupation shared by Diego Rivera and José Luis Cuevas. The women they depicted by the hundredweight represent not sexual exploits but partings. But whereas Rivera painted Indian women clutching armfuls of lilies, Cuevas drew whores with a moralistic eye: ever on the verge of decomposition, Cuevas's wenches are not desirable. In the early 1980s, Cuevas gave up drawing to devote himself to sculpture. Thirty years earlier, in 1955, he made a long trek with a girlfriend down Insurgentes to announce their engagement—as he told Juan José Reyes for an interview published in 1991 in the now defunct *Milenio*. María Asúnsolo, who lived at the bottom of Insurgentes, in Pedregal de San Ángel, was the last to be informed. On the return trip, Cuevas had a dark thought. On Insurgentes Sur, just before reaching the Monument to Obregón's Hand, Cuevas broke the engagement and walked on.

Two years later, beneath the mural adorning the façade of the Insurgentes Theater, Cuevas came across Diego Rivera, who was standing on the sidewalk and holding a gun.

"Good afternoon. I'm José Luis Cuevas."

Rivera's sole reaction was to point the gun at him. Cuevas backed off. Then, with a genial smile, Rivera demonstrated the workings of the handgun to an assistant who was sticking mosaics onto the image of some gun-toting Zapatista. Cuevas walked on; he didn't look back. Perhaps he remembered that the fiancée he left on Insurgentes in 1955 had tried to kill herself.

Félix Cuevas Avenue

Across the street from the large Liverpool department store on Insurgentes, there used to be a bakery and café called La Veiga, now shuttered. During the late 1980s it attracted writers, bullfight lovers, and shiftless conversationalists. It was the price of vodka shots—eight pesos—that made this mix possible and gave us an excuse not to leave the city.

In 1986, after the earthquake, everyone wanted out of Mexico City, a place that became synonymous with everyday monstrosity. That year we produced 4,000 tons of lead particles, 10,000 tons of sulfur dioxide, 48,000 tons of nitrogen oxide, 3,800 tons of carbon monoxide, 375,000 tons of hydrocarbons, and some 12,000 tons of garbage a day. It had begun to look a lot like purgatory. But where was heaven? Nowhere, or maybe in some bar that didn't yet exist.

Many people moved away between 1986 and 1990. Those who stayed were permanently tempted by two equally ludicrous options: to follow Insurgentes either down to Cuernavaca or up to Nuevo Laredo. South in order to breathe, north in order to work. In the late 1980s, the whole city found a way out of this quandary: to pretend nothing was amiss. Places like La Veiga came in handy for this purpose, while disaster reared its ugly head from under the sidewalks.

Why did we stay? Like Vienna, Beijing, or New York, Mexico City is an urban experiment. At its core lies a debt. We never knew whether we were the aftermath of a flood that had aged us or the prelude to some cosmic future. The wait has been too long. The city's glories do not exist. They are always already buried in the past. Fray Diego Durán recounts the arrival of priests and elders to a place where everything was white, reeds and snakes included. "We have found the promised land: there is nothing left to wish for." Reaching Mexico City was always a poor reward for so long a pilgrimage, and thus these streets reek of bitter nostalgia. We never got over being mistaken for Atlantis, or having been an empire.

We feel something vague is owed to us: honor, pity, or rancor. As soon as exiles, immigrants, or tourists set foot on this urban soil, they owe us something. Gratitude is not at issue. On the contrary, Mexicans will cordially efface themselves, but they will demand something vague in exchange, something so ambiguous that it becomes unspeakable. Mexico City is shaped by that vagueness: people ask for a trifling, but they hang on because they feel the city owes them something as large as it is unnamable.

San Borja Avenue

The Lara family moved to Mexico City from Real del Monte, in the state of Hidalgo, during the 1940s. Thanks to a startling resemblance to Jorge Negrete, the Mexican film star, Rómulo Lara married the owner of a restaurant called Los Guajolotes, which solved his money problems. In the 1950s, however, he was still toiling at the gas station next to La Fuente, the nightclub where in 1960 Ana Berta Lepe's father murdered Raúl de Anda's son. For Rómulo Lara, the glamour of Mexico's movie industry was routine: every day he pumped gas into the automobiles of stars like Pedro Infante and singers like María Victoria, Luis Alcaraz, Corona, or Arau. Everyone told Rómulo that he looked so much like Jorge Negrete, the intrepid national *charro*, that only the voice was lacking.

"You could be his double," suggested Luis Alcaraz one afternoon, as Rómulo was wiping his windshield.

One evening Jorge Negrete, the symbol of national manliness, drove into the gas station. Rafael called his brother Rómulo. Jorge Negrete looked at him: he stood speechless in front of his double. He scratched his head: Rómulo followed suit. It was the old gag of imitating the other's actions as in a mirror. Jorge Negrete went to the washroom and so did Rómulo. Jorge unbuttoned himself to pee: Rómulo was about to do the same but the game came to an abrupt stop. The miniature scale of Jorge's member was too pathetic. Now Rómulo stood stricken and speechless. Jorge Negrete threw him a sidelong glance and drawled: "If you're man enough to cut yours off, you could be my double." He drove off without leaving a tip.

Hotel de México

Between December 1966 and January 1967, a pack of builders and engineers stormed the old Parque de la Lama (500,000 square feet of birches and palm trees between Dakota and Filadelfia Streets, along Insurgentes), with the goal of raising a tower 720 feet into the air. According to the brochures, Hotel de México would boast 51 stories, lodging for 3,100 guests in 1,508 hexagonal rooms—including 1,188 bedrooms, 132 executive suites, 4 diplomatic suites, 3 ministerial suites, and 2 presidential suites—4 cafeterias for 800, 6 restaurants for 1,240, a revolving restaurant on the top floor, 14 private dining rooms for 850, a panoramic elevator for 100 tourists and 19 additional elevators for ordinary passengers and freight, 1 covered and 2 open-air panoramic terraces that between them could process 1,000 people per hour, 5 reception halls for 6,000 partygoers, 1 cabaret, 13 bars for 2,000 boozers, 1 convention room for 3,000 guests and services for up to 9,000 conference participants, parking for 2,000 cars, a customs-house-equipped heliport equal in size to that built by Manuel Suárez at Casino de la Selva in Cuernavaca, permitting the conveyance of 40 guests in two Sikorsky helicopters—plus a monorail for whisking clients to the aforementioned Casino in less than an hour—a health club, a spiral-shaped shopping mall of 21,500 square feet housing craft stores, banks, hair stylists, and jewelry outlets, the Siqueiros Cultural Polyforum with 50,000 square feet of mural paintings, a theater for 2,000 spectators, a museum with capacity for 1,100 people, and a hotel annex for chauffeurs, secretaries, and personal maids. The daily *El Universal* worked it out: "One thousand people entering the complex every 15 minutes."

Those were the days when there was a deadline for making dreams come true: before this presidential term ends, under this executive, right now, here's 165 million pesos, before I meet my Maker. In September 1969, when the project seemed unfinishable, Suárez remarked that he was "very keen to finish it before I die." He died eighteen years later, on July 23, 1987, and his Hotel de México was the tallest shell in the Americas, perpetually on the brink of either collapse or unveiling.

During the 1980s, Hotel de México was an eerie presence over the city, a symbol of the unfulfilled promises of a development perpetually derailed by a series of mammoth frauds, a shell of the Mexican Miracle's dream of "building the largest in Latin America." According to published records, the hotel's construction caused a dozen deaths, including that of Electa Arenal, David Alfaro Siqueiros's niece, on June 12, 1969, while the Polyforum was being built. Workers fell off their scaffolds and were splattered over underground tunnels that never opened to automobile traffic. These subterranean passages were filled with concrete and the hotel became a graveyard.

In November 1970, Manuel Suárez ordered a massive crypt to be carved behind Siqueiros's mural. Foreseeing that the complex would not be completed before he—or Siqueiros—died, he envisaged a group burial: he and Siqueiros would be buried together with painters Diego Rivera, José Clemente Orozco, and Dr. Atl, and engravers José Guadalupe Posada and Leopoldo Méndez. The crypt was walled up after a welder fell into it. Nevertheless, the existence of crypt and underground tunnels fueled the legend that life-size statues of Suárez, holding a sombrero, and Siqueiros, holding a paintbrush, were buried below, along with a much-discussed chess set featuring miniatures of contemporary politicians (Khrushchev was black, Mao was white).

Hotel de México was the joint venture of a dissident Marxist and an entrepreneur *alemanista*. Siqueiros emerged from prison in 1964, holding Suárez's arm and fearing death. The day the muralist was freed, Lázaro Cárdenas wrote in his diary, puzzling over the fate of political prisoners incarcerated during the presidency of López Mateos: "Why was Siqueiros freed, but not Campa or Vallejo?" Coincidences: twenty years later, Demetrio Vallejo was unable to attend a 1986 pro-democracy meeting at Hotel de México, an event that was canceled after right-wing extremists issued death threats against Heberto Castillo, the engineer who designed the hotel's framework on the basis, so he claimed, of Hegelian dialectics—supports grouped in sets of three, and by way of synthesis: nothing will fall down.

In 1964 Suárez dispatched the Communist painter to Cuernavaca, where he was to execute, for the sum of 20,000 pesos a fortnight (according to the contract signed on October 15), a mural titled *The March of Humanity* at Casino de la Selva's heliport. The mural ended up back in Mexico City, at the Polyforum, which was inaugurated on December 15, 1971, by President Luis Echeverría. But something had shifted in Siqueiros's state of mind. The first invitation to the opening ceremony, dated November 16, was sent to Dr. Paul Marcinkus of the Istituto per le Opere di Religione, a man who was later accused of brokering the deals between the Vatican's Banco Ambrosiano and the Sicilian Mafia. In this letter of invitation, as in those he sent to other Vatican officials—Monsignor Pascuale Macci and Commendatore Pier Paolo Morenda—Siqueiros writes about his religious stirrings ("the Polyforum broaches not only the problem of humanity, but also that of faith and salvation") and about the Christs he painted in jail. It was not a passing whim. At the end of his life, Siqueiros betrayed his own militant beliefs on at least two occasions: first, when he agreed to let his Polyforum work be hidden behind a wall—150 feet long and 15 feet high—making it accessible only to those who paid an admission fee; second, when he agreed to an exhibition advertising the Polyforum in Madrid which had been authorized by Francisco Franco, on the same day he ordered the arrest of art critic Moreno Galván to prevent him from giving a lecture on the subject of Picasso and *Guernica*. Siqueiros was afraid of death, and the Polyforum buried him, in some sense, the day of its unveiling.

Hotel de México was stillborn. In the late 1980s, when the various real estate and construction companies that tried to finish it for so long were exposed as corrupt, the giant tower was nothing but an empty shell, a steel and concrete cobweb that could be seen from almost anywhere in southern Mexico City. Neither hotel nor entertainment center, it was useful only as a point of reference for giving directions for getting to some new restaurant in Colonia Nápoles. It also served as a pollution gauge: as long as you could see the top, you were not in danger of keeling over in the street. Little by little, its outline has dissolved into the smog.

The North: The Poor

Ampliación Gabriel Hernández

Nobody goes north except for the poor. North is for begging miracles from the Virgin of Guadalupe, sleeping in unpaved slums, or lining up for some PRI handout. During the 1980s, when the rock-loving street gangs produced by the oil boom were broken up, what had been obscured by ragged rock concerts and skirmishes with the cops became all too clear: the isolation of barrio kids, *"chavos bien helados,"* as José Joaquín Blanco has called them. Nobody sees them, and yet these daylight ghosts haunt the sidewalks in search of a job, a girl, a friend, and are ultimately defeated (in advance), condemned to slouching against a wall and watching cars go by. The failure of the hopes kindled by urbanization is epitomized in that leg bent against a fence, those hands hidden in pockets.

These kids belong to the first generation that believed in the "Mexican economic miracle" and sought a place to enjoy the new riches. But things fell apart in the crisis. What are they doing here? No alienated *chavo* wants to be sent back to the country via the barrio; his family has been irrevocably expelled from the purgatory of country life. Incapable of associating, except down in subway platforms, alienated *chavos* lack even a barrio identity. The *bandas* identified with particular streets or with certain symbols (they called themselves sex, metals, punks, *locos, gallos, pitufos, pañales, calacos*), but isolated *chavos* have no name, nothing to say, nothing to reflect.

To what extent do housing projects in north Mexico City parody the barrio? Like vampires, northern kids don't show up in photographs; it's the blank space that denotes their presence. We recognize them by their contours; at their center there is nothing but silence. Urged to speak or to participate, *chavos cool* refuse to comply, with awesome poise (does being cool unify or isolate?). Their imperviousness to information is conveyed by *"no me chorees,"* don't fuck with me. *Choro:* snap trivialization of all the pollster's attempts to entice me. *"Te doy el avión,"* I'll play the game and tell you what you want to hear if you just leave me alone, I'll refract your words through my void and, never disagreeing, I'll neutralize your ideas since you don't get that I'm not saying what you hear me say. The icy *chavo* is always out to lunch.

Basílica: The Desperate

In 1984, three years before his disappearance, Miguel Angel Valesti unearthed a wooden Virgin of Guadalupe and cried to the faithful on the hill: "We'll build a new shrine right here for the *virgencita!*"

It never happened. He deserted the congregation that had attended his nocturnal sermons since the 1970s, standing on heaps of garbage lit by flaming torches. A visionary beggar, he defeated his loudest critics— garbage pickers—and gathered a flock of paupers who also went to mass at the basilica, around the corner from the site of his harangues. One day he vanished, never to be heard of again. People were left with the memory of a carved Virgin which Valesti claimed was a sixteenth-century original. Gone with Valesti was that uncannily poor congregation, reminiscent of the ravings of Nazarín.

Potrero: The Redeemers

A strike at the Pascual bottling plant on Insurgentes Norte marked the early years of the crisis: it lasted from May 31, 1982, when two men were shot dead by orders of Rafael Jiménez, the plant's owner, to August 6,

1986, when the first soft drinks cooperative in Mexico City was founded. In the interim, the sight of workers drumming up support all over town became part of the landscape. Their unionist stamina was stronger than murder, deceit, strike busting, and kidnappings, but above all, it outlasted time itself. Filiberto Bucio, a strike counsel, wrote of "the delays that disheartened those of us who had to watch every minute, hour, day, week, and month crawl by, whether standing outside the factories, at the Department of Labor, or at other government offices, Fonep, Fosoc, Secofi . . . It takes no time to say it, but we're talking about close to one hundred thousand man-hours."

Nicknamed El Pato, the Duck, José Antonio Palacios Marquina worked for two years at Pascual's northern plant before he was fired in 1982. He turned up at a workers' school in Tacuba, where he declared himself "sick and tired of the corruption and antidemocracy of this government, of the uselessness of strikes, and of left-wing parties manipulating workers' demands."

Early on May 1, 1984, after printing some leaflets at the workers' school, El Pato took two soda bottles, siphoned some gas from a parked car, and stuffed them with strips of his shirt. He packed the bombs in a knapsack along with a handgun he'd "expropriated" from a drunk by the railway tracks. At one twenty in the afternoon, as President Miguel de la Madrid watched the May Day parade, the first device exploded on the presidential balcony. Among those burned were Alejandro Carrillo Castro, director of Social Security for State Employees; Concepción de Oliveira, the Brazilian representative of the Latin American Workers' Unions; Ricardo García Sáinz, director of Mexico's Social Security; Jorge de la Vega Domínguez, PRI stalwart, and Rafael Cordera, leader of Havana's Central Workers' Union. After tossing the second bomb into the doorway of the National Palace, El Pato strolled down to Pino Suárez where he boarded a taxi back to the workers' school.

Next day, the sound bites were succinct. President de la Madrid: "We detect a foreign hand in these events. We will not fail to track down the enemies of the republic, and apply the law firmly and justly in order to safeguard our nation. No one will bring Mexico down." Secretary of State Manuel Bartlett: "The attempt at destabilization failed, as it will always fail, given the unwavering solidarity between the workers and the Mexican government." Fidel Velázquez, leader of the Central Workers' Union: "The CIA and international communism, in cahoots with leftist parties."

On Saturday, May 5, riot police raided both workers' schools. At Fresno, on Flores Magón and Insurgentes Norte, the search operation lasted four hours, until nine thirty at night, when the suspects were marched out in groups of five. The Tacuba operation started at midnight. By nine the next morning, the police had "permanently" occupied the premises. Two minors and twelve youths between the ages of eighteen and twenty-four were arrested.

On Friday the eleventh, El Pato and Demetrio Ernesto Hernández Rojas, "El Mao," both claimed to have signed their depositions under torture. Charged with manufacture and possession of explosives, damage to property, criminal association, possession of cannabis, and carrying a firearm without a license, El Pato declared from his prison cell: "I acted on my own. I did so in protest against the exploitation and want suffered by the working classes. I did not intend to injure anyone or endanger the president, but someone had to voice the workers' discontent. This time it was me, tomorrow it'll be others following my example. I expect nothing either from the government or from society. I will be freed by the mobilization of the working masses and the proletariat on my behalf."

Nostalgia for authenticity turned him into a savage, fleeing from urban barbarism. El Pato was a terrorist claiming his right to self-destruction. He could look in the mirror and say, "I am my country's worst nightmare." This was nothing new. Claiming the right to self-destruction had become commonplace under the Mexican system.

The first time he was jailed, El Pato was only twenty. He was sixteen when he left his mother's house in Ciudad Neza. He became a student, a worker, a terrorist, an inmate. When he was released in 1990, he thought it was all over. He was wrong. He was locked up again in 1994, for spraying pro-Zapatista graffiti on subway walls.

Rainy days are the echo of a greater punishment for the city. A burst of rain always swells into a churning flood. The streets become once more what they once were: lagoons, canals, fetid streams. People and buildings appear reflected as their own underwater doubles. Drenched by a downpour, city dwellers ask themselves the same question that obsessed Europeans as they wandered through the devastated Aztec city: what was here before? The answer, too, has been the same for centuries: the remains of a catastrophe.

Our city has always been seen as otherworldly. The theory of Mexico as Atlantis (Schopenhauer speculated on the etymology of Aztlán, Atlan, and Atlantis) has it drowned by an American flood that spared only the highest settlements. (According to Sir Francis Bacon, a thousand years after the universal flood came a "private" flood over this continent. Flocks of birds took refuge high in the mountains. When the waters receded, highlanders descended to the warm valleys, where they went about naked except for feather headdresses that paid tribute to birds, their plumed ancestors.) The esoteric tradition regards Mexico City as a degeneration of the red-skinned race (through miscegenation with Icelandic settlers who arrived by ship, and for lack of other nourishment invented human sacrifice, according to the nineteenth-century theosophist Antoine Fabre d'Olivet). Waterlogged and boggy, it is one great graveyard. Buried under its cobblestones, Salvador Novo wrote, are generations of people who perished to build Mexico City. Like Fray Marcos de Niza in 1527, upon unearthing a large horn in Coyoacán, Novo too might have exclaimed in surprise: "So they were unicorns!"

Santa María Insurgentes

Sometimes they blindfold the poor. It happened to Marcelo Moreno, leader of the surviving victims of the San Juanico explosion, between February 28 and March 15, 1985. "I woke up in a dark place. I couldn't see. I stayed there naked, unable to find any water to drink or to rinse off the blood. From then on I lost all notion of time. Two hours had gone by since they carjacked me on Santa María Insurgentes. Six men, one of them pointing his gun at me." The balance of this kidnapping: a broken nose and fractured left arm, bruises all over his body, anemia, and undernourishment. He lost twenty pounds.

The PRI Headquarters

No one knows how many people belong to the PRI. Inside the hefty fortress inaugurated by Gustavo Díaz Ordaz on November 20, 1963, in his capacity as "presidential candidate by popular acclaim," there exists no reliable register of affiliates. In the beginning, every fledgling workers' or *campesino* organization automatically belonged to the party of the Revolution; in consequence, many citizens are *priístas* without their knowledge, and should they belong to more than one union, their names figure twice—or more times—on the membership roster. That's why, when Díaz Ordaz and Alfonso Corona del Rosal, then president of the CEN, unveiled the plaque announcing that the monolith at the intersection of Insurgentes Norte and Héroes Ferrocarrileros had cost 2.4 million pesos, the two men were unable to hide their dismay. The inscription covers the party's ass: "This building was financed by the contributions of countless militants." But if the budget allocated to the construction company, Constructora y Edificadora Mexicana, to raise the PRI headquarters amounted to 340,000 pesos and 12 cents, how did the "militants" end up spending over 2.0 million? We will never know.

Another mystery: how did the PRI become its own shadow? It started out as a phantasm of revolutionary killings, replacing endless, random betrayals with the repetition of a mass melodrama: every six years, the PRI symbolically assassinates the president of the republic and displays, on the esplanade in front of the building, the next thug in charge. Horror stories: from being the revolution's phantasmic image, the PRI came to represent all that was unrepresentable—nation, unity, stability, national interests. Nourished on ghosts, the PRI became the biggest spook of all. As a phantasm for the nation, it denotes nothing but its own process of substitution. Everything can be translated into ever-changing, unintelligible terms (from the jargon of *cantinfleo* to that of Harvard technocrats: at the 1988 Congress, Socorro Díaz hailed Carlos Salinas as the "President of the United States of the Word," in involuntary homage to Dr. Freud). There is nothing external to the PRI (opposition always denotes a foreign plot), and "turn resistance into a form of support" has always been the formula for its omnivorous politics. The PRI: a machinery of ghostly names that functions out of pure habit and will continue sputtering even after all its members have died. Terror: how can a disembodied thing ever die?

Back to Edison Street

Despite appearances, writers never put embarrassing episodes behind them. Let's return to my grandfather. I run to help him get up; he's wet himself. Just minutes before, he was recounting the mythical origins of Insurgentes Centro. Now, I can only think of his death.

Years later, Grandfather felt death move closer and decided to write his memoirs in some notebooks I had given him. He filled up six of them and was starting on the seventh a few days before the end. When we opened them, they were covered in scribbles. Not one letter could be made out. We applied ourselves to quasi-paleographic methods of decipherment, but however we tried to sequence words—we used our imagination—nothing made sense; only Grandfather—and perhaps not even he—knew the gist of his scrawls. Something good must have come of the compulsion to write that occupied—however futile it might have proved—his last days. Grandfather's notebooks were cherished by his widow, for she believed in the power of their pages. I can't speak for others, but I suspect all of us wait for death by making, in one way or another, the same nonsensical doodles.

Zona Rosa, 1965

VICENTE LEÑERO

The Zona Rosa, or Pink District, is a cheap perfume in a fancy bottle. It's a chick from the sticks dressed as a chorus girl, a nouveau riche's daughter who pretends to be worldly but must go home early, so Daddy won't be mad. She's cute but dumb; elegant but frivolous. She's an uppity, greedy, affected schoolgirl.

To show off her dubious pedigree she commissions herself a coat of arms, displays her family tree, and buys sixteenth-century antiques at the Coloniart Boutique. She picks up a smattering of English, French, Russian, and Italian at the Berlitz School just to wow the tourists and sell them "Mexican curios" and little pottery idols down Génova Street. She outgrows her inhibitions by reading erotic literature at the Dalis Bookshop. An aspiring intellectual, she frequents the Souza and Juan Martín galleries, uttering "aahs," "oohs," and "aahs" in front of paintings by José Luis Cuevas, Alberto Gironella, Manuel Felguérez, and Arnaldo Coen. She's well versed in literature; she's chatted with Carlos Fuentes at Café Tirol; she's become a bullfighting buff after seeing Paco Camino leaving Hotel Presidente. She lives at Génova 20 to be neighbors with

Emily Cranz and Andy Russell, or at the Londres Residential to be on first-name terms with Gloria Lasso.

She buys her jewelry at Kimberley or Myro's—money is no problem—and orders her furniture from Chippendale and Cozy. Her fashion sense is kept up to scratch by Pilar Candel. She flirts coyly at the Lautrec Café, dines on steak béarnaise at Focolare, blows streamers at the Can-Cán, and dances till four—naughty girl wracked by guilt—at Jacarandas.

Illegitimate

The Zona Rosa was born suddenly, the offspring of a commercial venture, the fruit of an indiscretion committed in the nearby neighborhood of Colonia Juárez.

After forty painful years of mourning the *ancien régime* killed by the Mexican Revolution—years spent pining for their bygone power and glory—the distressed gentlefolk of Colonia Juárez faced a dilemma: either go on living in their gloomy old mansions, hungry but proud of their lineage, or accept the nouveaux riches' offer-you-can't-refuse of fresh power, new glory, and a bank balance in the black in exchange for seventeen streets and sixty-nine acres.

The conquistador prevailed, and so one day the ranks of gray façades with their diseased growths of columns, capitals, and curlicues gave way to sheets of glass and concrete beams surging from cellars and attics and hallways, trampling over bedrooms, giving shape and space to the aseptic commercial space of boutiques, beauty salons, gift shops, and bazaars.

Empire chairs, chandeliers, antique paintings, bibelots, velour drapes, and tapestries went from "family heirlooms" to "in-store specials" practically overnight. There was no need to move them—practically all these tchotchkes stayed put—only to add a price tag.

The Siamese cats that used to doze by the fireplace on cushions embroidered by the eldest daughter were scared away by the concrete invasion. Shamefaced, the daughter fled as well, usually to the top floor. She rented out the house. Tenants moved into the basement, the hallways, the living room. Eventually she sold the house and the land and went off to live in a modernist condominium. She couldn't bear to watch the construction of four- and five-floor modern buildings.

A handful of old mansions were spared and remain, as souvenirs, in Colonia Juárez. Some of them, islands in a sea of towers, weep behind lowered blinds and drawn lace curtains. Their owners have forsaken them, and now they are little more than the husks of legends. Who lives behind the weed-covered walls of Hamburgo 88? Could it be the ghost of Chabrier Lestrosne, a count fallen on hard times, disgraced millionaire, French refugee who was friendly with Dracula?

In the early 1960s, this patch of Mexico City was reborn as the "district of art, elegance, and good taste." That's how they christened her, with a dab of Parisian perfume. The father, a newly rich retailer, was raising her to be a sophisticated, extravagant gal who could hold her own with New York's Greenwich Village and San Francisco's Russian Hill. They forced her to copy foreign ways and the style didn't fit. Soon she was looking pretty threadbare and was nicknamed Zona Rosa. Too artless for red, too frivolous for white. Pink: just pink.

Xenophile

The music of an organ grinder standing outside Hotel Genève, or opposite the Golden Suites on Londres Street, disturbs Zona Rosa's slumber. She had tried to stay awake — it's so chic, so *épatant,* to party till dawn — but one martini at the Villa Fontana went to her head and made her drowsy, though of course she'll boast of having downed ten or twelve.

She gets up in a bad mood, annoyed that the organ grinder belies her vaunted love of jazz, upset that there's still a street market between Liverpool and Londres instead of a California-cool supermarket, bothered because she must go to mass at La Votiva and confess her petty sins (in English) to a Jesuit priest, and pissed, but really pissed, to see they haven't yet banned that obnoxious peddler pushing his newspaper-, bottle-, and old clothes-laden cart through the streets. She's from out of town; she's not a local. Why else would her stores be called Albert, Johnny's, Eddie's, Fanny, Gérard, Janna, Adorée, Andrew Geller, Jack Robert, Lila Bath?

Pretentious

Before the boutiques and galleries open, as she watches future *juniors* filing into Chapultepec Preschool, Zona Rosa breakfasts on a Boston-style hamburger at Aunt Jemima's.

It's time to check her reflection, coyly, on the shop windows, always free of metal shutters, day and night. Time to deposit yesterday's earnings at one of the eighteen banks. Time to fantasize about a trip to take her away from Mexico forever, as she pores through glossy brochures in one of thirty travel agencies or wanders streets that aren't named after European capitals for nothing.

By ten o'clock, Zona Rosa has decided she doesn't like Mexico. Buses ply up and down Reforma letting their passengers off at "Amberes, please," or "Génova's fine," or "Drop me at Niza." Young women in high heels click across the street to their jobs at hair salons, cafeterias, and bazaars. Others materialize under Insurgentes Cinema's great prow, simple girls from humble families transmuted into vampish, eyelash-fluttering coquettes, true natives of this sham Montmartre. Shop-owning ladies arrive driving their own cars. There are twenty-five parking lots to accommodate them. They open their boutiques, glance at their reflection in countless mirrors, cross and uncross their legs, parade their outfits and their hairdos. Sitting pretty—watching the world go by, being noticed and admired—is more important than the shop itself. That's why most of them are here. They were bored at home, so their millionaire husbands or lovers set them up with a boutique or a "beauty shop." No matter if the customers are few and far between. What matters is being close to Zona Rosa's imported designers. They have to compete, shamelessly ripping off Marisa Ruby's collection (my dear, she dresses Rita Hayworth!). They bask in the glory of Lily Ascheri, the famous soprano who never grants an encore or wears the same dress twice. They dress like Amparo and Jesusa, the empresses of Spanish fashion. And they steal customers from Les Hirondelles, where the budding misses, the daughters of society's finest, schedule demure fittings, stamp their feet, and demand a more risqué cleavage.

Haughty

Zona Rosa bewitches everyone. Those who don't know her, those who don't visit her, "are out of it," "miss the best of Mexico City." For this reason, at twelve o'clock publicists, architects, and youngsters from the French Lycée (Zona Rosa is the favored destination for kids playing hooky) sip coffee and orange juice at the Sanborns on Niza. At Café Konditori, best friends pour out their afflictions and secrets as they nibble on mocha cake and pray for a wink from some *junior*. The Spaniards, former regulars of Campoamor and Tupinamba, now meet at Restaurante 77 on Londres Street.

The nouveaux riches head for the fine fabrics of Telas Pani and the furniture exclusives at Chippendale, Cozy, Medina Peón, or Santoyo to spruce up their homes. Meanwhile the actor Che Reyes, dazed by Zona Rosa's scented venom, advises everyone to save their money, set up a shirt shop like his own, and avoid working for television. Mexican life is all here!

But neither at noon, nor at any other time of day or night—in sharp contrast to the proliferation of shops—do streets or stores boom with business. The great mass of shoppers, the housewives, the middle classes, remain faithful to downtown dollar stores and bargain basements along Avenida Insurgentes. They go to Zona Rosa for a stroll, to drop their jaws at the prices, or to ogle the assistants' legs, but not to shop.

Only cars, brought to a halt by a red light or a double-parked van, suffer from traffic jams. As night falls, parking valets whistle as they direct a sudden throng of Mustangs, Alfa Romeos, Corvette Stingrays, and Ferraris, all revving their engines as if on a racetrack. The proud owners of a new car must always take it for a first spin around Colonia Juárez.

Gluttonous

Counting cafeterias, restaurants, bars, and nightclubs, Zona Rosa has sixty-two different locales to indulge gourmet palates. She was taught to sample dishes from around the world, and every afternoon she invites the most discriminating diners—along with those posing as such—for lunch. In gastronomy as in all the rest: to eat in the Zona Rosa is "an unmistakable sign of good taste."

To close important business deals, there's El Chalet Suizo. Industrialists from the north prefer Cantonese delicacies at Luaú—breast of chicken with mushrooms and filet mignon in oyster sauce—not much better than the ones served up in Chinatown, but considerably pricier, to be sure. Executives and politicians lunch at Bellinghausen in the company of Luis Padilla Nervo, Marilú Elízaga, and Agustín Barrios Gómez. Bankers sip apéritifs at Delmonicos, keeping an eye on the New York–style board where a waiter chalks up stock quotes. And for the exclusive few—CEOs, business tycoons—there is the Key Club, in the passage between Génova and Londres, opposite Galería del Oso Blanco, where for fifteen hundred pesos Alex Duval can sketch your portrait in ninety minutes.

Affected

Jumping up and down, a scented Zona Rosa prepares to welcome the *juniors:* awkward Latin-lovers-in-training, failed gigolos, androgynous clean-cut youths parading as Alain Delon, Steve McQueen, or Peter O'Toole look-alikes.

You can smell them coming a mile away. Fragrant, they step from Salón Maxel after a twenty-five-peso "razor-sculpting" job, wearing Marqués de Larios suits, Leduc's made-to-measure shirts, and billing all expenses to Daddy's credit card.

They park the MG on the street, preferably under a No Parking sign, fully aware that this will lead to arguments, a lengthy recitation of influential relatives, and a last-minute attempt to bribe a law-enforcing, motorcycle-riding cop after he has already unscrewed the license plate and called the tow truck. But before this happens, the Zona Rosa *junior* stations himself at the corner of Génova and Hamburgo, staring covetously at other juniors sporting Italian-made clothes and sizing up women's curves. The girls studying English three times a week at the American Cultural Center are always in a hurry, and they scarcely have time to nod in agreement when they're asked out—if they're lucky—on an after-class date at Café Leblon or Café Kineret.

Studly *juniors* always top off a week of dates—or a rendez-vous with some American bird visiting Mexico as an exchange student—with a night out at Chipp's, the trendy bar. Inside there is a U-shaped bar and a lame jazz band that plays only till one, to the frenzied applause of Latin lovers who imagine they're being entertained by Charlie Parker or Miles Davis as they get tanked on highballs and ignore their dates.

Capricious

Sanborns is the headquarters of humbler juniors who don't hit the neighborhood in an MG or a Barracuda. Some have even made the transition from mere clients to maîtres of this crowded café. They show people to tables, bring them menus, take their orders, then stand around playing dumb and ignoring their client-pals, who must wait for the end of the shift to see the maîtres make a comeback to the neighborhood, either as rightful denizens or—why not?—as gang members.

Gangs? Of course: Zona Rosa takes pride in her Hollywood-style gangs: the members are karate wizards, as liable to be found kickboxing a rival as discoursing on experimental cinema. They read serious comics, write beat poetry à la Ginsberg, and use English expressions like "That's the way the bongo bingles," "Wear a safe," and "This is the way the world ends." And those who can't understand them are deemed to be pitiful ignoramuses, morons, *finks*.

Snobbish

Before night falls, Zona Rosa lets her hair down like Brigitte Bardot, removes every last trace of makeup, and changes into blue jeans. That's all it takes to become an intellectual and be admitted to Café Tirol.

It is here, and not at the U.S. Consulate's Benjamin Franklin Library, that one becomes cultured by listening to Luis Guillermo Piazza lecturing on American literature, Homero Aridjis expounding on erotic poetry, René Rebetz vindicating science fiction, and Emilio García Riera extolling the two films devoted to Zona Rosa: Ícaro Cisneros's *El día comenzó ayer [The Day Started Yesterday]* and José Luis Ibáñez's *Las dos Elenas [The Two Elenas]*.

Another clique—of painters—meets at Juan Martín Gallery, where the owner and namesake is not content with marketing and selling new, "nonfigurative" talents. He also takes them out to dinner at Pizza Real, counsels them through creative crises, and joins them in wondering why the hell so many ignorant and ill-informed foreigners still buy folksy dolls at Tamariz and waste money on Sámano's "Mexicanist" paintings at Firenze Galleries.

Café Carmel is the refuge of poets snubbed by the city's literary mafias—centered around Café Tirol and the journals *Revista Universal* and *La Cultura en México*—and writers who have nowhere else to go for dinner. Every night don Jacobo Glanz, the Carmel's proprietor, joins several tables so his friends can hear and extol his latest biblical poems in Yiddish. "Superb, don Jacobo!"

Prudish

Bright neon signs blink as Zona Rosa, draped in furs, feasts on coq au vin at the Normandie, chicken Kubla Khan and teriyaki mignon at the Mauna Loa; she takes in the magic of violins at Villa Fontana and dances under the shadowy vault at Jacarandas.

It is the sinful hour. And yet the mere hint of illicit pleasure sends her into a spin. She would be scandalized if a boîte ever dared to advertise a strip-tease — it is ab-so-lu-tely forbidden. The most she can aspire to — and this makes her feel quite worldly — is a poor, fluffy imitation of the Parisian Moulin Rouge at the Can-Cán, where a pack of chorus girls lumber through the same steps night after night, tripping over their feet, singing out of tune, and putting the tourists to sleep. Everyone is bored to death, but no one will admit to it for fear of offending Zona Rosa, who cherishes the Can-Cán as the crown jewel of her worldliness.

They'd rather drink — at whatever price — martinis and highballs and sing along under their ten-gallon hats:

"In-a-Chin-ese-foooo-rest, a-Chi-na-girl-was-lost . . ."

At four in the morning everything comes to an end. Home to bed then, after the required purchase of "violets for the missus" from a poor Indian vendor, slung with babies, who accosts the tottering die-hards of the night.

It is then that Rosa pines for her provincial roots. The Parisian gown doesn't suit her, and she's still hungry after dining on lobster Thermidor. Furtively, unseen by anyone, she sneaks away to the food stalls on Génova, and there, among the frying pans of La Tía Jesús and the stewing pots of La Bella Unión, she stuffs herself on chicken tacos, barbecued pork, brains, and innards. That's her true style. But hush . . . no one must ever know.

With a burp of remorse, she nods off at last. Her eighteen blocks yawn in unison as she rests her hexagonal, sixty-nine-acre body. Zona Rosa, the little provincial metropolis, the district of elitism, affectation and artifice, the phoniest address in town, is finally asleep.

San Rafael

GERARDO DENIZ

I met Juan Almela[1] in the first months of 1943. We were eight years old, and our eyes met when we both looked away from a live turtle that was having its shell wrenched off in the fish section of San Cosme market. The most appalling part was the creature's silence.

We never referred to the tragic turtle in later conversations, but our friendship grew and we were classmates for a while, as well as neighbors. I left the neighborhood of San Rafael at the end of 1951. He stayed on in the same house, where I still call on him, sometimes weekly, sometimes once a month.

Thirty years ago my friend told me of his intention to write a long and leisurely book about the neighborhood where he was born and has always lived. I, who had shared the place with him between the ages of eight and seventeen, endorsed his project. Years passed, then decades. My friend often talked about his book. I always responded enthusiastically, as though it were for real. But he never showed me a single page, never read me a single paragraph. I confess it: the book which over time I came to know, not like the palm of my hand (who ever looks at the palm of his hand?) but like the back of my teeth, that book became as real for me—despite its apparent nonexistence—as all the nonexistent books I have planned to write myself.

Seeking shelter from the rain, I dropped in on my friend Juan a few days ago. As on so many other occasions, he filled us two small glasses of a special, thick, yellow tequila. The tiled fountain spurted feebly in the small patio. Raindrops fell on the lilies. Above, a patch of gray sky. One by one, Juan's three stray cats, disappointed at the weather, curled up next to us.

My friend pulled up his leather chair, and we clinked glasses. Casually, he handed me a bulky envelope, as the rain pounded and the cats licked themselves clean. In spite of the drumming downpour, I understood perfectly.

"In case you felt like writing a prologue."

(I accepted with a single word, drowned out by thunder.)

And that's what I'm trying to do, with some anxiety. Because my friend, apart from being born in San Rafael and living there all his life, has figured out everything, has heard everything, and knows all there is to know. He comes up with the most unsuspected and unfathomable statistics, and collates a hundred years' worth of data (San Rafael celebrated its first centenary not long ago). He knows who was born where and when. The parade includes Victoriano Huerta, followed by Julio Torri, the Gorostiza brothers, Salvador Novo, Montes de Oca, Remedios Varo with Benjamin Péret, Renato Leduc, León Felipe. Uneven voices.

For almost thirty years, my friend has attended every one of the melancholy Pimentel Street fairs. What could I ever contribute to such erudition? A handful of disparate remarks. Since I want to avoid lavish praise, I fear I may sound grumpy at times; I know this is wrong, but consider the circumstances. Given my inferior stature, any opening must do.

Except for acknowledging the renowned musical masters who lived in the neighborhood, and the songs we were forced to sing in school (songs that are never forgotten, as my friend Miret rightly points out), Juan never mentions music in his book—he is an intellectual after all. I must painfully concede that he is right. There is no such thing as San Rafaelian music. Those of us who grew up here, listening to anything from Cricri to Prokofiev, associate certain tunes with certain streets, but these must be recognized as entirely personal, incommunicable chance occurrences. I thus have no excuse (though this will not stop me) for re-calling that primary school teacher of mine who on many afternoons in 1943, after school was out, would play and replay the only two piano pieces he knew by heart. One was a shapeless pounding called the "Ze-peda March," the other a sublime composition, which years later I found out was called "Íntimo secreto," by Alfonso Esparza Oteo. That waltz, heard at such an early age, in that place and at that time of day, marked my spirit forever; it branded me in scorching fire, like a heifer, with the shameful stamp of immobility. Apart from such uncanny expe-riences, the only other music I recall hearing as a native of San Rafael came from the Wurlitzer organ showroom on Rosas Moreno Street: a bellowing that often reached as far as my house.

Outside, the cries of street vendors were the epitome of unin-telligibility. I could make out, barely, the blind lottery-seller with his guide—"Nacional, forty thousand pesos . . . forty thousand for tomorrow"—but a certain Sunday-morning shriek took me a long time to decipher: "¡Flor de azucena!" The problem was I heard it from bed, and by the time I'd get to the window and look out, all I could see was the stately progress of General Heriberto Jara. It was during a San Ra-fael evening—around 1947—that I first heard the infinitely sorrowful whistle of the *camote* vendor pushing his cart through our streets, selling sweet potatoes—a sight that, fortunately, is still common in the neigh-borhood. Once, after spending weeks shut up in San Rafael, I ventured out to Parque México, and as I strolled I heard the piercing lament of that crepuscular cart. I feared he would never get back to my street in time for his usual round, tacitly supposing that in all the world there could be only one little pushcart graced with a bitonal steam whistle, and heaped with corn cobs and sweet potatoes.

In contrast to the very personal street cries, there was one hellish pe-riod toward the end of the 1940s when we suffered a plague of "sound cars." These nondescript old cars, fitted with powerful loudspeakers, would park at the corner and start blasting things like "*Naranjas, naran-jas* . . . Oranges, oranges, we're offering oranges, delicious oranges, come to this sound car and see, the oranges we're offering, at the in-credible price of . . ." (the exact figure escapes my memory), over and over again, at least a thousand times, for almost an hour. If we were lucky the car would then move on to the next corner and we could enjoy an encore of the whole performance, though now muted by a block's distance, for another forty-five minutes.

Suddenly there is a confused row down the street, an unmistakable drumming, and from patios to roofs the excited call is heard: *"¡Los perritos, los perritos!"* ("The doggies, the doggies!"). Outside, by the stream (they'd better mind the splashes when the Santa María–Tacubaya bus rumbles along), three or four hooligans of both genders dress four or five deplorable mutts in miniature sombreros and miniskirts. The leader of the troop shouts something incomprehensible through a megaphone. The drum begins its dreary beat. The clarinet joins in. And while one dog advances, walking backward on a rolling barrel, the others rise on their hind legs and dance. A wretched spectacle. And the music? Ten years later, we could still remember it; one day, while listening to the last movement of the *Fantastique*, I made my childhood friends laugh by whispering, at the point when the clarinet repeats its obsessive theme against a background of soft drumming, "The dancing doggies!"

San Rafael would have been a great place for evening church bells. But back then, the bells rang seldom if at all. One day, many years later, I drew my friend's attention to the peals coming from the church on Icazbalceta and Velázquez de León, but he cut short my nostalgic remarks by pointing out, "It's a recording." I should mention in passing that San Rafael's churches were terrible, with the exception of the one on Serapio Rendón, next to the Opera cinema (hailed, when under construction, as "the most stupendous in America"). But to find out all there is to know about churches (and cinemas decorated with plaster acanthus leaves), read my friend, who knows the lot. I also remember the eight o'clock morning whistle from the Larín chocolate factory, on Miguel Schultz Street. Larín! Now there's a fascinating history to be written, of which San Rafael represents only a bite.

There was no shortage of noises in San Rafael. Especially railway noises. There was always the engine's whistle, and some nights, depending on the direction of the wind, you could hear the very last beat of the train chugging away into the distance. When I lived there, locomotives still ran on steam, but they no longer rang those centrifugal bells.

I don't know why I am reminded, now, of that dark Saturday afternoon in 1964 when I sought refuge in my friend's tranquil abode after a family row. He was not at home. I was going down Miguel Schultz when I saw a strange bundle lying against the wall on the deserted sidewalk ahead. As I approached I recognized the blind man with bloodshot eyes, whom I hadn't seen for fifteen years. During my childhood he used to play an accordion, sounding a pair of tone clusters that only Bartók could have notated, and here he was repeating the action; but now the instrument only exhaled two alternate, still distinct, puffing sounds.

And what about the thunder of fire engines late at night? Now those were bells, ringing amid sirens and revving engines. The chief firefighter had the perfect fireman's name—Evodio—and was to die heroically in the course of duty. People like him still exist. There were daylight fires as well, but it was more impressive to jump awake, heart thudding, in the darkness. Sometimes the fire engine sped past me. Sometimes it slowed, along with the bells and the siren, and stopped neither far away nor close by. In his monograph, my friend naturally mentions the legendary neighborhood fires, but he does not dwell on their frequency, still unabated today. A flammable neighborhood, I always said.

Despite all this, during the 1940s the average San Rafael night was very quiet. A car might pass every five minutes. If a terrifying scene erupted outside, I would get out of bed, lean my forehead on the cold windowpane, and see, by the light of the streetlamp, a pack of cats rushing across the street. (It was most rewarding to examine that streetlight through binoculars, to discover the grainy texture of the glass and the tiny insects revolving around it.) Trams—essential elements of San Rafael's sound anthology—clattered down Artes Street until late at night. A sign on the front read "Artes"; then "2 Tacuba," then again "Artes . . ." My friend Juan has gathered all this information but he doesn't know that yesterday I trod on the curved rails that still protrude through the pavement on Icazbalceta and M. M. Contreras. There used to be a tram terminal there, centuries ago; I used to make my way there after wonderful concerts and dinners. When the trams disappeared, I took a taxi, and I could always tell the moment we left the neighborhood.

San Rafael's borders are well defined. My friend's book specifies all the relevant details. What remains to be said? Only that—at least during my childhood and adolescence—our relations with neighboring districts were thriving along three sides and absolutely nil to the west: Colonia Anáhuac was considered another world, for reasons of elementary Marxism. But Colonia Santa María, to the north, contained the old market, which was as much ours as theirs. Across the street, the south sidewalk of Ribera de San Cosme, a road that was San Rafaelian to the core, was taken over at night by the enticing sizzle of frying food. *Fritangas,* a name that says it all, and *churros,* defined by Spanish dictionaries as "fruits of the skillet." Between two stalls, a crouched figure sang

"Rumba-dancing skeleton," feigning nonchalance as a diminutive wood skeleton frolicked in front of him, on the sidewalk. You couldn't see the threads attaching the dancing figure to the vendor's jiggling knees.

To the east, across Ramón Guzmán, the street where Margarita lived with her piano, lay Colonia Tabacalera; here the transition was less obvious, though there was no denying that once you reached the Monument to the Revolution, San Rafael had been left behind. Pedro F. Miret, who spent nights thereabouts, assured me that sometimes he could actually hear the bustling sounds from the Buenavista train station (of course, it used to be much closer to Puente de Alvarado than it is today).

Ramón Guzmán was a wide and important boulevard, with its own distinct noises and trams, which it was not necessary to ride. There, one could also catch buses to Indios Verdes, along a thoroughfare that was then named no less than Calzada México-Laredo. One fine day, after minor demolition on the San Rafael side, Ramón Guzmán woke up with a new name: Insurgentes. Many people hastily call the section beyond the Monument to the Revolution "Insurgentes Norte," but they are mistaken. The correct name for the stretch running between the monument and San Cosme is Insurgentes Centro—a road that has even been improved, unexpectedly, by numerous trees that managed to grow on its central divider. At the south end of today's Insurgentes Centro, near a dismal horseshoe-shaped hotel, there was once a sign that read: "Doctor Ojeda—enfermedades de los ojos" (Dr. C. Eye, Eye Specialist). The right man in the right place.

To the south of San Rafael lay Colonia Cuauhtémoc, a delicacy. The change as you entered it was palpable, yet they were still family, with their leafy streets and slightly parvenu atmosphere. There is a park between these two neighborhoods, in what was once a station I never knew, and the book for which I am trying to write a prologue devotes a commendable amount of attention to it. So I shall not berate the author for withholding certain facts he is well aware of: that there we scampered and whooped and roller-skated (oh the clanging of skates, especially when you try to walk in them!); or that there I abandoned my dull pet chameleon when its brio began to fade; or that on that civilized grass I read passages from Alfred de Musset in tandem with Álvaro, a native of Cuauhtémoc, our low, guilty voices raising Gamiani's incandescence to positively obscene heights.

Unlike a certain Condesa, we were not loud in San Rafael. Only a seamstress who worked next to the beauty parlor would emerge at lunchtime to shout for her nephew from the corner: "Gilo!" And the most we ever heard through a wall was how Covarrubias's neighbor sometimes beat his wife, though moderately. A squalid, sterile couple they were, with faces as bitter as guayaca sap.

Note

1. Gerardo Deniz is Juan Almela's pseudonym.

Coyoacán I

GUILLERMO SHERIDAN

I've come to Coyoacán to have my shoes shined; I also suffer from nostalgia. I enjoy Coyoacán because it has survived the quick-buck facelifts imposed by city officials and the tiresome trends of fashion (which, as we all know, is so tacky that it constantly needs to be changed), and it has survived because the neighborhood is the perfect setting for wallowing in nostalgia. The plaza is a game, and whoever ends up with the most textual toys wins.

Three plazas, to be exact: three open spaces form one great plaza. The northeast plaza is the seat of political power, and is crowned by a palace that once belonged to Cortés but now houses government offices. A landscape of soporific bureaucrats—their torpor at odds with the frenzy of pigeons that turn every crumb into a casus belli—this plaza has been taken over by bureaucrats and loudspeakers operated by PRI apparatchiks convinced that their broadcasts will be made more persuasive by jacking up the volume.

On Sundays, if you're lucky, the plaza's kiosk comes to life as Don Gildardo Mújica's band drums its characteristic ta-thump, ta-thump;

otherwise you have to endure the howlings of a teenage starlet—
probably kept by a politician—improvising songs about the cause and
effect of impossible love. Tricycle-riding toddlers turn the plaza's paths
into preschool expressways; dazed newlyweds emerge from the registry
followed by crowds of relatives; two drunks stagger together in perfect
synchronicity, weaving a single zigzag, and—like the plaza—they move
neither forward nor back.

The little southeast plaza belongs to a more spiritual realm; the ancient Franciscan church rises over it, casting an aura of relative peace
and quiet. The church's former atrium—most people treat it like yet
another thoroughfare—still draws pious widows longing for gone-by
monasteries. Like hooded shadows, the old women march in procession, eating Sunday sweets, reciting litanies in response to mimes who
take them for easy prey, and staring—from the depths of their ancestral
boredom—at wannabe-dandies and matrons, guests arriving to attend
some hick wedding.

My shoeshine man works in the western plaza. It's mid-morning
when I arrive, buy the paper, and settle down for Don Gume's one-
dollar polish job with political commentary thrown in. He talks so
much, I consider him an example of what Quevedo termed the *parlaem-
balde,* the vain-speaker.

The western plaza fancies itself the liberal, postmodern, forward-
looking, painstakingly symbiotic sector. It's our local version of those
distant squares: Sloane, Washington, Tiananmen, Tlatelolco. The scene
is a ragbag of home-grown freaks, punks, and aboriginal skinheads
mixed in with candy-floss couples, zoom-wielding tourists, legwarmer-
wearing pan flutists, haggard gurus, caramelized socialites, Savater-
sucking intellectuals, snobs in search of Foucault's—*Fukó's*—pendulum,
panhandlers of every vintage, pomaded spouses, do-gooders with a
cause that needs *you,* and, last but not least, the last of the hippies—
jipis—still believing in Harry Krishna and talking groovy.

If the northeast plaza reeks of ink, *pulque,* and disinfectant, the
southeast smells of incense and dried flowers, and the west reeks of
sickeningly sweet patchouli blended with the neuron-busting spray
paint of the heavy-metal—*jebimétal*—artists. If the northeast throbs to
the megawatts—*megaguats*—of populism and the southeast reflects on
the *tantum ergo,* the west harmonizes Pink Floyd—*pinfloi*—and Andean
pan-flutes. People munch on democratic pork rinds on the bureaucratic
plaza, devour beatific *churros* on the next, and sip po-mo cappuccinos on

the last. They read Raúl Velasco's tell-all autobiography on the first plaza, the parish newsletter on the next, and *La Jornada* on the last. Cashmere, cotton, jeans. Hair gel, braids, dreadlocks. Et cetera.

But while the (ultimately eschatological) bureaucratic and spiritual plazas never change, the western square, though equally changeless, reinvents itself constantly. It has seen troubadours, mimes, jazz players, storytellers, ecologists, gymnasts, and Zen monks. The latest import is a splendid display of postcard-perfect pseudo-Aztecs who descend on the plaza every weekend in full regalia of feather headdress, cardboard breastplate, ankle bells, and rattles; after addressing Tonatiuh in Nahuatl, they dance and holler madly around a Styrofoam skull, their sandals stomping into the air a large percentage of the valley of Mexico. Compared to this kind of nostalgia, mine feels almost quaint.

Don Gume, the vain-speaking shoeshine man of clear Indian ancestry, confines his opinion to a single grunt between rubs of the cloth:

"Jerks."

I watch them skipping around and around. A stoned tourist calls "May I?" and joins the circle. Someone puts a headdress on him. The drumbeat picks up. The dance reaches a climactic rattling and ends with an epic group kneeling. The pseudo-Aztec closest to me opens his arms wide; he's wearing Calvin Klein briefs. The sky clouds over. In the northeast plaza, the loudspeaker starts again, a bureaucratic emcee vociferating:

"Let's all show we're proud of being . . ."

I can't hear what we're supposed to be proud of, because thunder rumbles and it starts raining. I pay Don Gume fast. The final image is a scuttling of bureaucrats, church ladies, hippies, and pseudo-Aztecs under the downpour.

All running in different directions.

Coyoacán II

JORGE IBARGÜENGOITIA

Coyoacán Square, my friends tell me, is one of the nicest corners in Mexico City. I stare, nonplussed for a moment, before conceding: yes, it is, inasmuch as any corner that might be called nice is a rare bird, and getting rarer. But deep down I'm fully aware that the square, the plaza, or *el mero Zócalo* as the taxi drivers call it, leaves much to be desired.

Let's examine the square. Coyoacán actually has two squares, one facing the church and the other next to it. The first is named Plaza del Centenario and the second, Jardín Hidalgo. Each of the two squares boasts a colonial monument. The first has the church gates, which in the absence of adjacent walls no longer open or close or lead anywhere at all. Three archways have been preserved as historic relics, as mementos of better days. The garden faces the single landmarked house in Coyoacán—the home of Hernán Cortés, no less. This building has housed government offices, a police station, and even a prison. Later it was abandoned, and now there is nothing but a courtroom and something that resembles a library from the outside (I've never confirmed whether it contains any books).

And of course there's the church, whose interior was remodeled back in the 1950s, to the point of making it unrecognizable. One can still take in the exterior of the church without feeling consumed by indignation: the façade and the walls of the apse, which lead to Caballo Calco Street, flanked by tamale stalls and juice kiosks.

Coyoacán Square, which was probably a nice corner during the seventeenth century, has fallen prey to the memory of its glory days. To understand its transformation, we might compare the square to a woman who was a devastating beauty at the age of twenty. She aged gracefully, feeling confident about her looks until she reached forty; from then on, she starts feeling ugly and takes action to regain her beauty by dressing not like a well-preserved thirty-something but like her former twenty-year-old self.

Something similar happened to the square. It matured naturally— that is to say, houses grew up around it that corresponded to what their inhabitants expected of a house—until the turn of the century. Then came the Revolution, which inspired landlords—who were never revolutionaries—to discover the beauties of colonial architecture. From then on, nothing has been built around Coyoacán Square unless it's colonial in style.

But like the lady in my analogy, whose efforts to regain her beauty are inspired by faded memories and made possible by the wonders of technology, the plaza's quest for colonial beauty has produced mutant styles and other aberrations.

One house, for example, was built in the late 1930s. This is a "colonial" example of Hollywood baroque. It was inspired—like most houses at the time—by the Pasadena railway station in California: massive, with fake tiled roofs, the walls painted pale yellow (now a cadaverous gray), its doors and windows framed by elaborate moldings.

The house stands in the center of the lot, surrounded by gardens, a design that would have been unthinkable during colonial times.

But then light dawned. Somebody (I think it was my Uncle Pepe López) discovered the "real authentic colonial style." And this is? Plastering everything with tezontle stone.

The houses went cubic. They might have a corner niche, for the sake of atmosphere, holding a Virgin of Guadalupe, and cheap, T-shaped metal windows. At street level, their storefronts were rented out to drug-stores, shoe shops, or whatever. Inside, the rooms followed no particular order, and if they got too dark, light wells to the rescue. The exterior was finished in tezontle, with pink stone trimmings.

Today, things have changed again. We've become more refined. Façades are now sober and whitewashed. A huge slab of a front door, filched from an abandoned church; next to it, a donut-shaped stone once used for tying horses. This ring, an owner confides, is strikingly similar to the hoops gracing pre-Columbian "ball courts"—whose pur-pose, it must be said, remains in doubt. Some contend they were used to play a game not unlike basketball, while others argue they were gallows for hanging the players of the losing team.

The city government—or is it the Department of Public Works?—has done its bit to embellish Coyoacán Square. They're done fixing up the garden—thank God—and they've started on the square. Something very odd has happened there. It was completely overhauled two years ago: iron benches, cobblestones, fresh trees, a new coat of paint for the archway, et cetera. It looked pretty nice. The odd thing is, now they're redoing it all over again. They decided to build a ledge around the path-ways, an undertaking that took three months, clogged the drains, and blocked access to the benches. Soon people were climbing over the ledge to get to the benches, scratching their knees on the way. Of course such inconveniences are to be expected on a building site. Appropriate measures have been taken, like ruining the gardens by hacking ditches to drain the walkways. But, hey, we're making progress. The stone to finish the ledge has already arrived. The square will finally have that un-mistakable colonial look, with a slight touch of Aztec architecture. But I wonder: Who instigates these works of embellishment? Who lands the contracts for providing the stone?

División del Norte

JULIETA GARCÍA GONZÁLEZ

The first time I saw the stuffed bear I was struck by the shade of its fur: the white, polar shine I always imagined in such creatures was sorely lacking in this specimen. An array of grayish, bluish, muddy stains covered the bear's great back and huge head. Standing high on its hind legs, front paws boxing the air, and jaws wide open to show its fangs, this polar bear was no more than the shabby shadow of what it must have once been.

For reasons that remain strange and mysterious, many of the kitchen- and bathroom-supply stores located on División del Norte, between Churubusco and Gabriel Mancera, have installed enormous stuffed animals by their entrance doors: two polar bears, two Bengal tigers, two lions, half a bull, and at least one zebra rise over the doors of shops with names so similar, one can't help thinking that they all belong to the same person. After passing by this menagerie day after day—I drive down División del Norte seven days a week—I felt irresistibly compelled to enter the shops and ask where the animals came from and how they wound up in such inappropriate surroundings; I could not for the life of me think of a plausible reason for placing these creatures on fiberglass stands and having them tower over people on the hunt for toilet seats.

When I started to ask questions, I was met with another surprise: the reticent attitude of the shop assistants. Young salesmen in loud uniforms, who spend their days convincing ladies about the virtues of bathroom tiles and the imperative of combining marble with Mexican ceramic floors, pass their free time playing with lions, tigers, bears, or whatever animal they "ended up with." They stroke hairy rumps and tousled manes, stick their hands into varnished jaws, and finger plastic dentures. They shake a bear's heavy paw and stick out their tongues at a bull staring them down from the store's upper level, next to a display of hot tubs recessed into the wall. These beasts are their toys: they hide behind the lion (or the bear or the tiger) and go "Boo!" to make unsuspecting clients jump; they rock the fiberglass stands, growling and roaring, to scare pedestrians away.

Sometimes they lean back against the beasts, elbows deep in mangy fur, to have a smoke. "We're used to them," said Alejandro Gómez, from El Cerebro de los Azulejos, a store whose name translates as Brain of Tiles, as he toyed with a fearsome-looking lion perched atop three bathroom sinks placed in the middle of the sidewalk. Gómez explains that "the animals attract customers, so we get to sell more." While there's no doubt that stuffed animals stop people in their tracks, I have serious doubts as to whether the sight of a big lion or striped zebra infuses passers-by with an uncontrollable urge to buy kitchen faucets or fog-free mirrors. But I keep getting the same answer, store after store. I start watching the customers: it seems clear that people come in with a set purpose. If they stop to look at the lion, bear, or whatever, that's because it's there, towering over the entrance. As far as I can make out, no one arrives with the express purpose of petting the bear, only to be immediately overcome by the need to buy a toilet.

At El Cerebro de los Azulejos, I am informed that the lion arrived about a year ago and that a man comes in to freshen it up every now and then ("about once a month," says Juan, another employee). He combs the mane, scrubs the fur manhandled by employees and customers alike, and polishes the false teeth. While I'm admiring the recently spiffed-up lion, a voice behind me asks, "Is it a he-lion or a she-lion?" The question seems pointless, given the beast's size and shaggy mane, but it turns out the lion is missing "something." Juan hastens to explain: "It's a he-lion, but they had to remove *that* because he was going to be on display. No way could they let ladies or kids see that, let alone touch it." That's the cue for another assistant to scratch the lion's empty crotch, the hollow arch formed by its legs, with a knowing grin, while the salesmen who are explaining the art of taxidermy, or just looking on, burst out laughing.

They fix up the lions, the bears, the tigers, and the rest to repair the ravages of living outdoors: urban grime, acid rain, mud splashed by passing cars. In spite of the care seemingly lavished on these mascots, and the desire to preserve them as bait for buyers, the stuffed beasts suffer far more than they should from the vagaries of the weather. I ask one of the salesmen why he doesn't bring the bear inside, explaining that people can see him just the same from this side of the door. But he looks away with a patient smile, as though telling me that it's only out there to lure customers, and when that happens, he and his colleagues receive bonuses: "The animals have to be outside." For him, the stuffed bear is an indispensable talisman.

"Can't tell you that. Why do you want to know anyway?" snaps the manager of El Gigante de los Azulejos—The Tile Giant—when I ask who owns the stores and the animals. I insist; he becomes extremely flustered and beats a retreat, waving his cell phone in the air. One of the employees comes up and asks me, half intrigued, half bothered, "Why do you want to know?" On the spur of the moment, I pretend I want to buy a polar bear of my own. "We're not selling ours, but one of the other stores had a lion up for sale. I think it was going for around thirty thousand pesos. That place over there, across the street." Refusing to add anything else, he turns around to show a young couple the latest mosaic friezes. I cross the street and ask if the lion—the one missing *that*—is for sale, and they say no. "How did it get here?" I inquire, and this invites a string of silly stories: "I shot it," "Santa brought it," "it was already here," "the owner bought it" . . . Who's the owner? Is he a hunter? "I don't know his name," says Juan, who is feeling helpful, "but I'll find out if you like." He doesn't have to; somebody else calls out the name: Raúl Martínez, a professional hunter.

They continue with a series of myths and rumors about the alleged owner and his trophies; some implicate the hunter and tile magnate in murky deals, while others uphold him as a hardworking, saintly figure who always pays his taxes. "It's all just talk," says Victor of El Mundo de los Azulejos—World of Tiles—seeking to reassure me. He sees the boss as a square and honest person who likes "big animals" and thought they might make good marketing props, bait to bring in the customers. Someone else observes that División del Norte is a fabulous place for tile shops, and that the owner, his boss, had the foresight to set up his business here, and that the said owner is simply a man with smart ideas, dedicated to his work. A positive genius when it comes to selling tiles and toilets.

But not all the salesmen at the tile emporium—let alone the competition—agree with this version. After telling me all about their weird, quasi-familial relationships with the bull and the lion and the tiger, a group of employees tell me that the much-named Señor Martínez owned a disco on the Periférico, near Naucalpan, famous for having lots of live animals running around. As a decorative addendum, the owner had procured the stuffed specimens which now grace his shops. One of my interlocutors adds that the owner was in league with a prominent politician—or more precisely, with the son of a certain prominent politician. A despicable dinosaur type, famous for his love of hunting down and stuffing endangered species, and pretty good at selling them, too. Another employee claims that the tile shops were mounted because the disco venture had gone badly wrong—"a girl was found dead and there was some other funny business." He also says that the owner's name is not Raúl Martínez but Alejandro Martínez, and I feel no more enlightened than before. Regardless of the exact name or business, I am still at a loss to understand the point of standing a lion on a bathroom sink.

The polar bear is celebrating summer. Someone put on him a pair of dark glasses that are too small. The employees celebrate the bear's fashion makeover, oblivious to the customers who wander in and out of the store, waiting for someone to help them. A young woman wearing a short skirt and looking like a second-rate model claps as one of the sales boys climbs up a rickety ladder to adjust the sunglasses on the animal's long muzzle. To keep his balance, the young man leans on a front paw and the whole bear staggers. One of his colleagues shrieks from below, "Don't break the sunglasses!"

The animals' garb changes with the seasons. In September they are dressed as revolutionaries (yes, revolutionaries) and sport huge sombreros with a horrible, hand-painted "¡Viva México!" They have patriotic paper flags taped to their claws, and their chests are crossed with cardboard strips representing bullet belts. In winter the bear (or the lion or the tiger) is dressed up like Santa Claus, with a red hat and permanently soiled white pom-pom, over a ludicrous robe. In February the animals clutch heart-shaped balloons (Happy Valentine!) which can also be tied around their necks or tails. When there's nothing to celebrate, their front paws are made to hold up all kinds of notices ("Female assistant wanted, good presentation," "Come In, Faucets and Basins on Sale!" and so on).

In what other city would a majestic polar bear wind up as an incentive to buy toilets? What makes us turn these splendid, magnificent beasts into female revolutionaries or props for useless bathroom fixtures? It seems that living in a city like ours forces one to give in to the whirlwind, to succumb to collective schizophrenia. The indifference with which people seem to accept that the appropriate habitat for a Bengal tiger is precisely División del Norte makes me think that the city has overwhelmed us, that we have lost our bearings. Is anyone horrified to think that these animals, instead of fishing in the North Pole or hunting in the savanna, gather dust on the street after being rejected as decorations for a disco? This could only happen in a place that has lost control and lost touch with reality. That's the scary truth of our overpopulated city, but no one seems to care.

No one cares. Not the tile salesmen, unimpressed by the daily sight of stuffed wild beasts about to pounce; they see them as no more than passing amusements, fit to distract a whining toddler or to entertain a bored girl while her mother examines no-slip linoleum. I feel as though I'm the only person to be surprised. I see these animals as the unfathomable excess of marketing ploys. I see them as a daily source of shock and anxiety, the outcome of abuses that were never punished, or even exposed. I see them as a window into urban madness. Why do I keep taking this road? Because I know that the animals in this impossible zoo will remain standing at their posts until their skin falls apart from all the touching and mending, or until—with the passage of time and the same destructive practices—some limb breaks off and they get thrown away. And until that happens, I will go on contemplating their open mouths, outstretched claws, and angry brows while they, mutilated, patched-up, and impassive, stare back at the monotonous stream of traffic.

Plaza Satélite

You can be born and raised in this city, vow never to leave it, and still hardly know it: to live here is simply to *practice* (*"ejercer"* is the dazzling verb employed by Salvador Novo) some of its locations, those that best conform to one's temperament. At twenty-three, Novo had never seen the sea; at twenty-eight, Carlos Monsiváis had never been to Europe; at twenty-nine, Héctor Aguilar Camín had never been to the PRI head-quarters. As for me, I belong to the more humble band of those ap-proaching the fateful age—twenty-eight—without ever having been to the Plaza Satélite Shopping Mall. This omission is due to my having frittered all my time contentedly away in shabbier but lovable and fa-miliar parts of this inefficient town: Colonia Roma, the old Centro, Iz-tacalco, the cantina-studded Zona Rosa, Nueva Anzures, San Ángel, Condesa . . . Until one idle Saturday afternoon in late summer I actually boarded a bus in Chapultepec Park bound for Satélite, determined to cross out at least one item on my list of places to know before turning twenty-eight.

I anticipated writing this text: on the way, I was practically giving it the final polish in my head. A diatribe against consumerism, aimed at a target so conspicuous that there was no need for insult: it would suffice to record, in all objectivity, some of its features. To be a camera, Isherwood-like. Sure enough, I jotted down the following observations in my notebook, using a medium, number two pencil: a place for car owners (in the huge warehouse-like parking lots, the pedestrian feels like a worm; he enters the mall feeling already diminished, almost mutilated, like a one-legged person in a sports stadium or a one-armed passenger in a packed, cruisy subway car). Satélite is a closed, covered mall; one is constantly treading on private property of some kind, unlike in the subway or even other malls, like Plaza Universidad, where the open-air sections allow some sense of the public street.

An ostentatious display of tacky luxury and "good taste" cultivated by an upper middle class with delusions of culture (cafés called Mozart, Beethoven posters hanging on the walls of electronics stores) and refinement (cheaply painted copies of eighteenth-century portraits; languid half-laced ladies in boudoirs, shepherdesses, et cetera). Aguilar Booksellers has a sign proclaiming "A Garden Full of Flowers, a Home Full of Books." Here the hairdressers call themselves, with a Hegelian flourish, Aestheticians, and hair is not cut but—oh Laocoön!—"sculpted." The mannequins in the windows are gorgeous and sophisticated, inaccurate mirrors in which gullible buyers see their own reflection. There is a fake marble floor, geometric metal sculptures, vast mirrors all over the place, decorative greenery in portable planters with brand-new fresh plants, no doubt destined to be thrown out and replaced the following week (Roberts advertises its suits religiously with little sprays of wheat), a glossy overall spotlessness.

Inside, this enclosed mall is fairly open-plan. Boundaries are vague between one store and the next, and it's hard to see where an aisle begins or ends; provided one is correctly dressed, coiffed, and molded—few fatties here—one can walk around everywhere unhindered. There are no policemen to be seen; no one is fighting or pushing in the lines for the cinema. For sale there are clothes, clothes, and clothes; jewelry, glassware, up-market crafts; appliances, appliances, and appliances. Everything is so extravagantly within hand's reach that it seems possible to purchase it all (how different from trashy stores, where excessive surveillance makes the products appear inaccessible). The unifying thought runs like this: "We're all rich here, so we have nothing to fear from each other: honest, clean, and polite; if any impudent riffraff would dare to come all the way here, an alarm would ring, sounding tunes from Bach or Vivaldi."

Things are planned—designed, painted, polished, positioned—with harmonious efficacy; the environment is tranquil, and it offers lots of room for children, the tame offspring of the shoppers (Disney characters adorn soda fountains, and there are toy cars and carousels for kids to ride while their parents shop at leisure).

I have never before seen such an expansive style of consumption. A German restaurant feels like an iced Hansel and Gretel cottage; a sea-food outlet disguised as a ship, with anchors and oars, rope ladders up the masts, and fishbowls behind the portholes. I encountered only one irony, involuntary, of course: the poster for a Shirley MacLaine movie that said, in English, "Generations change, but the choices remain the same."

But these jottings do not convey the shopping mall at Satélite. Though more concentrated and ostentatious, it is not *that* different from other fancy stores. What sets it apart is the people. Strolling around with such an arrogant display of health, hygiene, and fragrance; so sleek and flatteringly dressed; the families looking so homey, happy, and affection-ate, having displayed such lucidity when choosing the right products; the couples so loving and secure, the friends so exuberant together; the triumph of monogamy so spectacularly demonstrated in the bonding ritual between father and son as they inspect a surround-sound stereo. Unthinkable that anyone should ever fart, burp, spit, or scratch his balls. No utopia could rival Plaza Satélite: the Greeks would have envied this poise, this neatness, this restrained air of mastery, this serenity.

But this too fails to encapsulate the place. Again, it's only the de-gree of excess and ostentation that sets the mall apart from other places. Similarly unblemished shoppers, equally immune to trauma and to the printed word, no less relaxed and sporty, circulate through other malls, and I didn't have to travel all the way to Satélite to see them, or to muse despondently on how this class, financed by the hunger of millions of workers and unemployed people and overprotected by all the achieve-ments of science and technology, produces nothing, creates no culture, does not even design the things it consumes so naturally; it does not live, think, or feel anything without a clichéd recipe.

The most specific trait, I think, was the sense of impunity. To look at these people is to realize that democratic transitions or partnerships for development may come and go; crises, devaluations, centuries, dy-nasties may pass; atlases, cosmoses, and cosmogonies will vanish into air and others will carry on thinking and working on their behalf; others will fall sick, produce, despair; their enemies will be eliminated, while they float imperturbably on from store to store in all their gracious, re-fined, sovereign impunity, spared even the restrictions that other countries place on the fashion-plate sectors.

I slunk out with my tail between my legs, robbed of my feisty diatribe; in their weary futility, my medium, number two pencil and my notes (in Palmer script) seemed as foolish as the scenes in a photo-romance starring heartthrob Jaime Garza in a most photogenic pose, and read avidly by a stumpy, pigtailed girl riding in the crowded bus (besides myself, only laborers and maids traveled in the metallic belly of this speeding Leviathan). I retreated in defeat after traveling through the "opulence" of others.

I felt doubly defeated when I noticed the exemplary concentration with which an elderly workman read his book—encased in plastic protectors—a South American sociology manual, doubtless lent to him by a son or grandson hopelessly enrolled in some community college.

Las Lomas I

JOSÉ JOAQUÍN BLANCO

Toward the Hills I Go, Sweet Rest

Lomas is where the motherland stands tallest. There she glows, emblazoned and moneyed, ancient and modern, palatial and wooded; her proud lines belie any crisis, any threat of pessimism. There the nation blooms in all her changeless quintessence. The celebrated phrase "God did not concede its like to any other nation" should be applied, rather than to the Basilica of the Virgin of Guadalupe, to the wonder that is Bosques de las Lomas.

Fuente de Petróleos, the monument to oil erected by the administration of Miguel Alemán, is above all the landmark of a massive barrier that separates Las Lomas from the rest of the city: the long moat of the Periférico expressway. This side of the fountain, the traditional pedestrian city moseys on; beyond, there spreads a city of endless, winding, labyrinthine streets planned for cars and lined with a procession of enormous homes. Public transport is minimal, and taken only by servants (or rich juniors who are too laid-back or democratic to use any vehicle other than those belonging to Daddy).

At first glance, one might think that the early stretches of Reforma or Palmas Avenues betray a certain decadence. Many a mansion is labeled For Sale or For Rent; others have been torn down to make way for banks, supermarkets, and modernist office buildings. Quite a few have been converted into boutiques, beauty salons, private clubs, embassies, laboratories, or high-flying schools and colleges; there are financial companies, film studios, and even the odd den of pesky intellectuals, like the offices of the journal *Nexos*. During the interim months while the rental negotiations proceed, houses are turned into brothels and grand settings for clandestine parties, worthy of X-rated films; their leaseholders make the most of it, and I myself felt like a Visconti character one night at an illicit blowout among statuary, staircases, and coats of arms. Things can smell fishy even in Las Lomas.

But the decadence is an illusion. It's just that the traffic has increased, so the owners around there prefer to sell or rent out their properties and live somewhere quieter, like nearby Bosques de las Lomas. It is a spectacle of utter lunacy to see hundreds, even thousands of millionaires building the same palaces, all at once, on the same spot. Given such an outrageous potlatch of architectural excess, one falls to wondering about all this alleged "corporate belt-tightening" and the impossibility of raising wages.

Our affluent contemporaries suffer from lapses in taste; they consider the legends of ancient Babylon to be the last word in elegance and update them with a dash of Star Wars: an office block springs incongruously from a ravine; an ugly lumbering triangle is studded with stained glass by Vasarely; in the middle of the enclosed, high-rise mall (like the one in Satélite, but more luxurious), a vast light-well holds several levels of tennis courts. But this mall is teeming with construction workers hired to raise the palaces. Men who ventured far from the traditional city, with its bodegas, buses, soft drink stalls, and cheap eateries, are forced to buy food here, paying luxury prices on peons' salaries.

These *lomas*—rumps, or low hills—are filled in and coated with smooth and ornate stones to facilitate the rash of skyscrapers that remain, for some unknown reason, paralyzed halfway through construction. And that's not all. Just as in the old Lomas of thirty or forty years ago, but with the added havoc induced by science fiction and the itch to feel transported to planet Krypton, we have miniature palaces with monarchical pretensions, like so many mini-Trianons: stained glass, turrets, loggias, balconies, terraces, picket fences, columns, baroque staircases, coats of arms, gargoyles, pediments, friezes, parapets, gardens with their own promenades and benches—all relatively stylized so as to appear more "modern" than the ones in the parents' house—and yet, just like the parents' house, these vast homes could easily house a decent primary or secondary school, and, in some cases, even a whole university.

Our wealthy classes are still dreaming of fairy tales and building monster homes full of statuary and spurious coats of arms, with tiled roofs, Japanese gardens, and wide curving stairs (at a time when gowns no longer have a train to flow down them). The houses sometimes cloak themselves in greenery, with ivy-covered fences and stone walls, allowing only glimpses of the family chapel and its protruding dome.

Here and there, between the spectral, truly incredible confections built with no expense spared in Bosques de las Lomas, a sprinkling of makeshift dwellings has also appeared, shacks banged together with left-over materials by the construction workers themselves as a place to sleep or eat or drink or sell sodas and tacos. Lower down, in the old Lomas district, there are no street vendors; each home comes with its own storehouse, and it makes you green with envy to think of people who never run out of cigarettes or soda in the middle of the night and never have to trek out for supplies; they've got their own supermarket in the pantry.

In the peaceful, well-kept streets, leafy and almost lyrical, a doll-like child might suddenly surface, dragging his dog; but the habitual fauna consists of chauffeurs, maids in uniform, plumbers, and construction workers carrying loud radios. The owners of wealth are tucked away somewhere where they can be seen by no one but themselves.

Las Lomas is a city apart. No one has a reason to go there, and should the opportunity arise, there's no reason to be able to find your way around: on foot you get lost, and by car you will shortly find yourself escaping along some fast highway toward a less exclusive part of the capital. It is a sweet retreat, majestic and undisturbed.

And beware of hanging around the place to do journalistic research, beyond the allotted hour and without a car. Anyone wandering those seven-league drives by night is regularly accosted by police cars, whose drivers will demand ID and subject you to more questions than any journalist could ever dream—in the unlikely event of some millionaire becoming momentarily visible—of asking one of those Mexicans who have lifted the country to such dizzying heights, there on their own home turf:

hundreds of palaces being erected at once, from whose scaffoldings can be surveyed the ghostly sea, the swarming lights of the other city far below.

Reality Where One Least Expects It

In contrast to the older parts of town, which are places both of settlement and of transit, of commerce and of residence, and where social groups mingle quite naturally, the quiet streets of the new upper-middle class developments are reserved for the private use of their inhabitants—homogenized into a single income bracket and, more often than not, professing a single ideology, and sharing the same sense of fashion, customs, and mores.

The old concept of a public street that even Indians, paupers, and bums could tread if they pleased, where they might stroll or loiter to no one's surprise, is obsolete around here. Along these introverted drives (lined by houses or serial condominiums built for people who choose to be cut off from the city and, thanks to the car and the local shopping facilities, exist to some extent without even seeing it), intruders stick out like a sore thumb. For they have no business being here, in this street which is not a street, where no one can stroll or window-shop, and they immediately attract suspicious glances.

It's the morning after a festive night. The street is as empty as someone's backyard, and three wholesome children are playing with their skateboards. They come and go, doing pirouettes and balancing acts; on the fifth or sixth round, they become aware of a most unusual presence: a young woman, her head bowed, sitting on the fender of a parked car. The more they stare, trundling around her on their skateboards, the odder they find her.

Physically she looks like a servant, except for the way she's dressed and made up, revealing an attempt at style. Run-of-the-mill pantsuit of black synthetic material, with dusty smears on elbows and knees, spattered with mud around the ankles; pink blouse pinned with a brooch spelling Margarita in convoluted gilt letters. Tights with runs streaking from the big toe under strappy black high-heeled shoes; thick, worker's hands and tough nails covered in chipped red varnish. The caked, uneven foundation on her face is patchy with powder and smudged mascara. Under a salon hairdo that is beginning to come undone at the nape and over the forehead, her expression veers from gaiety to self-absorption.

Intrigued, the boys stopped skating and sat down five cars away, pretending to rest or fix their knee- and elbow-pads. The girl was leaning her head on her hand, muttering to herself, then tossing it back and laughing; she gazed into the horizon of neat identical rooftops and resumed her muttering, words cut short with little giggles, and fell again into blank absorption. One supposed she was some factory girl or maidservant who had saved up for months to buy these clothes for special occasions, like last night, and forced by some calamitous incident, she had wandered down here to greet the morning.

"She's wasted, man," one kid whispered amusedly. "Stoned, more like," said another, entranced to be using a word that quivered with forbidden adventure. "She's a loony," offered a third.

Fifty yards away a couple of ladies were standing having a chat, out with their pedigree dogs that were as handsome and healthy as the children. They found it strange that the kids had stopped clattering by on their boards. In their view, children should always be on the move; otherwise, if they were just thinking or talking, there could be only two explanations: lack of vitamins or impending mischief. So they strolled nearer, not really concerned, just to check up on some children who were as indistinguishable from their own offspring as they were from these boys' mothers. They were about ten paces away when they noticed the young woman. Now they were at a loss as to what to do. On the one hand, she wasn't doing anything wrong; she was taking no notice of the ladies or of the children. But still, she was setting a bad example, with all that mumbling and the unseemly traces of partying or disaster all over her, and caricaturing female elegance as she did.

But then again, she was in the street, which didn't come under any home jurisdiction of property, and so one could hardly ask her to move on . . . though this wasn't any old street, mind you, but a residential street in an up-market development, where surely one's children had a right to be protected from subversive, unsavory examples.

Only steps away from the girl, the dogs began to get nervous and tugged on their leashes in order to sniff her more closely. The ladies tightened their grip to prevent them from getting any nearer.

The dogs started barking. By now the children had dropped all pretenses and were shamelessly agog. The dogs barked louder. The girl jumped, saw the dogs, laughed, and started calling and clicking her fingers eagerly at them. "Here boy, hey pretty doggie. I won't do nothing to you, good boy, come here," she said, just as if there were no one in the street but the dogs and her.

The dogs didn't get it and yammered with redoubled fury. For fifteen tense minutes the young woman persevered in coaxing them, between incoherent comments under her breath. The children continued to stare; the ladies, transfixed, clutched the leashes tightly but neither moved out of range nor soothed their pets, which were now baying with brutal ferocity, slaver spurting between their fangs and glistening on their lips.

At last the girl gave up and cursed the dogs instead. She rose to her feet and set off down the sidewalk. Fifty yards later her slightly weaving figure dipped off-balance for a moment; she had stepped awkwardly and broken one of her heels. She removed her shoes and walked on barefoot until children and ladies lost sight of her.

The dogs, the ladies, and the children were still upset, however. Little by little they regained their composure. The ladies talked of other things and were kind to the children; they entrusted them with warmest regards for their families, made oblique allusions to the perils of talking to strangers, and withdrew in a haze of comments about the sorry state of neighborhood watch in this community.

The dogs had recovered their sweet natures, licking their mistresses and ingratiating themselves. The children returned to their skateboards, long enough to decamp a few blocks further on and start discussing a scene that was a rarity in their overprotected lives, an incident which, helpless as they were to interpret it, could give rise to the most extravagant fantasies.

Las Lomas II

DANIELA ROSSELL

Daniela Rossell had her first solo show in 1993, when she was barely twenty. It was held at Temístocles, Mexico City's most lively alternative space, housed in a condemned mansion in the ritzy neighborhood of Polanco. She showed portraits of various female family members posing in the garish bedrooms, terraces, and gardens of their suburban mansions, located for the most part in Las Lomas, Mexico City's answer to Beverly Hills.

Rossell's parents both came from families associated with the PRI — the political party that emerged from the Mexican Revolution, degenerated into what Octavio Paz once called a "philanthropic ogre," and ruled the country from 1929 to 2000. Her photographs provide a fascinating glimpse into the private lives of the rich and powerful.

Looking at these photographs, one is immediately struck by a certain gender imbalance: men are, for the most part, absent. We find traces of their existence—a silver-framed snapshot on a mahogany table, a painting dedicated to a certain Don Manuel, a stuffed-lion hunting trophy—but we soon realize that this is a world largely created and inhabited by women, the wives and daughters of mighty politicians and opulent businessmen. This feminine realm is characterized, above all, by what appears to be a fierce compulsion to fill every square inch with gilded mirrors, blackamoor sconces, crystal chandeliers, baroque self-portraits, lace curtains, Persian rugs, silver tea sets, and countless other tchotchkes.

In contrast to the exuberance of their surroundings, however, most of these women appear to be lacking something. They are not arrogant or haughty, snobbish or even wholly self-assured. On the contrary, it seems that they are suffering from an intense *horror vacua*, as if trying to fill an internal void through this compulsive accumulation of objects. Their wistful gazes betray a certain emptiness . . . is it loneliness? boredom? existential angst?

Inge, for example, a twenty-something aspiring model, appears in front of a pastel-colored, turret-filled mansion, posing next to a statue of Don Quixote. She seems completely unaware of the pathological excesses that surround her; ignorant of the fact that the family's fortune might have less-than-respectable origins, that a hundred-thousand-square-foot house might be an anomaly in a poor country. In another photo, Paulina Díaz Ordaz (a granddaughter of Gustavo Díaz Ordaz, the president responsible for the 1968 student massacre, and a step-daughter of Raúl Salinas de Gortari, the imprisoned brother of Mexico's ex-president) stands by a stuffed lion, a trophy from one of her stepfather's hunting expeditions.

Though most critics have read Rossell's photographs as critiques of the ills afflicting Mexican society—political corruption, social inequity, racial disparity—it is perhaps more interesting to examine them within the context of Mexican photography. Since the 1920s, photography in Mexico has been dominated by a marked ethnographic tendency: photographers from Manuel Alvarez Bravo to Graciela Iturbide have turned an exoticizing eye toward the countryside, documenting the lifestyles of impoverished peasants in the remote hills of Chiapas or the deserts of Sonora. Ironically, these photographs have become prized commodities, adorning the living rooms of rich Mexicans like those depicted in this series. Rossell's photographs use many of the same ethnographic strategies—she poses her subjects in their native environments and documents their daily habits and rituals. The difference, however, is that she focuses on those who until now had been excluded from the history of photography: the urban elite that is to blame for the sorry lot of the impoverished—but picturesque—rural masses.

Daniela Rossell, Untitled [Christian Gorging], from the series "Rich and Famous" (1994–2001). Cibachrome print. 76 x 101.5 cm. Courtesy of the artist.

Daniela Rossell, Untitled [Paulina Díaz Ordaz], from the series "Rich and Famous" (1994–2001). Cibachrome print. 76 x 101.5 cm. Courtesy of the artist.

Daniela Rossell, Untitled [Inge], from the series "Rich and Famous" (1994–2001). Cibachrome print. 76 x 101.5 cm. Courtesy of the artist.

Daniela Rossell, Untitled, from the series "Rich and Famous" (1994–2001). Cibachrome print. 76 x 101.5 cm. Courtesy of the artist.

Daniela Rossell, Untitled [Itati Cantoral], from the series "Rich and Famous" (1994–2001). Cibachrome print. 76 x 101.5 cm. Courtesy of the artist.

Daniela Rossell, Untitled [Itati Cantoral II], from the series "Rich and Famous" (1994–2001). Cibachrome print. 76 x 101.5 cm. Courtesy of the artist.

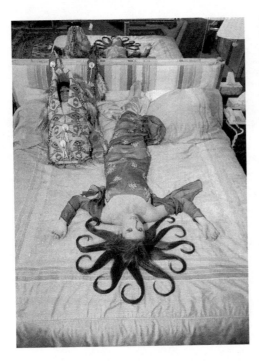

Daniela Rossell, Untitled, from the series "Rich and Famous" (1994–2001). Cibachrome print. 76 x 101.5 cm. Courtesy of the artist.

Daniela Rossell, Untitled, from the series "Rich and Famous" (1994–2001). Cibachrome print. 76 x 101.5 cm. Courtesy of the artist.

Daniela Rossell, Untitled [Inge II], from the series "Rich and Famous" (1994–2001). Cibachrome print. 76 x 101.5 cm. Courtesy of the artist.

Daniela Rossell, Untitled [Beatriz], from the series "Rich and Famous" (1994–2001). Cibachrome print. 76 x 101.5 cm. Courtesy of the artist.

3

The Metro

The Metro

JUAN VILLORO

Welcome to the Big Bang! In 1950 Mexico City numbered 2.9 million inhabitants; in 1970 there were 11.8 million, and by the year 2005 the population will be close to a figure that sounds like a doomsday emergency number: 30 million.

The only thing that mitigates such horror is the fact that Mexican statistics are as erratic as the scales used in its street markets. We'll never know exactly how many we are, for this city is, in the strict sense, incalculable.

In *Invisible Cities,* Italo Calvino says of the possibilities of urban design that "the catalogue of forms is endless: until each form has found its city, new cities will continue to be born."[1] The repertory includes, of course, the formless city, which aerial cartographers call urban sprawl and which flourishes under the names of Tokyo, Los Angeles, São Paulo, or Mexico City.

The megalopolis lacks a center, the logical core from which it once grew. In Tokyo, Roland Barthes was mesmerized by the central void, the city as ubiquitous periphery. Those of us who live in Mexico City understand this kind of fascination. The landscape overwhelms us, and the only way to make it cohere, to give it meaning, is to travel through it. The city works because it can be traversed.

In earlier times, a town's fame could derive from the roads that led to its gates. All Christian roads led to Rome, and Atlantis fascinates us because the roads leading there have been lost.

Shortly before his death, in the long interview published as *Life of Moravia*, Alberto Moravia observed that certain places preserve an aura of mystery because for centuries they remained virtually inaccessible. After negotiating the immensity of the desert, the traveler fell to his knees before Samarkand. Arriving was a prodigy in itself.

Mexico City captivates us for precisely the opposite reasons: here the challenge is not getting there but getting out. The megalopolis is built for internal navigation, like a sea without a port.

In *Die Unwirklichkeit der Städte (The Unreality of Cities)*, Klaus R. Scherpe maintains that the modern city relied on construction, whereas the postmodern version revolves around function (less an edifiable space than a setting for movement). Modern cities ravenously devoured empty space, but their postmodern equivalents remain indifferent to physical reality: they are complex sites where people and information flow like arrows in a chart.

Such changes in urban representation have their counterparts in literature. The nineteenth-century novel viewed the city as an entity that, though hard to grasp, was logically ordered. In *Notre Dame de Paris*, Victor Hugo tackled Paris as a Rosetta stone in need of deciphering.

During the first decades of the twentieth century, Alfred Döblin, Leopoldo Marechal, Andrei Biely, and John Dos Passos cast cities as protagonists in their novels. Berlin, Buenos Aires, Saint Petersburg, and Manhattan became polyphonic characters in novels that were necessarily fragmented because they aspired to portray chaos. Large cities lack a structured language; they can only aspire to a broken language, a mosaic fragmented by limitless growth and exuberant chaos. Lost in the maze of Brandenburg, Döblin understood that "Berlin is largely invisible."

An image common to all these novels was that of the "concrete jungle." The city became the place to lose one's bearings. Babylon, Sodom, and Babel are other names for this topography of disorientation and disgrace. Iron-and-mortar jungles threaten morals and are cursed as "monsters," "hydras," "whores." Citizens are imperiled by "bad" neighborhoods, hemmed in by walls, dehumanized by machinery, depersonalized by crowds, alienated by labor. Roberto Arlt, in his intense 1931

novel *Los lanzallamas (The Flamethrowers)*, denounced the urban plight as
follows: "In cahoots with doctors and engineers, they proclaimed: man
needs eight hours' sleep. He requires such-and-such a number of cubic
meters of air in order to breathe. If he is not to putrefy and, what would
be even worse, to putrefy us along with him, a given number of square
meters of sunshine are also necessary. And in line with these criteria,
they made cities. Meanwhile, the body suffers."[2]

The city that devours and obliterates its children inspired many literary creations, from Robert Musil's scatological "Kakania" to James
Joyce's triple D: "Dear Dirty Dublin," not to mention Karl Kraus's
apocalyptic "Laboratory for the End of Time."

Irrigated by a corrosive, corrupting sap, the urban jungle grew to
boundless proportions. Postmodern cities—oceans, infinite zones of
passage—signal a shift from verticality to horizontality, and a change of
moral perspective: they are no longer seen as malign entities.

Today's megalopolises face such grave problems that it is a miracle
they can function at all, and contemporary fiction has moved from con-
demning them to exploring their modes of working. Take Tokyo or
Mexico City, cities so ungraspable that their writers must renounce the
project of painting an all-encompassing fresco. Since critics cannot treat
the city as an external landscape, they must operate from within its
boundaries.

One of the pioneers of this approach was Elio Vittorini, author of a
classic novel whose title, *Cities of the World*, belies the impossibility of its
completion. Despite the title's claim to universality (a theme which is
also present in the other title considered by the author, *The Rights of
Man*), the book's originality actually lay in its use of an entirely local setting. The characters in *Cities of the World* never set foot outside Sicily as
they travel through deprived, isolated regions of the island, but in each
place they discover the rest of the world. After decoding the logic of the
place, we realize that Módica is Sicily's Jerusalem. The title proves ac-
curate after all: the Italian island is a miniature of the world.

Vittorini's method consisted in observing minute details; Calvino, his
disciple, took the opposite approach: he describes what remains unseen.
Since every place is shaped by a set of functions, one has only to decipher
a city's modus operandi in order to anticipate its geography and the customs of its people. Such is the principle that governs *Invisible Cities*.

Ricardo Piglia's novel *La ciudad ausente (The Absent City)* takes this pro-
cedure further: the plot and characters furnish the clues for the reader

to infer a place that is never described. In the best of 1990s urban fiction, territoriality is omnipresent, but it must always be inferred, like the megalopolis that surpasses us.

The City and Its Mechanisms

How is Mexico City different from other oceanic spaces? Amid the steam of tamale stalls, the smell of epazote, and the cries of street vendors, there's a sense of deferred tragedy, our preferred strategy for coping with chaos. Today the impressions recorded by Bernal Díaz del Castillo ("Tenochtitlan is a second Venice") or Alexander von Humboldt ("a city of palaces") take on the appearance of sarcastic prophecies, not to mention the exalted kitsch of Bernardo de Balbuena in his *Grandeza mexicana [Grandeurs of Mexico]:* "A Rome of the New World, in its golden age . . . an Athens for science, and in treasures, a Thebes." Those of us who live here know that our city is a disaster: daily, Radio Red's yellow helicopters broadcast warnings that the ozone level has once more surpassed 300 points, and scientists enumerate the catastrophes that threaten the city (in *La superficie de la tierra [The Surface of the Earth],* José Lugo Hubp presents a catalogue of disasters that includes floods and earthquakes, not to mention mudslides, and possible ice meltage from volcanic eruptions).

As though a fabulous algebra constantly nullified the sum of negative values, we have become experts in degeneration: we compare our rashes, discuss the lead content in babies' blood, and mention the deformed placentas of pregnant women. It is not ignorance that keeps us on this carousel of rats and stray dogs. To be honest, we like Mexico City. Like Don Juan in Stravinsky's opera *The Rake's Progress,* we have fallen in love with the Bearded Lady at the circus. And leaving aside the matter of our dubious taste, how to explain the lack of fear, the incapacity to be terrorized in the face of such blatant horrors? Carlos Monsiváis has written about a "postapocalyptic" attitude shared by the inhabitants of Mexico City. We are the result of a catastrophe, but we act as if the worst has passed. Besides, it would be impossible to trace the nuclear fallout, the massive earthquake, or the ruthless epidemic that did this to our city. What matters is that we've left our misfortunes behind. To "defer" tragedy by relegating it to a hazy past is our best therapy. The city before us is the end result, not the cause; the aftermath to catastrophe, not its harbinger. Extreme danger exists only in flashback, and should it ever become necessary to sit through that part of the movie, most of us would elect to stay for the show. An aphorism by Monsiváis captures the logic of the postapocalyptic mind: "There is no worse nightmare than that which excludes us." Let's stay here.[3]

Although all cities are bastions against nature, few have matched the destructive fury of Mexico's capital. The struggle against the elements has been pursued with fanatical thoroughness. The floating empire of the Aztecs, whose waterways Renaissance cartographers compared to Utopia, was reduced to the rotting canals of Xochimilco. Having done away with water, air was the next target. The urban landscape is marked by these two crucial losses: traffic lights blink over a drained lake and airplanes disappear into the thick scum that was once blue sky. At a recent exhibition of children's art, I found that none of them used blue for the sky. They used their crayons to convey a more realistic hue, a kind of celestial brown.

We've run out of water and air, but the dynamic city keeps growing. But where is it headed?

All thumbs point downward. Mexico City's prime engineering projects have been underground ones: the subway and the drains. Our last frontier is underground.

During his visit to Mexico, Humboldt reflected on the quarrel between Neptunists and Vulcanists. Do minerals originate from marine deposits, or from the earth's igneous core? In a landscape dominated by volcanoes, he understandably felt drawn to the latter hypothesis. Could there be some tectonic principle, some primordial magnetism that explains our antipathy to air and water?

In Mexico City, breaking ground for a new building always requires archeological skills, since foundations, telephone lines, and sewers have to skirt buried Aztec ruins. But aside from bumping against pyramid steps, building downward precipitates an encounter with a symbolic order. As Enrique Florescano reminds us in his essay on "Mesoamerican Myths": "The dominant concept in Mesoamerican creation myths is the notion that the center of the earth enclosed a cave, where essential foodstuffs were stored and life was regenerated."[4] Guillermo Bonfil Batalla's expression "el México profundo"—*deep* Mexico—can be applied literally; the dead and our origin are buried underground; the most important Indian legends—Quetzalcoatl, the prodigious twins of the Popol-Vuh—recount journeys to the underworld.

In 1994, we, descendants of the Seven Caves, live in an environment marked by journeys. According to Paul Virilio, the pulse of the postmodern city can be measured by recording how time triumphs over space. The main goal is no longer to build, but to move fast. Mexico City grew against the waters and the heavens; it is governed by the imperative to grow and transport; its last frontier lies underground (future takes us back to the origin). No place defines such a city as appropriately as the metro.

The City and the Lions

In Mexico City, all limits are purely symbolic. *"Desierto de los Leones"*— "desert of lions" —is an apt name for one of its fringes, for this area is neither a desert nor populated by lions. The name may refer to a land where pumas once roamed, but in any case the lion brings to mind those old maps where a chubby Aeolus marks the direction of the winds, and a Latin inscription signals the end of the known world: *hic sunt leones*, "Here be lions."

The lion has symbolized not only the unknown but also what was known but couldn't be accepted. In *The Indians of Mexico*, Fernando Benítez writes that colonial maps used the legend *"hic sunt leones"* to denote indigenous lands. The lion as a racial symbol even appears in blues music: Alain Derbez's radio program "This Train Ain't Got No Lions" takes its title from Big Bill Broonzy's song about segregation. Lions have always represented geographic or cultural margins. We thus should not be surprised to find an entire Mexico City metro station devoted to this animal. Get off at Etiopía and you will see countless stone tiles, all insistently engraved with the image of this beast.

Before returning to the lion we must venture further along the subterranean network. In an essay titled "U-Bahn als U-Topie" ("The Metro as Utopia"), the Russo-German philosopher Boris Groys reflects on the Moscow subway, which played the same role in the Soviet collective imagination as the metro did for Mexico City.

Incapable of constructing an egalitarian utopia, Stalinism churned out a wide-reaching industry of simulation. Each turn of the cog stressed that the ideals of the October Revolution had been fulfilled. One of the most efficient of all such compensatory devices was the Moscow metro: the Revolution was electrified, and it ran underground.

Utopia means "noplace," and so its designers had to seek

compromise solutions and intermediary zones. "The appropriate strategy for the construction of utopias," writes Groys, "consists in finding an uninhabited and preferably uninhabitable site in the midst of a populated area."[5] In the early twentieth century, the Russian *disurbanist* projects failed due to their radical negation of reality. Their alternatives to the urban jungle included outer-space cities, movable houses, swimming pools that adapted to the swimmer's rhythm . . .

The metro, on the other hand, can fulfill several utopian requirements right here on earth: its growth is potentially limitless; it is completely dependent on a superior order; and it is a controlled space where passengers catch glimpses of the edifice while the landscape remains obscured. "Though the metro is part of the reality of the metropolis, it continues to exist in the realm of the fantastic; its totality can be conceived but never experienced."[6]

These features are common to all subway systems, but what set Moscow's apart was its capacity to defy time. In its tunnels, socialist-realist portraits hang on marble walls of palatial splendor and are lit by sumptuous chandeliers. Façades can be Islamic, Roman, or Renaissance; proletarian overalls contrast with the subway cars' austere futurism.

Most science-fiction utopias conceive time in linear fashion; their landscapes are too new to be convincing. A true utopia would be beyond time. According to Salman Rushdie, the film *Brazil*'s greatest merit resides in its portrayal of an aged future. Typewriters and clothes appear older than ours and thus acquire an eerie realism: the future seems more credible when it already looks worn out.

By recreating an impossible period, the Moscow subway reinforces its utopian condition. But it is closer to Orwell's dark dystopia than to More's Utopia; its spatial and temporal alterity produces repressive effects. "The masses do not enjoy the luxury afforded them by the metro. They are unwilling and unable to savor its art, to appreciate its elegant finishings, to decipher its ideological symbolism. They are deaf, blind and indifferent as they file through countless treasure chambers. The metro is not a serene paradise of contemplation, but an inferno of perpetual motion."[7] This is, needless to say, Groys's version, the assessment of someone who stands outside the apparatus. Inside, the metro produces a frictionless sense of estrangement, for it is a place where the citizen cannot rise to "the level of his hatred," to borrow a phrase from E. M. Cioran.

The subways of Moscow and of Mexico City display some odd simi-
larities. Both are packed with the symbols of failed revolutions and perform a clear compensatory function as "underground heavens." Perhaps it's not a coincidence that both were inaugurated one year after
the crushing of dissident movements. The Moscow metro opened in
1935, a year after all Soviet artists' and intellectuals' organizations were
disbanded and their members forced to regroup under a single state-
controlled body; the Mexico City metro, opened in 1969, was the first
major public work unveiled after the Tlatelolco student massacre of
1968. Totalitarian states create an "impossible," atemporal zone to replace lost freedoms.

The most forceful coincidence between the two systems, however,
is surely their exploitation of the past. Pictographic signs are a striking feature of the Mexican project. In 1969, the images representing
the stations along Line 1—white figures against a "Mexican" pink
background—were designed as a modern codex with a twofold purpose: proving that pre-Columbian culture was alive and well, while acknowledging that many of the riders were illiterate. The icons' discur-
sive level varies in complexity—a cannon represents the fortress near
Balderas station, also alluding to the Revolution's "Decena Trágica,"
while the pictogram for Chabacano station, whose name means apricot,
merely represents an apricot—but they invariably seek to represent
something national, autochthonous, Mexican.

This appropriation of the past becomes explicit with the use of
Indian motifs on friezes and low reliefs (Insurgentes station being the
most monumental example of this tendency), the recreation of pre-
Columbian displays (a pyramid in Pino Suárez station, stele in Bellas
Artes), and the naming of stations with Aztec words like Tacuba, Mixcoac, Tezozomoc, or Iztapalapa. At Panteones, the stop for the city cemetery, an Aztec sculpture is graced by a label reminding us that the
earth is "both womb and tomb," a humid primeval cave, and that
Mictlán is the Aztec land of the dead.

Bastion of the country's informal economy, hall of exhibitions, concerts, and book fairs, land of sex-cruisers, suicides, and premature
births, the metro is a city on the move. As in *Brazil*, or in the subterranean passageways of Moscow, everything contributes to temporal confusion. The trains are a polished show of imported technology (French-
Canadian, as it happens), and the modernist design of certain stations is

so bizarre that they have been used as sets for science-fiction films: *Total Recall* was shot in Insurgentes and Chabacano (where traces of fake blood still streak the vaults, like souvenirs from the future). As for the past, you can find it in the friezes, station names, and pictographic signs. It all adds up to some unthinkable pre-Columbian modernity.

But it is not the metro's architecture that makes the deepest impression; it's the men and women traveling with expressionless faces, as though they had been bribed to ride it. Mexico City's metro carries five million people a day. Despite their numbers, they have been unerringly selected; to descend the escalator is to cross a line of racial segregation. The underground city is populated by—pick your slur—*nacos*, Indians, Mexicans. *Hic sunt leones.* It is not a coincidence that the lion is the icon of Etiopía, a station that by one letter, the U that in other languages symbolizes the subway, misses being called Utopía, Utopia. But it's better this way: Etiopía, our bid for Africa.

For those who own the surface, the metro is something you'd take in Paris. Below, the masses circulate at postmodern speeds. It would be paranoid, and indeed too generous, to suppose that this negative utopia— refashioning history, rotating myths at sixty miles per hour—was planned as such. City planners could never be so ingenious.

So why does no one pull the red emergency handle? Does accepting an adverse habitat create new modes of conformity? Does the displacement of tragedy, the assumption that disasters have been left behind, leave people with no energy to complain about anything else? Does our postapocalyptic ecosystem turn us all into wimpy passengers?

What's certain is that two axes of Mexican life intersect underground: a rhetorical recuperation of the past and functional racism. The metro as a model of injustice does not make motorized city-dwellers lose any sleep, accustomed as they are to tiny Otomí girls peddling chewing gum at traffic lights. The indifference above is greater than the mineral resignation below, at least while temporal confusion is not matched by geographic disjunction: imagine what Chiapas station, Mexico City would look like.

Landscapes, signs, lions, postmodernities, all move through this ever-expanding city. "The only thing we know about the future is that it is unlike the present," wrote Jorge Luis Borges. Where is the underground tempo headed? Where is it taking these drowsy, robotic, mute masses? Perhaps the one real compensation of the subterranean world is to picture the surface from down there. Perhaps the lesson of the tunnels is to bestow a different value upon the streets, to demonstrate, in secret, that the city is the heaven of the subway.

"Let us take heaven by storm!" cried an unrepentant utopian. Mobs advance into the subway cars' fake daylight. Outside, virtual and powerful, the city waits for them to resurface.

Notes

1. Calvino, *Invisible Cities*, 139. Translation modified.
2. Arlt, *Los lanzallamas*, 22.
3. Monsiváis, *Los rituales del caos*, 21, 250.
4. Florescano, "Mitos mesoamericanos," 31.
5. Groys, "U-Bahn als U-Topie," 1.
6. Ibid.
7. Ibid.

Voyage to the Center of the City

RICARDO GARIBAY

Choose the day and the hour, accept the urgency of your daily grind, decide to save some time—"for the metro goes much faster than any vehicle rolling over the surface of the city"—descend into the nearest station, and step, for your misfortune, into the deep expressway of neurasthenia. The Mexico City metro has ceased to be a joke and a boast. You will emerge black and blue, smelling to high heaven, your clothes in rags, your money gone, your umbrella and briefcase gone after it, half-suffocated, furious, frightened by what you've seen down there, and grateful to have resurfaced in more or less one piece: a miracle wrought from sunrise to sunset, seven days a week, for one and a half million riders living in this unlivable city.

Let's focus on our underground system of mass transport (and mass hostility), and speak only in passing of the city above, jammed with cars—thanks to an incompetent Traffic Department—and helpless before leisurely rubble-builders: bridges that take years to reach the other side, fossilized mountains of sludge, impassive skeletons of iron turned to rust and mold by five rainy seasons, labyrinthine detours leading to the middle of nowhere—or worse, leading back to the same highway you were struggling to leave half an hour ago.

Last week it took me one hour and twenty minutes to drive from Thiers to the Excelsior building—at five thirty in the afternoon. Two hours and thirty-six minutes from Satélite to the Churubusco—at 8 A.M. Two hours and forty-seven minutes from Politécnico to Colonia Hipódromo. On Thursday, under heavy rain, I went from Monterrey to Chilpancingo (just over a mile) in . . . two hours and twenty minutes! We had to charge onto the sidewalk in front of the Ignacio L. Vallarta School, flattening the shrubs, running over two small trees, and lopping the exhaust pipes off fifty or a hundred cars in order to escape the traffic around the roundabout. It's been this way for two years, maybe three. The population is multiplying at a truly barbaric rate, there are more and more proletarian districts, every month some twenty thousand cars join those already on the road, there are too few buses (and most are ready for the scrap heap); trains mosey along like retarded slowworms. Leaving home for an appointment is a hair-raising race against time, and meanwhile the city government bureaucrats are leisurely pondering our future advantages—the benefits of that ever-receding future "when the works are completed"—and bemoaning the setbacks unavoidable in any great city in the throes of development.

But to get back to the metro: was it not billed as our salvation?

This article is dedicated to the "sensible city officials" responsible for so many mishaps, and it bears only my signature because it would be impossible to include the names of the twelve million people who live in the metropolitan area.

During the space of five days, accompanied by photographer Ignacio Castillo, I spent six hours daily traveling on the metro. What follows is a short compilation of sights, sensations, and dialogues culled from that experience. If I seem restrained, it's because I do not wish to sound alarmist. The article was specially commissioned by my editor, and I agree with his philosophy: the purpose of journalism is to point out the wound and rub salt on it, to help run the city by exposing deficiencies and mismanagement, and to do so in the name of all those who lack the means and ways to protest.

Monday, 8:15 A.M.—*Tacuba station.* There are at least five hundred people on the Zócalo-bound platform. Here comes the train. They brace themselves as though preparing for a guerrilla raid. The doors open: join in the fray, if you have the guts! An instant, savage free-for-all. In twenty seconds the bell will ring, the doors will clamp shut, and the throngs will squeeze no matter what, shouting, elbowing, pushing, shoving, trampling, stampeding. Twenty or thirty bodies crowd around every door, vying to be swallowed at a gulp; in they must go, all at once, and now the doors shut; those who got in crush together against the glass; those left behind jump backward, as the hissing snake of orange coaches pulls away. The platform remains almost empty for a couple of minutes, but in a fell swoop it fills up again. Here comes the train, I can hear it. The crowd surges forward. A woman with four children in tow struggles toward us, looking worried:

"Please, mister, are you in charge here?"

"Of course, ma'am. What's the matter?"

"Nothing, I just wondered if you could help me out. With these four there's no way I can get on, I've missed several trains already, they were supposed to be in school by eight, no way, I don't want my kids to get squashed, if you'd be so kind as to help . . ."

On Wednesday we are to witness an almost comic scene: shrieks from a woman already inside the subway car while a baby is hurriedly passed from one pair of hands to the next along the platform, like a football, fumbling hands, face up, face down, this way and that, and the woman must be the mother and no one can figure how the baby got away, and just as he makes it inside the car the doors slam shut and his diaper gets caught between them: a shit-smeared, yellow, dripping diaper.

Now we are traveling from Tacuba to Zócalo, carrying two of the first woman's brats, while the other two, slightly older, way down there, close to the floor, raise beaming faces obscured by skirts and pants.

"This is just about okay," Ignacio tells me, "because Tacuba is the final stop; the in-between stations are the rough ones."

Monday, 12:30 P.M. —*Pino Suárez station.* This is a madhouse of a market. Two or three thousand people charging down the stairs, up the stairs, rushing through the tunnels, running along the platforms, lining up impatiently at ticket booths, thronging out to the street, pouring in from the street. The hubbub is deep, deafening, and incessant. It dazes and dizzies you, jangles the nerves and quashes the soul; it makes you want to escape onto the blessed repose of the rowdy, rabid street above that at least opens up to a brown sky of smog. Down here you can buy whatever you like, from an aspirin to a poncho, from a pocket compass to a pound of Arab tortillas. Ah, the joys of the big city!

"Mind you," says Ignacio, "it's the same in every subway around the world. You've been to New York or Paris or Moscow . . . In all honesty, I think this is better."

"My dear Ignacio, I don't give a damn about Paris and New York. I care about my world, my people. Sure this is better: it stinks less than those other places—though it's getting pretty bad—and it's less filthy dirty. But in other places you don't have to walk past vendors hogging all the floor space, vandalized photomurals, escalator handrails slashed to ribbons by switchblades. Other places might have suffocating crowds as well, but here it's the inadequacy, the congestion which sicken me. In Paris you can traverse the whole city in every direction, you're always a block away from a subway entrance; but here, three subway lines for one of the largest cities in the world? Three subway lines for twelve million people in the metropolitan area? The inner-city expressway they're building will do nothing to relieve the pressure, on the contrary. Wouldn't it be better to dig more metro tunnels than to slap on all those underpasses and monolithic bridges? Isn't the carless class the fastest-growing sector of the population? Is there room for more bus lines? Call this a life, this grinding ordeal of passageways, corridors, and staircases?"

"What most intrigues me about doing a story on the metro," my editor Julio Scherer had said, "can be summed up in the following question: is it possible to live spending several hours a day in a foul mood? Because when I go down there, everything flies in the face of my senses and against the *joie de vivre* they are supposed to afford me; my eyes, my ears, my fingertips, my nostrils, the taste in my mouth, all are painfully overwhelmed as soon as I set foot on that underground space."

"That's the crux of it: the space," rejoined Alvarez del Villar. "Studies show that human beings require a certain amount of space for everyday life, a minimum area to ensure the proper functioning of body and spirit, you know? Without it, people are thrown into an airless proximity to one another that chafes and incenses them against their fellows. Too much rubbing of shoulders turns everyday conviviality into a pinprick torture."

Tuesday, 7 A.M.—San Lázaro station. The feel of the station varies—along with the look of the people—according to the neighborhood it services. Around Chapultepec or Insurgentes, for example, the atmosphere is lighter, and there are pretty faces, gaggles of college kids in cashmeres, blouses, and airy skirts. But Tacuba, San Lázaro, and La Merced have been taken over by the masses and their fried-food stalls: a heaving agglomerate of tousled heads, brown skin, malnourished faces, dense pigsty odors. Boarding the train, jostling to get in or out, are feats worthy of pirate legends, cavalry charges, and medieval insults. Crowds, crowds, crowds. Bedlam unleashed amid denim and polyester and string bags, while a tangible reek of rotting vegetables hangs on the air at nose level.

"Is it fair, mister?" demands a girl in a thorough state of decomposition: her skirt is twisted backward, her shirt minus two buttons, her hair hanging in sweaty tails. Angry and desperate, she continues: "Look at my arms! Pinched to death, and I won't say where else their fingers went. Hell, it's the same thing day after day, and wherever you go nothing but riffraff. I ask you, is it fair?"

Tuesday, 2 P.M.—Bellas Artes station. Ignacio photographs a pair of teenagers who claim to be students.

"Nah, I live in Mixcoac and he's from Tasqueña. It's just that we're coming from school, like, P.S. 6, huh? Yeah, well, we first go to class then we come down to the metro. Whaaaat? To grab around, that's what for, when it gets supercrowded. This guy's the one to watch, man, he's gross, me I'm more laid back, like. Just a pat, that's right. One o'clock—one isn't it, dude?—when the pussy come out, course some come out before and some after that. Wuhzdat? Sure there's times we get lost, he's gone one way and me another what with all the people messin' round. Wuhzdat? Me? Me I'm just . . . What you saying 'bout me? We're all in the crowd. Hey, it's like back, wheeee, sideways, uh-oh, when it stops when it gets going, your hands just end up full of pussy, no sweat! But you gotta watch out for the queers, see, loads of queers around . . . The best deal is the line to Tlalpan or Chapultepec, or round here. This guy's a freak, he grabs everything, *nacas*, trash or whatever!"

Wednesday, 7:40, Tasqueña station. A bureaucrat from the treasury. He carries a sandwich and a thermos bottle in a canvas bag, and sports a shiny suit and plump tie.

"Yes of course, by all means, I always say we citizens have a duty toward the public servants affiliated with the media. Excuse me? Yes, of course, I believe mass transit is a top priority for any major city, and the planning in terms of government budget allowances. Oh yes, no, mornings and evenings every day, because I'm fortunate enough to have a family and the overtime . . . Sorry? Yes, of course, the metro, yes, I consider it very favorably, it is a hygienic method of transport, it moves fast, it connects one to the nerve centers of the city. Oh, pardon me, I only wanted to expand on . . . No, not at all, nothing to complain of, though I'm not saying I wouldn't like to own a car, like yourselves, who are only putting up with this for the experience, am I right? Here I am trying to explain and you keep interrupting, you want the nitty-gritty, don't you, the unvarnished, eh! Well I have nothing more to say. I'll keep my gripes to myself until I can keep my own car waiting while I tell them. If you'll excuse me, here is my train. Some of us have work to do."

Thursday, 7 P.M., Moctezuma station. A woman on a double seat, with two small sleeping children.

"Go ahead, sir, no bother at all, take all the pictures you like. Yes, put it this way, we should have got off two stations ago, but I thought best to go on to the end of the line and wake them up then, and it'll be less trouble to take the . . . ? You're telling me, imagine, with them half tottering and the mobs of commuters pouring up and down. . . . Early mornings I drop them off at the nursery and then at noon I take them to the place where they're kind enough to watch them for me, till around now every evening when I come get them . . . Yes, absolutely, but what am I to do?"

Friday, 3 P.M., outside Tacubaya station. A euphoric Ignacio Castillo fires his camera at the milling crowds.

"Know what, sir?" he calls out. "In case you wanted to compare, how about a tour on a second-class bus?"

"And where would we go, Ignacio?"

"Pantitlán, La Aurora, or behind La Villa, if you felt like it, so as to investigate the diff—"

"This is a story about the metro as an indicator of national development, Ignacio. Not a story about destitution. We went out to look at people packed to a pulp due to the shortage of public services, not at people who haven't enough to eat. I'm already smelling and hearing the metro in my sleep! Another time we can go down to Mezquital and stare at thirty-year-old senior citizens, okay? That's enough for today!"

Metro Insurgentes

JOSÉ JOAQUÍN BLANCO

Some of us may remember the propaganda blitz that preceded the construction of the great sunken plaza at the Insurgentes metro station. Geometric abstraction was then all the rage: the Olympics posters, the sculptures dotting the "Route of Friendship," buzzwords like "abstract," "kinetic," or "computation"; electronic, hallucinatory compositions and disintegrations were everywhere. The desire was for a smart, ultramodern capital on the lines of science fiction. Skyscrapers, plate glass, metals, plastics: the massive nudity of unadorned concrete surfaces to build an austere architecture of monumental curves and straight lines, all with a simple design. In the much-vaunted maquette, the subway plaza was to ignore the decrepit buildings around it and allude instead to extraterrestrial models, like the cities in Superman or Martian comics: circular roads, split levels, vast open spaces.

Ten years later, one can sit on the edge of the dirty, dried-up fountain that borders the rounded entrance to the metro and watch the comings and goings of intermittent multitudes one has seen before in San Juan de Letrán. They scatter across the plaza; some knock aimlessly back and forth or herd together in groups; others home in on a waiting girlfriend, kiss her, and lead her away; the ones with a schedule disappear swiftly through the tunnels on the outer ring.

Like everywhere else in this city, there is a predominance of dark-skinned youths uniformed in the trendy gear that conceals their lack of gainful employment: satchel with protruding book (anything from Mao to Og Mandino, from the *Communist Manifesto* to Kahlil Gibran, from *Jonathan Livingston Seagull* to Herman Hesse); jeans, sneakers, the sporty look and laid-back swagger that give the impression of some kind of student of something; T-shirts with cosmopolitan phrases like *"Voulez-vous coucher avec moi ce soir"* and—in English—"I'll try everything once" (this on the front, on the back: "Maybe twice"); *"¿Qué me ves?"* ("What you staring at?"), *"Je suis MAGNIFIQUE";* or even *"Gallina vieja hace buen caldo, Usted decide si la embarazo"* ("Old hens make the best broth, You decide if I make you pregnant"). They are aged thirteen, fifteen, seventeen; they hang out in packs at first, happy as truants, telling themselves the world belongs to them and sooner or later they'll escape from the crowded family apartment on the outskirts (where they're a growing burden on the wage or subwage of the sole family member with a job, who supports ten people). They wear faded, frayed T-shirts adorned with colorful patches, torn flaps, necklaces, funny buttons.

The older kids roam solo. Their faces are more serious, their gaze more purposeful; scamming, dealing, whoring, brawling, and cadging after months or years of unemployment. A dime novelist might compare them to the hieratic figures of savage Aztecs. Their remote features delineate another form of consciousness, in which survival means contemplating life from beyond good and evil, beyond the feelings and manners cherished by those with sufficient income. And just as they were brighter and smarter than middle-class kids of the same age, so by their mid-twenties they are prematurely aged, thickened and gap-toothed, their bodies scarred by accidents, illness, and fights.

The city (its poverty, its overpopulation, its barrio ways, its violence) turned the futuristic set of the Insurgentes metro station into just another plaza with a holiday feel: soiled, crowded, many-colored; despite its aristocratic contours it's nothing but an outpost of Garibaldi Square. The bars became demoted to cantinas. The fancy restaurants with their outdoor terraces wearily embraced their fate as snack bars, after their plates and bowls were showered with cigarette butts, garbage, and grit from the perennially congested highway above (an expressway that is constantly jammed around the rotunda, making it the roundabout that isn't one).

Metal ducts ripped from somewhere are lying around. The tunnels behind the shops are the lairs of homeless people who are regularly moved on by the police: Indian children wrapped in blankets, crawling around their timid mothers; men encrusted with the grime of months, starved into imbecility, dressed in tatters, and tormented by all sorts of tics and itches. The shrubs in the planters have succumbed to the perpetual onslaught of trampling, pissing, and littering; they wither away near healthy, blooming pots with sophisticated plant combos that are trucked in for special events. The smell of urine intensifies in the vicinity of stairways and tunnels. The human mass struggles in and out, automatically dodging obstacles such as beggars, loudmouths, vendors, secret agents, dealers, rent boys, prostitutes, and pimps. The stores have gone either down-market or bust; some storefronts sit empty for months. The city government had to step in. It opened branches of its bureaucracy—bearing names like Conasupo, Injuve, and Boletrónico—and mounts exhibits of amateur photography or children's art. To relieve the social tension, it hires bands to play mariachi or pop music, like a festive counterpoint in the background.

The Insurgentes plaza has not contaminated its surroundings with futurism (although here and there a tall building tries its best to match up); no interplanetary epics could be set in the streets that radiate from it. It is overlooked by a broken skyline of truncated towers, amid brick walls plastered with showy geometrical murals that do little to stop the place from looking like a bomb site. The environs are barnacled with stalls and bus stops and coated in posters, notices, flyers, and ads for obscure learning centers. These exploit the despair and joblessness of young people with guaranteed job placements as IBM technicians after some "fastest courses, lowest rates." Or how about Dianetics, typing, intensive English, a correspondence course in accounting, your high school diploma in a year, commercial draftsmanship, radio and TV repair, or "agronometry: the career of the future"? Half-smothered under layers of offers, this sentence: "You know what Jesus expects from you!"

Past midnight, when the masses have drained away into the last metro convoys of the evening, the plaza begins to look like itself again, reverting to the model some of us remember. Night erases the traces of those who have passed through it, and the floodlights—in the style of the light-and-sound show at the Teotihuacán pyramids—bring out the lines of its stark circular construction, like a planetary monument or some very ancient pyramid. The isolated, almost insignificant social outcasts

of the day trickle through: drunks, lovers, petty criminals, junkies, senti-
mental loners—all keeping an eye on their watch and their wallet.

The plaza seems solid, unrattled by shouts, sudden noises, bursts of
mysterious laughter. Dark shapes drift in the darkness: clumps of policemen. The uniformed silhouettes seem to be in their element here, and
the curved wall by the mouth of the metro would suit a firing squad.

Spacious and solitary, the plaza by night would provide the perfect
setting for some climactic moment of peril: it recovers its ceremonial
feel, that of a temple consecrated to violence in whose shadows the
cops—clubs hanging, revolvers in holsters—smoke and talk, waiting for
their cue to officiate.

The Metro

A Voyage to the End of the Squeeze

CARLOS MONSIVÁIS

Every day, close to five million people make use of Mexico City's metro, fighting a vicious battle for oxygen and millimeters. Long gone are those old film scenes showing countless individuals squeezing into a ship's cabin or a taxi. That was surreal metaphor, in any case; this is something entirely different: chaos in a nutshell. The city—its essence, its idiosyncrasies—plays itself out in the metro. Riders are sullen or raucous, rueful or exasperated. They burst out in choral monologues or keep quiet (doubtless in an effort to communicate telepathically with their inner self). Reluctant paragons of tolerance, they boast the energy to remain upright in a stampede, to slim and instantly regain their customary body types with each squeeze. The close proximity to so many bodies breeds—and cushions—impure thoughts. In the metro, the legacy of institutionalized corruption, ecological devastation, and the repression of human rights is formally passed on to each passenger and to the legions he or she potentially contains (each rider will engender a carriage-full). They keep this heritage alive: it's the "humanism of the squeeze."

While one cannot claim that what feeds ten people will also feed eleven, one can assert that where a thousand fit, ten thousand will be crammed, for space is more fertile than food. In all the world, there is nothing so flexible as space; there's always room for one more, and another and another, and in the metro, human density is not a sign of the struggle for life, but of the opposite. Who said two objects cannot occupy the same space at the same time? In the metro, the laws of molecular structure lose their universal validity, bodies merge like spiritual essences, and transcorporeal graftings are commonplace.

One can attain pluralism by venturing into the metro at peak hours (feats of warlike retreat, already calling for their Xenophon), or by venturing into public housing projects where privacy is a matter of weaving and dodging, a pretension contradicted by packed streets and families breeding in front of the television set. There are so many of us that even the most outlandish thought is shared by millions. There are so many of us, who cares if the next man agrees or disagrees? There are so many of us that the real miracle is getting home, closing the front door, and seeing the crowds magically diminish.

How could one not be a pluralist, when subway trips teach us the virtues of unity in diversity? How could one not be a pluralist, when identity is constituted by pushing and shoving, and maintained by the mysteries of population explosion? Prejudices become personal views, demography takes the place of tradition, and we remember this about the past: there used to be fewer people, and the old minorities (in contrast to the current majorities) counterbalanced their numerical handicap by spending time outdoors. Claustrophobia rose—hunger for fresh air, for a life that could never go underground and could never be compared to a descent into hell—and street life prospered. Then came the metro, and agoraphobia became fashionable.

Is it possible to score in the metro? Many say yes, it's a piece of cake, because if the metro represents the city and recreates the street, it must by necessity contain sex—all kinds of sex. Packed into subway cars, humankind reverts to primal chaos, a *horror vacui* that is fertile ground for propositions, the rubbing of bodies, lustful advances frustrated by lack of differentiation, surreptitious grinding, blatant grinding, risk taking, and other transgressions. It's all the same in the end. The metro abolishes singularity, anonymity, chastity, desire—mere individual reactions that become insignificant in the larger scale of things, in which a former "many" is the only precedent for the current "too many." It's all the same whether one enters or exits.

The metro's perpetual novelty consists in squeezing the entire country into one square meter. A feat of hospitality, each carriage becomes a biblical metaphor, generating space for loners, couples, families, tribes, progenies. The metro dissolves the boundaries between bodies; there is room for everyone, after all.

4

Monuments

Monuments

GUILLERMO SHERIDAN

I love monuments—statues, fountains, palaces—those periods marking the end of every paragraph in the urban text. They are my now and my nostalgia.

The first to leave its trail in the path of my memory is the Monument to Álvaro Obregón in San Ángel. My grandfather, who had been a staunch enemy of the general and had been exiled by him, used to take his grandchildren to eat ice cream at a place with a good view of the hideous gray tower. Inside that gray tower lay *The Hand.*

We would slurp up our banana splits with gusto while Grandpa chewed on his rancor, glaring at the monument. Sometimes he would hiss sourly under his breath, without taking his eyes off it: "All that's left of you is your hand, you traitor, and look at me, alive and kicking, having me an ice cream!"

My grandfather always spoke in exclamation marks. If we asked him what a "traitor" was, he'd reply: "A traitor, as the word indicates, is a scoundrel who betrays his nation and its sacrosanct values!" When we asked what "scoundrel" meant, the answer was, "A scoundrel is anyone who is an enemy of your grandfather!"

Sometimes he took us inside the monument. He paid the entrance fee and ushered us along to the fateful display case. We were shaking, but he was convinced that a sight of *The Hand* was essential to fortifying our civic consciousness. When we got to it, his face was twisted with rage and his voice shook.

"There is the hand of the scoundrel who tried to kill your grand-father! Don't you ever forget it!"

How could we? It looked as though five prawns had organized an orgy in a small jacuzzi. Hovering in some Lovecraftian substance, *The Hand* was crooked into a virile gesture that sought to grasp the reins of the Motherland, or at least to scratch his stomach, as he must have often done in between battles. *The Hand* was horrific.

My visits to the Obregón monument made me think all monuments contained a hand, or some other piece of a hero's anatomy. So I concluded, for example, that the Latinoamericana Tower—the only sky-scraper in the city at the time—was a monument and that, given its size, it must contain offcuts of Pancho Villa's entire army, horses and all.

The Monument to the Niños Héroes preoccupied me somewhat. That there might be boys who, besides being boys, were heroes, added up to a pressing demand on my own potential heroism. Many a time did I dream of myself duly chopped up and distributed over several monu-ments for having defended the peaks of the Popocatépetl to the end from some foreign scoundrel and announcing to the enemy general at the mo-ment of surrender (because it was assumed one always surrendered): "Though I be vanquished, traitor, I still have not claimed defeat!"

I also visited one monument that still exists: a fountain in Parque México, in Colonia Hipódromo Condesa. It represents a voluptuous In-dian woman pouring water into a pool, from two pitchers that are ren-dered slightly superfluous by their proximity to her enormous breasts. I was convinced that this was a monument to my mom in a permanent state of lactation. Hence I was affronted to see the local kids groping her stony tits. There was this red-headed boy who actually managed, for a brief moment, to get his mouth around one of her nipples. He paid a heavy price for this presumption, since he fell head first into the pool and tinged the water the color of his hair, to the indifference of the statue, who was the only adult in sight.

I loved the monuments along Paseo de la Reforma. The Angel of In-dependence, Cuauhtémoc, and Christopher Columbus were sequential landmarks leading to the Caballito, a rearing equestrian statue whose distinguished balls we admired from inside the car as we sped by. Diana, the huntress, was our favorite of course, that round butt of the roundabout, strong and curvaceous, that virgin rump capable of engendering whole tribes. I was initiated in the equestrian arts astride the lions gracing the monument to Juárez on the Alameda Gardens: I slid down the marmoreal volutes of their dais. I think Reforma, watched over by so many heroes, has always given me a feeling of safety.

We love statues because they are points of reference, places to meet, and ideal spots for traffic accidents. We love them because they belong to everyone; they have a place in the city and also in the image of the city we all have. Every inhabitant of Mexico City harbors his own private Paseo de la Reforma. La Diana, Cuauhtémoc, and the other monuments are the postcards of this personal voyage through a city that is also our memory. That's why I'm fearful that one of these days someone may decide to change this street. Some committee or other has already proposed modifying Reforma, adding or removing statues as though this were not an avenue but the living room of a bored housewife. Besides, the thought of changing avenues around in the midst of the current chaos is like that Laurel and Hardy scene in which, after having smashed a whole crockery set, Laurel picks up the one plate that didn't break and concentrates on polishing it to a shine.

Some years ago, the city fathers wanted to relocate Diana on the grounds that the woodland goddess belonged in a wood, not in an avenue full of killer buses. This argument struck me as fool's logic. If we follow the same reasoning, the Caballito and other equestrian statues should be packed off to the racetrack, the Angel shunted still higher, to above the clouds, and the Fuente de Petróleos returned to Wall Street. It was proposed that Diana should be replaced by a work of sculpture with the alarming title of Monument to Mexicanness. A Mexicanness so insecure that it needs to pay homage to itself. Addicted to superficial changes (substantial ones being beyond them), the city authorities imagine that herein lies their passport to a posterity studded with ruins. Can anyone picture Londoners moving Nelson around, or the Parisians transferring Joan of Arc?

Let's leave the city in peace, along with its heroes and goddesses. They all worked too hard to be what they are—city, hero, or goddess— and they don't deserve fanciful makeovers. If inside each monument lurks a hero, then the monument to disaster that is Mexico City contains quite a number of them. Several million in fact.

La Diana

VICENTE LEÑERO

Diana's buttocks are stupendous, there's no other word for it. At 21 inches across, you'd need arms five and a half feet long to hug them. Besides, they're made of bronze, as is the rest of her. Two tons of metal to produce a hollow, eviscerated body, the perfect female chassis according (so they say) to the tastes of the average Mexican honcho who likes them chubby, with generous helpings above and below, and proper legs. As far as measurements go, this one amply fits the bill: 42 inches around the thigh (both right and left), 27.5 for the calves, 17 at the ankles. All this thanks to her towering stature: nine feet high, practically twice the average height of our national dwarfettes.

In terms of the vital statistics favored by beauty competitions (bust, waist, and hips), Diana the Huntress could represent all of Chapultepec Park quite confidently with her 61-45-65.5 (quantities in inches). Adjusted to the proportions of a real female body 5 feet 8 inches in height, this translates as 34-25-37. Not bad. Lupita Elorriaga, Miss Mexico 1974, was exactly that height and her beauty could be computed as 36-24-36, that is, two inches bustier than the bronze goddess, but slimmer around the midsection and hips. It comes down to the same in the end. Both are way out of reach for the city's philanderers, who must content themselves with a look and a wish.

They've had long enough to look at her, at any rate. Save for short periods off-duty when she has disappeared, whisked to a secret location for the purpose of cleaning her pedestal, undressing her, moving her to a different spot, or heaven knows what, Diana has remained steadfastly at her post over the fountain for thirty-two years. Six long presidential terms of maidenhood, aiming her arrowless bow at the North Star under the libidinous gaze of Chapultepec's bronze lions; still waiting to be written up by Carlos Monsiváis, who left her out in his survey of Mexican camp. Or maybe a literary wink from Carlos Fuentes, or Octavio Paz, or any of the many scholars who claim to be so turned on by "Mexicanism" but have only theories for the Aztec goddess Coatlicue, the Virgin of Guadalupe, or the lovely Pepsicóatl when it comes to chin-stroking about our matriarchal fiber. Not a word about her, oh no. Her, Mexico City's sweetheart since 1942, solace of late-night drunks, patron saint of pubescent lusts, peerless rival of unliberated wives, touchstone of scandal for decent citizens; brazen virgin, shameless hussy, porno sculpture, whore of Babylon, tramp, courtesan, slut, loose woman soliciting right in the middle of Paseo de la Reforma: "See you by the Diana," "Four o'clock at the Diana," "One peso to the Diana please."

Ignored. Slandered. Blessed. All in all, important. Her story is worth telling. So here it goes.

Something Simple and Bucolic

As metropolitan journalists are fond of saying, those were tough times for Mexico and the world. During the second year of General Ávila Camacho's presidency, our country declared war on the Axis powers, apparently because they had sunk our ship *El Potrero del Llano*. A national emergency was declared, and a law was passed making military service compulsory. It was 1942, the year that saw María Félix's lovely face fill the screens for the first time in *El peñón de las ánimas (The Mountain of the Spirits)* and the release of Rodolfo Usigli's play *La familia cena en casa (The Family Dines at Home);* the year a forty-five-year-old sculptor from Guanajuato, Juan F. Olaguíbel, applied himself happily to the task of modeling and casting the bronze effigy of the Archer of the North Star at his studio in the neighborhood of San Bartolo Naucalpan.

The idea for the statue was born months earlier, after Olaguíbel completed his demagogic, fifty-four-foot tall monument to the popular hero El Pípila in his native Guanajuato. Himself as distended in conceit as the colossal statue (which he considered a masterwork of stone), and no doubt striking much the same triumphant pose as he gave to the legendary hero of Mexican independence, the sculptor proclaimed his intention to gratify Mexico City with a sample of his talent.

Whatever you say, maestro!

Exploiting his recent success in Guanajuato, he pulled enough strings to obtain an audience with the then-mayor of the capital, Javier Rojo Gómez, the one who cut through the city with expressways, to the disgust of Salvador Novo, and revolutionized Avenida Revolución.

It would appear that Rojo Gómez was all for it, and in an extra fit of magnanimity offered Olaguíbel's art a huge space at the classy end of the Paseo de la Reforma. There was nothing there but a large gas station for the new rich of Las Lomas; today the Fuente de Petróleos occupies it, a sculptural ensemble that was eventually entrusted, much later, to the same Olaguíbel. But at the time he found the site too large, and turned it down, along with the architectonic scheme proposed by Vicente Mendiola to commemorate the nationalization of oil, which had just been completed in 1942 with Mexico's agreement to pay twenty-four million dollars in restitution to American oil companies over the following five years. Olaguíbel reckoned this monument could wait (as indeed it did), and explained to Rojo Gómez that what he had in mind was something simpler and more bucolic, on the lines of an Amazon frolicking in a grove.

"Okay," said Rojo Gómez, swapping one end of Reforma for the other and offering the last available roundabout, right by Chapultepec Park's lascivious lions. Not daring to refuse twice, the sculptor refrained from pointing out to the regent that his grove concept would have been more at home in the middle of the park, for the sake of atmosphere, and besides, an anonymous Amazon was hardly the appropriate climax for an avenue flanked by busts of historical notables. He bravely bit back his misgivings, slapped down his modesty, and undertook to put her there, outside the wooded park, crowning the ungainly fountain, which was—of course—designed by Mendiola.

A Thousand and One Muses

It was time to get down to work. Olaguíbel withdrew into communion with himself.

Right. An Amazon.

Like, how?

Like, naked.

Naked?

Of course naked, like those classical statues that sing the splendor of the human form, blah, blah.

All right, naked. What else?

Doing something.

She could be, um . . . flexing a bow!

Just the ticket, flexing a bow. An archeress of the heavens aiming at the North Star. In which case, to be conscientious, we'd have to face her in that direction, though that leaves her buttocks pointing at the Ministry of Health across the street. Oh well, can't be helped.

Now that the grand overarching plan had been decided, the sculptor embarked on a quest for the model. "As my master Rodin was wont to do," he smugly told the journalist Guillermo Zetina of *Excelsior*, many years later, "I set off to seek her in the streets."

Though we cannot take the sculptor's version of events at face value, it is necessary to repeat it. First let us picture him, age forty-five, tramping the sidewalks the length and breadth of town, staring at all the pretty girls. A happy task, endorsed by duty and the example of Rodin.

"At last I found the ideal woman on an avenue," said Olaguíbel to Zetina. And from that moment on, according to him, everything was a piece of cake. The fortunate elect was no professional model; she was just a homemaker, who by 1970—when the *Excelsior* interview took place—was safely married and the mother of two children, though she remained "as svelte as ever."

On the occasion of that historic meeting in 1942, the young woman agreed straight away to pose nude for Olaguíbel. He brought her to his studio. "And I must say," he remarked, "she collaborated in the task very enthusiastically from the word go." Olaguíbel completed thirty-two sketches; thirty he gave to his muse, and two he kept.

However, this story of a single model runs counter to earlier declarations made by the artist, who seems keen—perhaps wisely—to sow maximum confusion. In 1967 he told another reporter he had used eighteen models as a basis for Diana, and that any other versions floating around were prosaic, mischievous horrors.

The gossip thus referred to involved the names of certain national movie stars and even politicians' mistresses. "Come off it, what wouldn't so-and-so give for a body like that?" objected the counter-gossips. "And it's certainly not whatsername. It would be great publicity for thingamajig, whom no one takes seriously any more . . ." Horrors indeed. Ugly and prosaic, as Olaguíbel rightly said.

Speculation continues to this day about the identity of the model. Some speak of a single muse, a flamenco dancer named Blanca de los Ríos. Others whisper about a Sunday painter, who shows her work at San Ángel's "art garden." There's also talk of two girls who posed in tandem for the statue: the first—according to confidential information from Héctor Pratt, who worked for Pemex, the state oil company, under Mendiola—was a top executive at Pemex who lent her top half to be copied; the second was a humble clerk at the Treasury, whose lowly condition was no obstacle to other virtues: she had a traffic-stopper of a body and legs that inspired Olaguíbel to mold the eleven inches-worth of calf displayed by his Diana the Huntress. May God preserve her in fitness.

Clothing the Nude

For six months our sculptor was at it: April to October 1942. Not a soul dropped by the workshop; no one took the smallest peek at what was inside. Busy as they were, solving the country's problems, neither top politicians nor the city government employees seemed aware of the gradual genesis of the bow-pulling maiden that emerged one day, cast in six parts, from the toasty bowels of Olaguíbel's furnace. "Awe-inspiring, a thing of beauty," corny journalists would gush. "Sock it to me, big mama!" foul-mouthed drunks would call out.

But they were not to see her as she was. No sooner had Olaguíbel sent word to Rojo Gómez to the effect of "Finished!" than scandal erupted. Some say the fuss was stirred up by the members of the Morality League, headed by the ineffable Núñez Prida; others, that it originated from the First Lady, Mrs. Soledad Orozco de Ávila Camacho. Whoever started it, the upshot was that the nation's moralists—en bloc—howled with outrage at the news that a bronze female, privates and all, was due to preside over the entrance to Chapultepec Park—Chapultepec, for pity's sakes! The paradise of Mexican children, the playground of our daughters, the healthy hike of unsullied youths who have no need to acquaint themselves prematurely with the topography of women in their birthday suits. To cap it all—please try to understand—there's, well, the coarseness, the depravity of the pose! No shame, none, and to think it's the portrait, so I've heard, of that missus, what's her name, the unsavory one . . . Really, this is going too far.

"And it cannot be allowed!" cried the Morality League. "No way!" agreed the authorities, turning their thumbs downward, as in, go to hell.

Olaguíbel pleaded as best he could: Hadn't Vasconcelos sprinkled statues of naked ladies throughout Alameda Gardens? Didn't Michelangelo's *David* expose his tackle? Weren't the cherubs in the cathedral without a stitch? Wasn't the Venus of Milo . . .

Hold it right there. "Let her be like the Venus of Milo, then," conceded the moralists magnanimously. Covered up from hereabouts to down there, where it's most sinful to be looking. When he met with Olaguíbel, Rojo Gómez put on a regretful face and pointed to heaven, indicating that the order came from above. The sculptor duly found himself molding a special loincloth for the Archer of the North Star. But he cheated, of course. Confident that morals—like life—change with every new presidential term, and that someday the clamor of public opinion would restore his work to its pristine state, he gave Diana a dinky pair of panties held on by just "three spots of welding," heh heh.

So it was in her undies that the Amazon was hoisted to the top of her fountain, welcomed only by a grudging snarl from the disappointed lions. There was no unveiling ceremony. No crowds. No panegyrics to the artist's talent. Not even a fanfare for Diana. Only the delivery of a check for six thousand pesos to the sculptor, as a symbolic advance— they doubtless told him—on the reward he truly deserved: immortality.

By dark of night, with the sheepishness of one attending the wedding of his firstborn to a hooker, the city government gave Mexico City its love goddess, its sex symbol, its concubine. Her name was a gift from the people. Against the intentions of Olaguíbel, who had engendered her as any old Amazon with a long and cumbersome title—the Archer of the North Star—the metaphysical city dwellers elevated her to divine status and identified her as Diana, daughter of Jupiter and Latona, Roman goddess of hunting, who obtained permission from her father to remain unmarried, and whom Jupiter—god of heavens, light, time, and thunderbolts—made goddess of the forest. Diana the Huntress she was called, from the first dawn, by the grandiloquent city dwellers. Diana of Chapultepec, Goddess of the Grasshopper Woods.

Such was her fame that she was soon inspiring other sculptors to make copies of her: the Diana of Ixtapan de la Sal, patron saint of rheumatics, or the Diana of Acapulco, hostess of tourists. Rumor also has it that Olaguíbel cast two identical copies: one is owned by a high-ranking functionary—a lead yet to be investigated—and the other belongs to Mauricio Urdaneta—a story yet to be confirmed.

But Chapultepec Park owns the real Diana, the one that took her place in Mexican history on an October morning of 1942, perched atop the fountain that instantly began to spout its symmetrical jets. The arcs of water were later colored, thanks to Mayor Emilio Peralta Uruchurtu, by colored lights as they danced, never splashing a drop onto the statue's feet or sturdy legs (and still less onto the notorious bronze panties held in place, heh heh, by just three spots of welding).

Approaching Striptease

Time passed. Out went Rojo Gómez, from the mayor's office to his ranch back in Huichapan. In went Casas Alemán and swiftly out again, crestfallen after a failed bid for the presidential chair. At last behold Uruchurtu, who came and remained, aspiring to eternity.

Nothing much happened to Diana during adolescence and early adulthood. Amusing anecdotes, at best. The racy quips she drew from inebriated nocturnal gentlemen, the occasional crazed suitor clambering into her basin to bathe with the goddess, or the aborted disrobing, one night when Olaguíbel himself, egged on by two friends and three drinks too many, attempted to remove the loincloth that marred his creature.

"I was unlucky," said the sculptor. "A policeman saw us and made us come down."

There was a nice joke, too, in *Los caifanes*—that Felliniesque film by Juan Ibáñez—which fulfilled the loony desire of millions of capital dwellers: to climb up and cover Diana some more, magnifying the act of censorship. It never happened except in that film narrative, where, at the climax of a most gladdening sequence, a group of exuberant characters manage to strap a white brassiere onto the statue.

In fact, over the twenty-five years that Diana remained sheathed in her decorous briefs, city dwellers grew used to seeing her as she was: censored. There were no campaigns to demand her disrobing, no decent protests against decency. Such an embarrassing state of affairs was a boon for the moaners and groaners, who railed against "the regime of censorship running this pious country." "How dare they preach about voters' freedoms and responsibilities," thundered the misfits, "when there they are, Diana's panties, undeniable proof of the government's savage prudery!"

When Diana's fountain was damaged by the 1958 earthquake, and the statue had to be removed to reinforce the pedestal, new hope stirred for Olaguíbel and the members of nudist groups. What an opportunity to have her do a striptease in the name of freedom! But Uruchurtu was adamant. He hid the huntress where Olaguíbel and his followers could not find her, and reinstalled her—if anything, cleaner and shinier than before—as soon as the base was repaired.

More time passed. Nine years, from 1958 to 1967. Women had won the right to vote and Diana had come of age. She was twenty-five, the age of fullness, when suddenly talk of undressing her began.

Apparently the pressure came not from below but from above, from the aerie whence the metropolis was governed by General Alfonso Corona del Rosal, Esq. They say his aides prodded him as follows into Operation Clothes Off:

"The Olympics are approaching, your honor, sir. Visitors from all over the world will converge on the City of Palaces. What will they think of Mexico, your honor, sir, when they see this censored Huntress? Furthermore—and this is strictly between us of course—election time is also drawing near, and it is none too soon for any gestures that may arouse popular sympathies, Sir."

We cannot be absolutely sure that the suggestion came from above and was not a petition from below, from Juanito Olaguíbel's workshop. We do know, however, that one morning the sculptor celebrated his seventieth birthday by sending this plucky, if ill-written, missive to Corona del Rosal:

> Most esteemed and discriminating friend (colon). On the occasion that by order of the authorities of the city government the statue popularly known by the name of Diana has been taken down, for the purpose of checking the pedestal on which it was stood, by virtue of the fact that

it seems it was not properly set on it since the last installation, a defi-
ciency that has gotten worse with the passage of time, I venture to address you with the respectful request that, making the most of this occasion, I might be permitted to restore said sculpture to its original
form. Indeed, it was approximately twenty-five years ago that as a result of certain circumstances I will not bore you with, the aforesaid
sculpture was ruined by the addition of a certain completely unsuit-
able garment, which not only distorts its artistic purpose, but also
makes it quite ugly as you must have noticed. My humble request does
not offend morality, taking into account the lofty artistic nature of the
sculpture. There are many precedents we might cite: at the Palace of
Fine Arts and in the Alameda Gardens, a considerable number of figures in a state of undress have been publicly exhibited for years. Beyond our borders, and I mention this for its great relevance, at the
Vatican Museum the love of art annuls the low pettiness of other sorts
of thoughts. I am quite sure, esteemed Head of the city government,
that the whole city will applaud this decision. (Paragraph.) Please accept my fulsome thanks in advance. Yours faithfully (Paragraph.) Juan
F. Olaguíbel.

Corona del Rosal's reply, dated November 30, 1967, was somewhat
longer and more literate. Beginning with the same invocation to an "esteemed and discriminating friend," its central passages ran as follows:

> I am pleased to inform you of my favorable decision with regard to your
> request, and in light of the reasons you have verbally put before me,
> you are free to proceed with whatever works you deem necessary to re-
> turn the Diana to the original form in which she was conceived and ex-
> ecuted by you . . .
>
> My decision is based on a range of candidly reported opinions, as
> well as comments which I have solicited from a diverse cross-section of
> figures including artists, intellectuals, teachers, professionals, journal-
> ists, writers, etc.; I believe this survey can claim to be a valid reflection
> of public opinion.
>
> There are, moreover, legal arguments of note. The Federal Copy-
> right Law exists to protect the artist from any deformation, mutilation,
> or other unauthorized modification of his work, as well as from any ac-
> tion which may undermine the prestige of said work or lead to the di-
> minishment of its honor or repute.
>
> More broadly, we observe that mankind has always reached out to
> the highest values. One of these is beauty, and, in striving to materialize
> it, the greatest artists have turned to the human body, the nude body,

for its expression, and in objectifying their ideal they have not confined themselves to the physical attributes of womanhood but have elevated her into a goddess: Aphrodite, Venus, Diana, etc.

The letter closed with this moving paragraph:

As you have explained, your renowned Diana constitutes a well-deserved homage to Mexican womanhood, for like the artist you are, you have poured your vision into a splendid statue which cannot be immoral when it exalts, in its nudity, the most prized qualities of womanhood presented, and rightly so, in the form of a goddess.

Twenty-five Years of Tears

At daybreak on December 6, 1967, four years before his death, Juan F. Olaguíbel personally supervised the return of the Diana to her pedestal on Paseo de la Reforma. She swooped from the sky, hanging from a mighty crane, swaddled in white cloths that would compound the emotional intensity of her ceremonial striptease.

It had taken only a week for Olaguíbel to undo the three stitches of welding that held the loincloth to her body, and now here she was, the goddess revealed to her worshippers for the first time, completely naked.

The crowd massed around the roundabout took the event as a cabaret act, cheering wildly as the performance reached its glorious climax. Juan F. Olaguíbel was overcome with feeling:

"At last art, progressive culture, and the open-minded sagacity of our officials have carried the day," he intoned, "after twenty-five long years of travails, bitterness, and tears."

There was nothing more to say. As a matter of fact, nothing was added on the subject of Diana for seven years, until a few days ago, when the city government announced that due to the construction of the overpasses required for an inner-city expressway, Diana the Huntress would be relocated to another roundabout, at the intersection of Reforma and Mississippi.

Once more, though this time without fanfare or polemics, the goddess descended from her pedestal and went meekly into storage at the

Department of Sanitation, where she remains, pending accession to her new throne, within reach of every lecherous paw wishing to size up the twenty-one-inch spread of her majestic buttocks.

No one seems to give a damn about this relocation, except perhaps the bronze lions crouched over the entrance to Chapultepec Park. And even the lions are getting old, too old to muster up a sexy snarl.

5

Eating and Drinking

The Chinese Café

JOSÉ DE LA COLINA

Like a magical, secret flower growing in the sorry neighborhood of San Miguel was Rosa Li, my love never conquered and forever lost. I would like to tell this story as Thomas Burke might have done when he wrote about London's legendary Chinese quarter in *Limehouse Nights*.

At the intersection of Isabel la Católica and República del Uruguay or El Salvador, there was a narrow, deep, dismal Chinese café owned by a tall and taciturn Cantonese man, frequently absorbed in a newspaper with Chinese characters, and his plump Mexican wife, always dozing behind the register. The only one who seemed to do any work, waiting tables, carrying chop sueys and milky coffees and buns, was the daughter of this interracial marriage, ah, the sweet, slight, lovely, demure, quiet, serious girl of rare smiles, whose smile was like a knife, a flower, a yellow rose, like nothing else in the world; ah Rosa Li, how you glided and meandered through the restaurant, as if a bubble of silence protected you from the jukebox blasting *ranchera* songs ("You, you alone are the cause of all my tears, disappointment and desperation, and to forget you I plunge into drink, into perdition") and boleros ("That last night we spent together, I try to forget it and yet I can't, and those short

moments that you were mine, I long to forget for the good of my soul"),
and polluting the air with merciless sentimentalism, and how you
moved toward the booth where we were sitting at nightfall, Arturo
Pérez Hortigüela, Fernando Toba and I, friends since our school days
at Colegio Madrid and the Politécnico, and you, in a soft voice graced
by the liquid vowels of a Chinese language that you probably couldn't
speak, you asked, bending your pale oval face and high cheekbones and
very slanting eyes toward the young man that I was—dazed to find you
so close to my eyes, so close to my desire, and so remote from my life—
"What would the gentlemen like to drink?" And I, instead of ordering a
milky coffee, was so pierced by desire and wild, sudden love that I requested a "Chinese coffee" to the mirth of my friends, who elevated the
expression into a pet joke ("We were having a Chinese coffee in a cof-
feehouse of the same ethnicity"), and perhaps you did smile, Rosa Li,
upon hearing my slip, ah your faint and pure and fleeting smile killed
me, revived me, finished me off (and the man who is remembering you
now, Rosali Rosalovely Rosaliquid, the paunchy balding shortsighted
fellow who thinks of you and attempts to pin you down on the page, that
man has been in love, has been through many loves, reciprocated or
otherwise, happy or painful, but has never ceased to be secretly in love
with you). The three of us, though I swear none more than I, were fasci-
nated by her, and we dared one another to ask her out for a walk, a
movie, anything at all, and wondered who would be the first to coax a
kiss from her, or something more, with a bit of luck lovemaking between
the sheets, a feat that would enable the victor to ascertain whether Chinese girls have a slanted sex or not; like all youths of that age, we used to
exchange boastful tales of instant, earth-shattering, extraordinary erotic
exploits, but only Hortigüela managed to emit a brusque, awkward stab
at an invitation, putting on a pseudo-Mexican swagger of "Hey chula,
so when are you 'n' me going to the movies?" which Rosa Li fended off
in silence, with a slightly longer smile than usual and a little sideways
turn of the head.

One evening Rosa Li was not to be seen in her parents' dingy locale,
nor was she there the following evening, or ever again, and though we
still went there hoping for her reappearance, patrons were now served
by her plump mother, who was somewhat less drowsy than before, while
the father, having renounced his vow of silence, leaned over the counter
chatting with Chinamen, three or four of them, all uttering the same
thin, shrill, unintelligible profusion of tones and vowels, those constant

Chinese vowels rattled out like notes struck by a maddened virtuoso on a xylophone, and we were sure they were discussing the unknown whereabouts of Rosa Li, her unknown fate, for perhaps she had been spirited away by some sinister individual belonging to the mysterious and tentacular Chinese underworld, a master in the cunning arts of stealth, intrigue, and torture, some diabolical Dr. Fu Manchu of the kind that we pictured, our minds fueled by Sax Rohmer's thrillers, pursuing evil ends behind the honest façades of Chinese stores along Dolores Street.

Some months, maybe a year later, Hortigüela said to me: I found Rosa Li. You're kidding. No, I know where she is. Come on, where? Guess. No idea, where? Where do you think? Give me a break, I don't know, in a Chinese coffee shop on Dolores? Nope. So tell me. In the Meave whorehouse. No way. Yes. Where's that? On Meave Street, off San Juan. I don't believe you. You don't believe me when I tell you that's where Rosa Li is? But what's she doing there? What do you think? A whore? Well, she sure ain't a nun. But how can she? Who knows, must have gotten a bad case of harlotry. Fuck you, Hortigüela, I don't believe you. Fuck you, De la Colina, wanna bet? Take a chance on the chink. Let's go there on Saturday night, deal?

It was like a dagger blow because I was so genuinely, romantically in love with Rosa Li that I never even profaned her by using her, as my desires urged me to do, during those sessions of solitary pleasure that would leave me more perturbed than satisfied. However, arming myself with courage, I went along with Arturo to the house on Meave Street, a one-way alley off San Juan de Letrán, between El Salvador and Vizcaínas. The brothel was a large apartment cut up into a warren of little cubicles, all disposed around a central room furnished with half a dozen tables where the girls applied themselves to getting as many shots as possible of (false) tequila, rum, or so-called brandy bought for them by railway workers from Nonoalco, or by bingeing campesinos looking as though they had just come out of the bush: men who were all reeling from an equal number of shots of (real) tequila, rum, and so-called brandy. A mellifluous, spongy bolero was playing, one that was famous for poisoning unwary souls ever since my days in La Merced ("When the silver threads of youth are blooming . . ."), and had now resurfaced with lethal force, damn it, from a giant jukebox twinkling with tiny lights. We had gone to see Rosa Li and if possible to possess her. Sure enough (even today, some forty years later, it saddens me to remember it), she was there that night and other Saturday nights too, a blossom of the mire, of the most bemired melodrama of Mexican cinema, always gay and in the company of some client; Rosa Li, more beautiful, more desirable, more cheerful than ever, seemed not to recognize us even though her table was so close to ours. It was unmistakably her, a princess turned prostitute, visibly glad to have abandoned her kingdom of milky coffee and chop suey, though not the jukebox's malevolent influence. (It was perhaps the jukebox in that Chinese café that was to blame for Rosa Li's undoing!)

I got around to sampling the services of other Meave ladies, thin, long Sonia for instance, who was much in demand and specialized in the dreadfully named "doggie" trick (consisting in a spasmodic contraction of the vagina), but I never dared so much as to come near Rosa Li. I don't know why, perhaps because I was always waiting for her to approach me in her undulating sliding style, for her to face me, with that face that defied oblivion, whoredom, and death, and ask, "What would you like, sihl?" And to cap it all I had to put up with Hortigüela's merciless sarcasm, fueled by what I suspect was his hidden love for the debased princess, as he insisted on singing a version of the much recycled "En un bosque de la china," with lyrics altered to fit the circumstances: "Entre putas de Meave / Rosa Li se emputeció / y pues soy un putañero / nos encontramos los dos" ("In the Meave whore grounds / Rosa Li became a whore / And since I'm a whore hound / I'll meet her for sure").

Then, one afternoon in 1987, I was at the movies watching *The Last Emperor*, the story of the last Manchu ruler Puh Yi and of his first and second wives, when suddenly I was struck dumb, breathless, overwhelmed because there on the screen I saw Rosa Li, I saw her youthful cheeks, her own elegant swaying walk and the wrenching sweetness of her smile, transferred by the industrial wonders and wily arts of film onto actress Joan Cheng, and from her onto the character of Wan Yung, first wife of Puh Yi and last empress of China.

Armando's Tortas

JORGE IBARGÜENGOITIA

One of the greatest inventors in the history of Mexico City has been Armando, peerless creator of *tortas,* or Mexican sandwiches. His influence upon the culinary evolution of the Mexican people has been so profound that no one remembers what a torta tasted like before the advent of Armando.

Legend has it that Armando's career peaked when he was sent on a diplomatic mission. On the occasion of some important event—the centennial of Mexican Independence, perhaps—it was resolved that the Mexican embassy in Paris would throw a mammoth party. In order to ensure the highest quality of service for diplomats and top officials of the French government, Armando himself journeyed to France by boat, carrying a crate of avocados.

Armando's torta is a baroque creation requiring the coordination of approximately twenty-five elements—including the sharpness of the knife and its operator's lettuce-chopping skills—in rigorously choreographed order. If the sequence is altered in any way—by adding the chipotle before the cheese, say—or if the quality of any ingredient is below par, like a mushy avocado, then you're not eating a genuine Armando's torta.

Armando's tortas were made from cuts few people care for these days—tongue, brains, or liver—and were to be consumed with a glass of local liquor and the spicy pickled vegetables provided in ample supply on every table. I know at least one client who had a near-death experience after overindulging in these powerful appetizers, but he survived and lived on for forty years, which he spent recounting his prowess.

Armando's torta was a classic, and as such it has gone down in history. The complexity of its design, the array of ingredients, and the rigor of its preparation paved the way for its demise. Unable to adapt to either market forces or the demands of modern life, this majestic torta was eventually replaced by a more straightforward invention: the hot turkey torta.

The hot turkey torta is dazzling in its simplicity. It requires nothing more than a few slices of roast turkey and a dollop of guacamole. The inside of the roll is smeared with gravy. Usually garnished with pickled onions and chilies, this torta reached the pinnacle of its popularity during the presidency of Miguel Alemán, and its rise thus coincided with the beginning of Mexico's industrialization and also with the generalized, but short-lived, conviction that no meat is more succulent than a turkey's.

The hot turkey torta was soon replaced, in turn, by the hot pork torta. Its status began to rise toward the close of the Ruiz Cortines presidency and peaked under López Mateos. The only difference between this torta and its predecessor lies in the animal supplying the meat.

Pork tortas are still eaten today, but they are clearly on the way out. In keeping with the observed trend, we can safely predict that the next step will lead to an even larger animal—from turkeys to pigs, and from pigs to cows—and a corresponding reduction in the complexity of preparation. Slice a roll in half, drop a steak in the middle: the torta of the future is a beef sandwich.

Once, when I was a kid, my grandfather came to visit and solemnly announced, while removing his gloves, that he had just seen, at the corner of 16 de Septiembre and San Juan de Letrán, a group of men selling tacos that were wrapped in a kind of "red poncho."

"I had three, and they weren't bad at all," he said.

The arrival on the market of *tacos sudados*—steamed tacos—marks one of the climactic moments of Mexican technology, as momentous as the invention of the automatic tortilla-maker or the creation of the very first *taco al pastor*. The steamed taco is the Volkswagen of Mexican food: good, reliable, and affordable. No more than five minutes need elapse between ordering your tacos and wiping your mouth in satisfaction. They held center stage for more than six presidential terms, and their recent decline is due solely to the neurotic but fashionable fear that any food not cooked in the diner's presence is bound to be poisoned.

As for *tacos al carbón*, let me just say this: it's a shame that it took Mexicans four hundred years to realize that beef, too, can go into a taco, and that this realization came at a time when there are almost no trees left to feed wood-burning barbecues. Technologically, these tacos are a step backward. But though a technical disgrace, they are a marketing wonder: a tidbit designed to double the prices while persuading the client he's eating for free.

"Man, a steak and two tortillas for three pesos! How lucky can you get?"

Vips in the Early Morning

JOSÉ JOAQUÍN BLANCO

He has grizzled hair and a bad case of inebriation. At this time of night (3:30 A.M.) the staff at Vips doesn't know what on earth to do with him; they have already threatened to call the cops, to no avail. It's a weekday and freezing cold; in about an hour, through the great expanse of the restaurant windows, the gray, damp, steamy streets will begin to fill up with the outlines of construction workers, servants, and other early laborers ready to crowd into early morning buses.

The gray-streaked, fifty-something drunk sends all the employees to hell and goes back to sleep, his (spittle-streaked) face resting on the counter's brown formica top. The floor manager can't decide whether to carry out his threats or wait until the booze wears off a bit; maybe he'll leave of his own accord. In the meantime he busies himself, putting out menus, napkins, and garishly folksy cards advertising real Mexican dishes on bare tables. After all, some deadbeat or another always washes up on these cold mornings, and most of them—drunks, freaks, sad loners—leave quietly in the end.

You can always tell cold mornings by looking inside all-night restaurants: the insomniacs of the cold are completely different from the late-nighters of warmer seasons. In summer, the early hours are full of laughing groups, juniors showing off, blissful young lovers. But on chilly nights there are few cars, patrols, or pedestrians about; stray dogs become more visible—millions of stray dogs, some marauding in packs, fornicating, threatening; others down-and-out and solitary, numb with cold, whining dully, sniffing out human trails leading them to irascible or fearful persons who shoo them away. Parks, traffic islands, parking lots, construction sites: so many campsites for mangy dogs. Under the shadow of tall buildings, the leap and scurry of rats. And the cats: on thresholds, windowsills, hot tin roofs, under sheltering trees, in their own still shadows, projected on the glossy asphalt by the streetlights.

On cold mornings the spacious, bright restaurants might stand empty for hours, except for yawning waiters, until some oddball like this one wanders in. He arrived, wearing good clothes, trying to act out the level gait and gracious demeanor of his normal self, but succeeding only in a halfway decent parody of them. He ordered some food, a drink; well before they were brought, he'd gone to sleep. The waitress surrounded him with steaming dishes. The man was oblivious.

Nothing distinguishes this fellow from many others who have good jobs, a house, a wife, children, credit cards, assets, fixed opinions; his car is probably right outside, badly parked. He seems to be in a crisis: he's never gotten plastered by himself before, or only once, but so long ago that he kind of forgot about it. A journalist in search of a story sizes him up over from behind a novel he is reading, in English: *Kalki*, by Gore Vidal, "His Most Outrageous Bestseller." He thinks it would be fun to play television reporter and march up to the fallen man, cameras behind, microphone to the fore, firing intrusive questions at him: How does it feel to be in this state? How come? Why is that? Wouldn't you be ashamed if your chubby little kiddies saw you? Et cetera. The man would tell the reporter to go to the same place he sent the waiters, and when he saw himself on the news, he probably wouldn't remember being filmed.

The reporter would lead in with some kind of introduction: "Upstanding men who have made sacrifices all their lives in the name of order, and done their best to fulfill the roles expected of them, can suddenly explode. Some trifling triggers a shouting match with his wife, and unforgivable accusations fly across the table; a bad day at work upsets—if only for a few hours of raging or bingeing—all the values that had seemed so solid and immutable. Anything at all can unexpectedly tear a good man from the golden cage of his life for a few hours. And here is a typical case before us. Excuse me, sir, can you give us your name? Will you answer a couple of questions for our television . . . ?"

There is a strange beauty to the lost denizens of the chilly hours. Look at this one, for example, slumped over the counter. His suit is not yet crumpled. His tie is tasteful and well designed. His shoes are still shiny. His manicured, plump hands sport two modest rings. A pair of spectacles—thick, respectable lenses—pokes out of the breast pocket. Finally, when it starts to get light out, the manager will have no choice but to call the police. He does this two or three times a week. In fact, the kitchen boys are already here with the buckets, wiping and mopping, cleaning away the leftovers of the early hours so that the restaurant looks neat and virginal when the first batch of bureaucrats arrives for a business breakfast. It would not make a good impression if they saw this sodden wreck, who will soon wake up on the back seat of a police car, on his way to the station, as the sun rises; straightening his lapels, smoothing down his salt-and-pepper hair, negotiating a bribe with the officers. At some point he will descend from the police vehicle and take a taxi to his home or to wherever it was he left the car (if he can remember), exuding an authoritative, confident air, and with explanations prepared.

Then he will look back on the binge: thoughts, feelings, nightmares. The things he's always known but can only enumerate, with precision, on such occasions. The possibility—drooling head against formica counter—of sending the whole caboodle to hell. The experience of loneliness, the sense of uselessness, all that; so many other anxieties, wrinkling the expansive smile (he practices it in the rearview mirror) of the prosperous, mature man, the boss, the head of the family.

Cold mornings leave no trace in all-night restaurants, and yet such locales are inseparable from the icy hours. At those very tables, in those chairs where lovers linger, bureaucrats breakfast, and friends meet for lunch. In the darkest hours before dawn, insomniacs have mulled over crimes and suicides, plotted schemes, wrestled with their consciences; they have read or scribbled all sorts of things, have formed or discarded all sorts of complicities.

The icy early mornings of Mexico City are often plotted in such overlit, artificial surroundings. Sometimes one is there, as a protagonist. On other occasions, one just glances in, like a tourist, just checking out the destinies of others.

Nightlife

CARLOS MONSIVÁIS

We are the bed's recurring dreams.
James Merrill

The light of day falls harshly upon individual or collective traits: grotesqueness, bad taste, physical imperfections, high risk. But while daylight exaggerates—it's class conscious and catastrophist—nighttime proves more level headed. Night obliterates flaws, smoothes incongruities, overlooks danger (no use in staying home all the time, as if home were some nunnery or prison), redeems what was made ugly by God—or by lack of exercise—softens the extremes of under- and overnourishment, and makes lust dance to rumba beats. All this, needless to say, *after a certain hour.*

The people's night belongs to those who balk at excessive security, dislike consumer society (bourgeois discos), and are uninterested in scrutinizing the way others dress. Not all participants lack buying power: many are middle class—there might even be a stray bourgeois or two—but most are subject to perennial budget constraints ("I'll be back next payday") and the anxious desire to catch something—anything—before youth dries up. (And youth dries up when one no longer aspires to remain awake forever.) In the past, before television, before crime, the people's night was a requisite rite of passage—and a lesson in urban consciousness—for youths with little money; now it's been taken over by married men in search of an affair (preferably with a total stranger): people are now scared of doing anything with their own partners in spite of—or because of—twenty or thirty years of marriage.

The Geopolitics of Partying and Desire

Mexico City is home to between fourteen and twenty million people, but its more extreme offerings *(Get your kicks at knock-down prices!)* add up to two or three thousand cantinas, a few dozen clubs—with or without table dancing—two or three variety theaters, thirty or forty gay bars, one plaza full of mariachi bands . . . and the thirst for freedom and experiences that were hitherto inconceivable (or unrealizable because they were unnameable). This geography of desire and eagerness might be called the *new people's night,* and it was born in the early 1990s, not because anyone willed it so, but as a result of the obvious: there are fewer night owls now than in the past, but their extreme malice and recklessness—in contrast to the bygone innocence—make up for their small number. No one is shocked by anything anymore; no one is scandalized by the widespread incapacity to be scandalized. The survivors of this journey to the end of the night are looking for action, and only a hangover or a mugging can coax them back into the fold of repentance. *I was such a fool to abandon my TV!*

There are no more old-fashioned shows. Why leave the maternal womb just to snooze in front of some frivolous act, with actors standing up there and us sitting down here? Impresarios now peddle interactivity, or whatever one calls the audience's active participation in the show. If you aren't joining in on some level, you feel like you're sitting in front of a broken TV. Inhibitions crumble and the dread of *what will people think* is relegated to the past—a happier time when others cared about our actions. The authorities now understand that prohibitions merely multiply the censored act—or, in a more malicious reading: they understand the profitability of corruption—and thus they let people enjoy themselves (with the help of some external stimulus) at those unthinkable spectacles.

New Species: Live Sex

By 1995, the brief desperate moanings that constitute *Live Sex* prospered in spite of Mexico's economic crisis and the peso's devaluation. *Sexo en Vivo, Live Sex!* Here were orgies within the budget of every student. Downtown, in the Centro, a number of dives—La Chaqueta, La Corneta, La Diabla, La Bruja, and El Catorce—specialize in shows encouraging audience participation. Their clients are amateurs, eager to strip and to prove the last axiom of the millennium: the mysteries of the body are more complex than the mysteries of the soul, since the latter's sins can be forgiven any day, while the former has only a limited time to benefit from the penance of gyms and diets. Live sex brings about an inversion of spheres: the private becomes public and the public, which was so private only hours or minutes before, is celebrated by boastful participants and ignored by the rest of the audience because it physically excludes them. Live sex in Mexico City is not, as in other world capitals, a touristic-commercial fact but a touristic-commercial project, undertaken by an ephemeral community that imbues it with theatricality, with a sleazy and degenerate but still relatively spontaneous character.

Eje Central: The Lumpenization of the Future

Most of the downtown clubs are on or near Eje Central, a wide road that gobbled up streets formerly known as San Juan de Letrán, Aquiles Serdán, and Santa María la Redonda. This area was considered picturesque; now it looks more like the bastion of the unredeemable: street vendors, stalls peddling food that is as dangerous as urban crime, errant drunks known as *teporochos,* and packs of youths in search of a miracle—getting plastered for free. On these streets you can buy any number of horrors. Buyers of the world behold: pirate videos and tapes, bargain-basement clothing, heaps of socks and T-shirts, perfumes and deodorants, CDs, design-free sweaters, Christmas specials in July . . . People with an air of defeat about them: buyers and sellers are interchangeable (some sell what they don't want to own, others buy what they don't like).

El Catorce: Advantages and Disadvantages of the Present

You dance on a whim for the youth's conceit . . .
Salvador Díaz Mirón

If anyone is still searching for good reasons to justify the rain of fire that will destroy sinners, the end of the millennium offers a good one: the proliferation of gay bars. Years ago, before these locales acquired a proper English name—they're known as "bares *gay*"—they were subjected to incessant police raids: every three months their liquor license was suspended and put up for expensive renegotiation. Now the city tolerates—as though under the counter—the existence of a plentiful minority. Take, for instance, El Catorce, also known as Las Adelitas, a bar located on Ecuador Street, on the former site of a public bathhouse of ill-smelling repute (one can still intuit the spectral scent of towels and soap). Here's a den of modern permissiveness, a magnet for all sorts: men with eyes like computer scanners, women who cannot, for professional reasons, choose their partners (i.e., whores), gay couples who lost their air of ambiguity when they left the closet, sensation seekers, reporters on the trail of a great story about subalterity, UNAM students writing hard-hitting theses, and a sizable horde of young veterans. And why not? The cast is predictable because when that which is forbidden ceases to be forbidden, it becomes uncontainable. *Come see the fun we never knew! Come see how you'll see yourself, once you open your mind a crack!* It's fashionable to encourage tolerance, although tolerance itself is out of fashion.

El Catorce—the name means "fourteen" in Spanish—is a tiny dungeon that unintentionally recreates a 1940s cabaret, in cheap Mexican film style, with its corners and crannies lit by bulbs so faint they only deepen the darkness. There is no cover charge. A beer costs sixty cents US. There are tables, a few photos depicting Pancho Villa with his wife Luz Corral, a bar, arcade games, and one or two posters of well-endowed men (obscene in their record-breaking proportions) . . . The place is a cross between a disco and a cabaret, and on weekends it buckles under the pressure of up to a thousand regulars.

The Catorce gets so crowded that it's often impossible to move. Most patrons are young, and—judging by their appearances—at least half are soldiers, construction workers, or mechanics. A handful of women move among the crowd of men, giggling at their newly found minority status. Forty or fifty couples on the dance floor barely exchange glances as they dance to the rhythm of techno, pop, cumbia, merengue, redova, and salsa ("Oh tropics! Why did you curse the masses with the movements of ardor?"). There's no tension in the air, perhaps because cruising no longer produces sexual tension: it no longer matters if someone accepts or rejects you; who cares, there are billions of people having sex right now, and just as many who're lasciviously fantasizing about it. Cruising loses its cabalistic dimension to enter that unacknowledged department of love: statistics. ("I get excited just thinking about how many people are doing it.")

As the superego's censorship recedes, those present engage in a kind of exhibitionism that would be unmentionable in their village or at their parents' house: they grind, dance like there's no tomorrow, and are unfazed by the morning after's moral hangover. They've come here to do one thing: to come. Even clubs—former temples of the pick-up cult—have been secularized. Getting off is no longer a devotional rite, as it used to be when a Night Out was a great psychic reward; it has now become a business that increasingly demands market research and sex workshops. Although the patrons might not realize it, the threat of AIDS opens a parenthesis between desire and fulfillment, between enjoying one's freedom and paying in advance for the privilege. Judeo-Christian guilt has been replaced by fear of forgetting to buy condoms.

Lust conquers all, but sexual incontinence is kept in check by fear of the consequences. Who would have thought it? A small safety device has come between pleasure and its enjoyment. With or without brochures, AIDS has assumed the censor's function and is now responsible for turning sex into drama, complete with morning-after panic. To parody a famous Mexican song: *"Sin condón la vida no vale nada"* ("Without a condom, life's worth nothing"). Voyeurism, formerly a classic symptom of frustration, has become the epitome of safe sex. An unholy exhibition of inhibitions! A sinning spree stopped short by a bingeing virus. Not the most cheerful of topics for a nightclub. The sensible patron will alter the bolero's lyrics: *"Yo sé que soy una aventura menos para ti"* ("I know that I am just one less fling for you"). Otherwise he will plunge into the abyss because he already lives on the edge: *I don't take precautions because no one cares if I live or die; I don't use one because sooner or later we'll all die; sex is like Russian roulette.* And what do tonight's revelers know about the "plague of the century"? Do they read up on protease inhibitors, drug cocktails, and special diets? Or has their courageous irresponsibility inoculated them against information? Ye gods! *Volverán las oscuras golondrinas* but the carefree, unwary days when latex did not cast a film over the world, *those will never come back.* If sex is a risk, AIDS desexualizes lewdness.

A New Species: Los Chacales

A strange term flies around the club: "Look at that *chacal!*" "That's some piece of *chacal!*" So what's a chacal, and what's behind the zoological comparison to a jackal? In gay slang, chacal refers to a young proletarian with indigenous (or newly mestizo) features belonging to that historical invention the "Bronze Race" (sardonically and onomatopoeically renamed as "Bronze Race, Clang, Clang!"). Broadly speaking, the chacal embodies working-class eroticism, gestures eluding any complacent decipherment, a body sculpted by the gym of life, hard work, the dust clouds of inner-city soccer, long marches, military drills, and crawling through the rain to surprise an enemy who's always on the verge of materializing. The chacal's superb shape is the product not of aesthetic concerns but of manual labor.

Even when no one looks at him, the chacal acts as if everyone wanted him. He struts through the room, assimilating the lust of others, pausing to field lewd vibes, or walking as though he needed extra space for a body swathed in the desires it arouses. This is a common occurrence in racist societies: natives are desirable sexual objects because it's so puzzling that they're the majority and because they're just like us but poor. As for the chacal, he never looks, so as not to give away his gaze for free, but he allows himself to be ogled for the sake of his self-esteem.

It took a long time for the chacal's desirability to be generally accepted. At first it was the whim of an elite in search of class contrasts, the thrills of slumming it, and the myth of the Noble Savage. For over fifty years, hot, working-class *nacos* were the rare but prized trophies of sexual hunts. But then advertising turned to sports, soccer, exercise, and the codes of male beauty started to be publicized everywhere. Working boys appropriated sexy looks, started wearing tight T-shirts and strategically torn jeans, and perfected a glance that may be hostile or indifferent, but always enticing. Hundreds of thousands of teenagers from working class barrios and rural areas adopted the time-hallowed motto of sex: "exhibit and thou shall sell." And thus the chacal was born, neither for hire nor off limits, as an indigenous alternative to the Greco-Latin model. Chacals draw a considerable audience of risk takers who remain cool even when, laying eyes on a chacal, they experience a fatal premonition. Of course, the brave man knows that mixing social classes is to be done *at one's own risk*. But who ever disputed the machismo of victims?

El Catorce: "Are you wearing that to show off?"

Suddenly the river of the street is filled by thirsty beings . . .
Xavier Villaurrutia

It's two thirty in the morning, the dance floor clears, and there remain only three girls who look like hookers and seem apathetic to the sexual tension surrounding them. They look bored but that's just part of their act. The master of lubricious ceremonies asks someone from the audience to come up on stage and, as if by spontaneous generation, four chacales appear. There are no preludes and no striptease niceties: Shazam! In two seconds the boys are stark naked. That's better. Instant delivery is more appropriate for the end of the millennium.

With no regard for the protagonists' egos—and with no fears of retribution—the audience approves or disapproves of the genital offerings on stage. Occasionally someone wins a round of applause or a burp of appreciation, but jeers prevail:

"Think you gonna conquer the world with that?"
"It came up to let us down!"
"It's not there, it must be out to lunch!"
"Were you late when they were being handed out?"
"File a complaint with God!"
"It must be having a bad day."
"Try vitamins!"

The nudists ignore these mortal darts against their manhood. The emcee yells out his repertoire of jokes. Of all his lines, the one most favored by the audience is the one announcing live sex:

"Aaand here's the milkman!!"

Patrons rearrange their chairs, ready for theater and for more porn wit.
"Come on, scrub out that pot!"
The young prostitutes gyrate under the lights, bored by the routine. Encouraged by the emcee, the men get progressively bolder:

"She wants one guy, and over here, she wants two."

One girl, completely naked, wanders up and down the stage, uninhibited by love handles. The emcee pursues her with a cry that is like a floral tribute:

"*Ca-shon-da!*"

"She's hot and wants a man!"

With great virtuosity, the girls snap condoms onto their respective partners-for-a-night; they consent to a moment of fellatio or to grinding onstage. Their foreplay is lustful but serene (if such a thing were possible, like a carefree bolt of lightning). After more grinding and humping, copulation begins in earnest. "What happened to intimacy?" I ask myself rhetorically, while the kids onstage fornicate in accordance with the rules of "get in there while you can" and rush to orgasm, the *petite mort* that dissolves into sleep.

If he is of a moralistic bent, the visitor to Las Adelitas will find it all pretty disturbing, but what kind of moralist would descend nine (or fifty) circles of hell to recoil in horror at the sight of sin? And after three minutes in the place, who would dare to expel the money-changers from the brothel? For the moment, nobody's abandoning the Cave of Abominations, no one seems upset by the sight of live sex. Things would be different if we were watching a film or video, since pornography is an anti-utopian device: one would think the splendid bodies of porn stars would help the Solitary Vice rid itself of its bad rep, for why project desire onto bodies that do not deserve it? Perhaps, for that reason, it is not altogether appropriate to speak of *pornographic* shows. On a video or in a magazine, pornography creates fantasies but also a structure; live sex, on the other hand, might not ruin sex for good, but it does render spousal obligations unpalatable. And such is the delayed effect of censorship that watching a couple in full genital mutiny seems like an act of virtual porn.

The Bad News: The Loss of the Night

> To dream, to dream the night, the street, the staircase
> And the cry of the statue unfolding the corner . . .
>   Xavier Villaurrutia

In the language of cities, Night has been defined as the realm of time reserved for chance and recreation. Until a few years ago, Night was limitless and going out always left one with a sensation of transgressive plenitude. To "get lost in the night" meant breaking with routine and exorcising the predictable; anyone who woke up at noon wondering whose apartment he was in, convinced of having ruined his prospects forever, had made excellent use of nocturnal time. "That night, last night, what a night that was last night!"

Not anymore. Urban violence and crime have laid siege to Night. Going out, even in the safer areas, is risky: you might wake up at noon, wondering which hospital you're in. Bunkered at home, under lock and key (and burglar alarms), the losers of Night idealize and demonize it by turns: "It was a waste of time / Yeah, but the best waste ever." And nothing has taken its place, for it was the supreme domain of voluntary risk, of unknown pleasures. Its tombstone: a television set left on until dawn.

El Catorce: To Battles of Love, Fields of Latex

> Live prey! The beak bloodied!
> The wing swift! The surge of flight!
> And a madness of peaks and sparks . . .
> Porfirio Barba Jacob

He who fornicates in front of a crowd publicizes the most detailed account of his personal technique and renounces mystery forever, giving up the enigma of intimacy that once depended on the (not impartial) testimony of a single witness. That was long ago, when we entrusted others with our intimacies. Never again. It's *my* intimacy and I'm going to show the world. Before live sex, in the days when boasting of amatory prowess was selling one's soul to the devil, inhibition would have made a mockery of public (or pubic) displays, and a failed attempt at becoming aroused in public would have been met with laughter. But the abolition of privacy increased our powers of concentration, and teenage copulators are blind to the world because in a megalopolis, all that is not family or fiancée or friends appears like a remote landscape. Sure, it's tricky doing it on a dance floor, but these kids who sleep in tiny rooms with eight or ten other relatives have seen it all, and they know all about the pathetic sounds of lovemaking. In a world of thin partitions, the sounds of sexual grappling are equally meted out to all. The end of privacy came long ago for the poor, and no one living in cramped quarters ever demanded that you "close the door because I want to be alone with your kisses."

The soldiers at El Catorce never bother about their surroundings because their surroundings never bothered about them. They are here to let off steam and pick up whatever's available, if "whatever" submits to being fondled. They lose themselves in the beat, in the frenzy, in the horny camaraderie, in the urge to give their libido a chance. They don't think of themselves as gay; they'd beat the life out of anyone who ever called them *that*. They just follow their instinct to avoid turning into pillars of salt.

Here on stage everyone fucks with fury: I don't give a damn, it's their business, all coitus was created equal, just imagine how many people are at it right now in China. And the audience: if they deign to look on, they don't ogle the fornicators with savage glee, but view them rather as part of some *National Geographic* or Discovery Channel documentary. Permissiveness can be overdone, and onlookers end up staring at the most intense sexual acts as if they were episodes of bureaucratic life in Borneo. The message is loud and clear: sexual feats that exclude *me* are tedious spectacles.

The couples here are homo and bi, with a sprinkling of hetero, in line with the Napoleonic Code and its variants, which refrain from specifying the gender of companions on the dance floor. The great majority are gay men who alter the mechanics of unsatisfied desire with a penchant for dark places. They dance to music that was fashionable months ago in the glitzy discos of Pedregal, interspersed with anachronistic hits like "La Macarena," a pop-banalization of flamenco that was very popular at one time, or Caballo Dorado's Spanish rendition of "Achy Breaky Heart." Ah! Techno mechanizes movement and modernizes the soul. Ah! The apogee of ghetto discos becomes clear: they are the modern version of old-style dancing clubs, minus the technological wonders that dazzle patrons who pay colossal bills in bourgeois discos.

It's not only poverty that emerges as a strategy for resisting the uniformity spreading over our planet. A life lived in cramped quarters— combined with a historical lack of job opportunities—imbues teenagers with the will to convert uninterrupted dancing into a way of life, something requiring more than skill, something that is more than a way of passing time. They don't live to dance; they dance to experience what will otherwise never come within their grasp: a modern, psychotechnological fever that sets the stage alight.

New Species: The Stripper

Which came first, the gym or the stripper, the barbells or the youth bent on turning narcissism into a career? Without biceps, triceps, and pecs, there's no way a body can be rented out for lustful purposes. The male stripper, a species of ten years' standing, fulfills the requisites: an agreeable or tolerable face, evidence of regular muscular exertion, choreographic energy (not quite the same as dexterity), minimal sensuality in the whipping off of garments and—so as neither to please nor displease—permission for quickies given by an emcee: "OK, give him a feel, but no long-term parking allowed . . ."

The stripper may or may not be gay. He must be, however, a product of that assembly line of hard bodies called the gym. Pumped up by weight training and priapically advantaged (optional), the stripper's job is to make his nudity as offensive as possible to all spectators, male and female. "So how come I never get this type of flea in my mattress? Why is mine a bad deal?" (There's nothing more attractive than a body that insults by comparison.) And like all new species, the male stripper has gone from better to worse. When he first appeared, he was a rarity and always welcomed with applause. Chippendales was just starting, and every stripper made the audience cheer. Eventually, the opening of both gyms and minds produced a glut of hunks, and made sex-symbol status a prerequisite for any attempt to conquer the world. "If they're hot for you in private you might as well be invisible. You've got to be publicly appetizing," was the message dominating casual conversations held in the antechamber of experience. Apart from good pay, which is always useful, the great advantage of wholesale male nudity is the re-elaboration of desire, as articles, plays, films, and TV programs never tire of pointing out. By current standards, the body is not just the mirror of the soul but the soul itself.

There are risks to this. Recurring spectacles are bound to turn spectators into critics (if Lady Godiva strolled by naked every day, villagers who initially averted their eyes would bounce back as implacable juries). But it doesn't matter. The stripper's nudity signals availability. Even if nothing actually happens, stripping evokes quickies, rolls in the hay, back-in-a-minute acts, profferings of "I couldn't deny this or a glass of water to anyone." And such a leap from the concealed to the attainable cheers the new generation of Tarzans in this concrete jungle.

El Catorce: Permission for a Slight Tremor

Now altogether nude, the stripper works the stage with aerobic vitality to the beat of Proyecto Uno's hit "El tiburón": *"No pares, sigue, sigue"* ("Don't stop, go on, go on / Don't stop, go on, go on"). Ay, my friend Onan is in sore need of company! He may have a fine time on his own, but there's no one to listen to his feats. All songs speak of sexual urgency to please the new mainstream—people who dislike ambiguity and see music, both between the sheets and on the dance floor, as the great spur, the arbiter of life's boxing match. And the lyrics are, who could deny it, both technical and philosophical: *"Un poquito más suave / Un poquito más duro"* ("Bit softer / bit softer / bit harder / bit harder / bit harder").

The stripper persists in his calisthenic circuits, and two girls and a boy lick his dick, just like that, on the run, in an act of fetishism that anticipates sexual intercourse. These simulacra of fellatio are the perfect combination of audacity, symbolic ritual, denial of ancestral inhibitions, and (in the case of the more informed and perverse participants) a rehearsal of *Antaeus and the Earth*. The stripper looks a little bored; he probably hoped to be recruited by a classier joint, a disco where he could pose as a Greek statue covered in gold dust, or chat with the audience, or be desired in the old-fashioned way, that is, with politely repressed panting.

Massification of a Species: Transvestites

> What you see, a bright deception . . .
> Sor Juana Inés de la Cruz

Of all their talents, transvestites are especially adept at one of women's most essential skills: show business. Women, we hear, are no longer founts of suffering, tenderness, or uncomplaining maternity. Today, the most womanly woman is she who draws the most floodlights, she who neglects the kitchen but cherishes the stage. Contrary to what many suppose, transvestites don't imitate Woman (a creature, since Eve, in search of a room of her own) but the Successful Woman, a very different animal, one worthy of praises, parodies, and recreations. In *La Cage aux Folles* the chorus sings: "We are what we are, and what we are is an illusion." Yes, but in the realm of deceptive appearances, the illusion is not of womanhood itself, but of an enduring fantasy about women. A drag queen wants to be the woman who bewitches the audience, the one who's an expert in the suspension of disbelief, the one who mesmerizes the audience, the one who becomes a cult figure. Among all female attributes, the transvestite selects those belonging to a victorious minority: women who, being ensconced at the top, escape the destiny of most women.

Transvestites have proliferated since the 1980s. We see them on TV, on the street (working it or simply partying), and acting in hotels, discos, and clubs. Faced with such an explosion, I wonder: might not working-class transvestism—the only kind available in Mexico—be an indirect attempt at fame? Today the human heart aspires to new heights codified in the *Guinness Book of Records* ("Believe me, I am the humblest and most unassuming person on earth"). To be a celebrity is the universal ambition, and transvestites who parody celebrities, enact a psychic appropriation of fame: "I will possess this celebrity's soul for five minutes."

It was not always this way. In the past, certain styles became divine, and hence the imitations of Bette Davis, Joan Crawford, or Marilyn Monroe. Later, when transvestite shows became legal in Mexico, there was a fad for international divas like Donna Summer, Madonna, or Grace Jones. Mexican divas followed, usually taken from television shows (the small screen is the fountain of the three wishes). Not only did mythic *ranchera* singers like Lola Beltrán and Lucha Villa enter the repertoire, with their deep voices and over-the-top folkloric attire, but also modern singing stars like Mónica Naranjo, Ana Gabriel, Yuri, Thalía, Fey, or the nouveau-martyr Selena. To do Mónica Naranjo, for instance, is to be transported to Madrid's Movida without budging from home; it's to clothe oneself in the gestures of free women.

What is it with transvestites? They don't make up even 1 percent of gay men, we are told, perhaps .005 percent, but they are easily the most conspicuous members, and bigoted minds identify the part with the whole. But they are certainly the ones who have suffered the most and still do; the ones who renounced individual identity to gain a modicum of acceptance. They perpetually appropriate what they are not, always playing feminine roles with reverent irony or respectful sarcasm. They embody the scientific method of makeup, the supremacy of embroidery, the transfiguration of dreams into costume, the high-heeled pump, fake breasts. They reproduce, exactly and cartoon-like at once, voices, gaits, looks, and mannerisms expropriated from women.

Behind the stage, behind the pageantry and delirium of disco nights, lurk personal histories marked by humiliation and blows and family and the feeling of being different and marginal in every respect. Transvestites take risk to extremes: scores of them have been bashed, tortured, or murdered. They are the objects of jeers and derision, and their survival implies a wholesale acceptance of the debasement imputed to them: "If I call myself every possible name, they can't call me anything." This leads to drunken binges, drug addiction, the suicidal abuse of silicone implants, the whole pitiful exhibition they make of themselves "because it's expected of us." But all they have been through—sniveling mothers and violent fathers, upset families and housing projects—fades away when the emcee announces: "And now, ladies and gentlemen, sensuality itself in female form . . ."

El Catorce: The Clientele—Yesterday Is So Long Ago

The transvestite doing Lucha Villa is so perfectly female that she doesn't even resort to playback. At first I thought I was watching a real woman who couldn't land another job. *Victor Victoria.* Let's face it, the drag queen look is easy to copy: you simply have to look female in a passé sort of way ("energetically languid" it might once have been called), and then impersonate a society lady with a penchant for imitating Hollywood stars. I refine my theory: it's a transvestite pretending to be a woman pretending to cross-dress. *Victor, Victoria, Victor.* Another deranged theory occurs to me: what if it's a straight male delinquent on the run who has disguised himself as a lesbian who goes in drag to conceal her inclinations? I stop, on the verge of losing myself in the tangle of identities, and acknowledge the virtues of the voice, whatever its gender.

These songs provoke runaway community bonding. The audience sings along without stumbling, and one can't help wondering where people find the time to memorize all those lyrics. Have they been fitted with a brain chip containing a century of Mexican hit parades? Ask anyone about any song and she'll tell you the composer, singer, and record label; and if you insist she'll come up with the exact month and year of the original release. One thing is certain: the people's night is blessed with a good memory. And clever. A girl who claims to be an economics student and is here with her pals from organic chemistry gets into the unfathomably repetitive Lucha Villa song *"¿Para qué, para qué, para qué, para qué llorar?"* ("Why, why, why, why cry?"), altering the lyrics to bring out their obscenity: *"Tú me la vas a hundir"* ("You / you'll sink it in me / I swear by my mother / you'll sink it in me"). She roars with laughter, as if she were teasing her high school teacher.

A few yuppies always show up at Catorce and similar dives, after dropping off their girlfriends or exhausting their appetite for chicness. In the past, tuxedos were compulsory, but current crime levels have become a deterrent against pretension, and the yuppies make do with tacky blazers and a readiness to score—a symptom of late-night fearlessness. How strange! The "private" is hardly an endangered species, quite the contrary—witness all those fortunes made by robbing what belonged to others—but where eroticism is concerned, the private is losing ground. The couple at the next table tell a friend they come to El Catorce to bank sexual stimuli for later. "It's like this. He likes guys, so when he feels them coming on to him, that's when he pays attention to me. But it's a bind, because if he shows up with me then they ignore him, and then we both get frustrated." And who cares about society, when these days people only whisper during commercial breaks, and between visits to the kitchen. Haven't you noticed that serious gossip only blossoms far from television sets?

A New Species: The Güigüi

A sequin of honeyed lights . . .
Enrique Molina

Two young men ritually animate the street. They are always on the lookout, these hawkers of other people's charm, these bawds of industrial sex. They are the *güigüis*, the newest night animals, the most aphoristically inclined PR men in town, instant psychoanalysts who can detect lustful impulses lurking behind a prim façade, spot hesitancy posing as leisurely strolling, and curiosity on the brink of overcoming indecision. The goal is to turn the passerby into a client through an enticing offer: Come on in, or you'll miss the best of the greatest. And what's that? Well, if you don't know at your age you'll never find out.

"We're open, sir. The show is about to start."

"Come in, come in, it's deluxe, if you're not satisfied we'll return your orgasm."

"Nothing to be afraid of, this black hole won't eat you."

"Pleasure to measure! The client's wish is our command."

"Blondes by the bucketful, never seen so many blondes. Not a peroxide among them."

"Tanga show, my friend. Topless and thongs, what else do you want?"

"Take a girl home with you, you can even take the cashier."

The güigüi does justice to his name, which derives from gua-gua-guá, a slang term for babble. He throws himself at cars, prowls the corners, presses leaflets into hands. He is the snake charmer of the urban pit, fighting your indifference with pushiness, handing skeptics and ditherers a program offering a couple of glorious hours. A street publicist and a night-errant, he summons up the spectacle long before the audience arrives. By touting the imminent show of human flesh, the güigüi has, so to speak, ripped off most of the clothing worn by the objects of his recommendation before they even turn up for work.

The Table Dance: "To the Client's Taste"

> There are days when we are so, but so lubricious
> That a woman's flesh would be offered in vain.
>   Porfirio Barba Jacob

In 1991, table-dancing clubs appeared in Mexico. Their aim: to speedily put the client in touch with the frontal charms of late-night courtesans (note the tribute to censorship in this turn of phrase). Table dancing is a visual and tactile idea whose time has come; it originated in Zona Rosa's tourist strip and from there it spread quickly throughout Mexico City and the provinces, where it comes up, sad to say, against merciless prosecution by right-wing mayors who cannot stomach naked ladies, dirty old men, or even an insomniac paterfamilias. In Monterrey, Guadalajara, and Mérida, right-wing PAN mayors have closed down bars, harassed their owners, and lectured society at large . . . yet they are being defeated little by little. Table dancing is repugnant indeed, dear ladies, but if anyone has a mind to sample it, let him enjoy it as long as he's of legal age.

In Mexico City, matters are simpler. Ah, faithful parishioners of El Caballo de Hierro, El Florencia, El Keops, El Evento, El Quid, El Olímpico, El Folies Bergere, El Cadillac, El Baccará, El Manolo, El Rey!

Here at El Keops, for example, the protocol is to arrive late, well fed and . . . alone. The girls will be more than happy to indulge lonely patrons by offering their companionship. They may be stark naked—just like God brought them into the great table dance of the world—or wear a modest tanga.

A solitary middle-aged man ogles the girls with a tenacious gaze. He is—like all of us—prey to devastating appetites, but here the lack of social pressure augments the visibility of his desires. His lust delights him and revitalizes him. In a post-Freudian world, sexual hunger does not lead to complexes but to befriending our own frustrations. Maybe our traumas are our only true family . . .

What is the most significant change in all this? Little remains of the former repression of sexual freedom; now it's fear that prevents us from enjoying ourselves. The table dancer performs with mechanical diligence for the patron, and denies him the right to a systematic feel-up—which is like forbidding a hanged man from kicking the air. But there's a difference between lunging at one of the girls—only to be brushed away—and paying for a private table dance (a compromise that would be tantamount to breaking the rules of the game by giving up the pleasures of stealth and daring). Table dancing only works if it implies bottling up desire. The rules of a game that does not distinguish between voyeurism and carnal urgency—look but don't touch, touch but keep your hands moving, keep your hands from the pleasures of artful caresses—turn table dancing into a party of men condemned to going through the motions of repressed desire.

A pair of gentlemen who look like bureaucrats cast aside their fatigue and start enjoying the show. "She's pretty hot!" they enthuse almost in unison, pointing out two girls. Oh my God! Both of them are staunch believers in their own sex appeal, or so it seems from their sudden burst of confidence. *Down the road that quivers / to the rhythm of his wallet.* A chick dressed in nothing but a dash climbs on the table. Now you see it, and now you see it again. Eyes widen. We are a long way from Gypsy Rose Lee. The transaction will be straightforward and "organizational," as the jolly bureaucrats say, thinking that they have their arms around the bombshell already. Her attributes are within reach of sight and touch and taste. Makes me think of what they used to call "lunchtime," in the Tijuana and Ciudad Juárez bars of the 1960s: midday breaks for punters to sample the gastronomic delights of the female organ. Lunchtime! Lap up your scrumptious *mole.*

In the people's night, a table-dancing joint is strictly speaking a show of hands. If the bureaucrats are in seventh heaven, it's not because they think grinding—or a good rub or the scent of an imminent genital meal—is the ultimate experience, but because the high-speed pampering neutralizes the round of tedium and resignation that tortures them from Monday to Friday. Oh my God!

"Don't Pull on Our Blanket"

Unhampered by economic crises and unemployment, the new people's night—lascivious, exhibitionistic, and helpless—sustains one of Mexico City's essential traits: the ability to transform impotence into hallucination, a feat that rises above the swindling, exploitative character of gangster dives, and one which goes beyond the creation of new spaces for minorities. In a city as large as ours, partying becomes the great vernacular of survival. Now that nightlife has diminished, the city relaxes her moralizing drive. The city will be tolerant as long as we let her be indifferent, and she's indifferent only so as not to be reminded that she has become overtolerant . . .

And all this, remember, *after a certain hour.*

6

Urban Renewal/
Urban Disasters

Call the Doctor

JORGE IBARGÜENGOITIA

Years ago, when I was a boy, I was proud of this city. I think we all were proud of this city. I can still remember how delighted I was to find it in my geography book, listed among the cities with more than a million inhabitants: considerably smaller than London, a little smaller than Buenos Aires and Rio de Janeiro, but slightly larger than Sydney or Melbourne. I can also remember a time when we were proud to exclaim, "Why, I used to play football here, and now it's a neighborhood of two-story houses!"

What happened to our city is rather like the story of the woman who gave birth to a huge baby. All her friends cooed, "Goodness! What a big boy!" And as time went on, they'd ask, "How's the child doing?" And she'd say proudly, "Growing and growing, can you believe it?"

And so on, until the boy had grown to ten feet by the age of eighteen months, and the family had to tear down part of the house and turn it into a duplex. Nobody asked about the boy, and the mother was no longer eager to report his continued growth. He had to sleep on three beds, and couldn't take a walk down the street because he'd get tangled in power cables. And still nobody said a word, until he ate the maid, and someone mustered up the courage to ask his mother: "Look here, has he seen a doctor?"

That's what's happened with large cities, and not just with this one. Barely thirty years ago growth was a badge of pride; now it's a terminal disease.

Or rather like having a monster at home; we have to live with it and understand it in order to avoid being crushed to death. I thus intend to write a series of articles on the subject, with the goal of putting my own thoughts in order, and I'm going to publish them hoping the reader will find some use for them.

First, let us take note of the following circumstance: Mexico City was founded seven centuries ago, in the middle of a lake, by one of the most belligerent tribes in history. The surrounding waters served as a moat in wartime, as a thoroughfare in peacetime, and as a source of sustenance all the time. Without the lake, no one would have thought of building a city here, and without hostile tribes all around, it would have been pointless to build the city in the center of the lake. Eventually the lake dried up, and the shore tribes mixed together and lost their hostility. What remained was mud, unstable ground, and dust clouds. So our first conclusion can be that the city is here because it was put here, although there's no good reason for its continued presence on this spot.

If the Aztecs had not had an empire, the Spaniards would have built the city closer to home, somewhere on the Gulf coast. Mexicans would have been great navigators, and hence great tradesmen, cheerful beach dwellers gazing at the central plateau as if it were some forbidding desert. History would have been otherwise. But it did not happen thus. The Spaniards drove deep into the mainland and, by this fact alone, determined one of the most salient traits of modern Mexico: its self-centeredness.

Second, we have to examine the causes of the city's rampant growth.

Some villages turned into cities because of their location by a fine bay or a mighty river; others grew because they were in the middle of a major agricultural zone, because mineral deposits were discovered in the area, because they stood at an important crossroads, or because they were located halfway between sources for two raw materials that go together, like iron and coal, thus becoming an ideal center for steelmaking, and so on. But none of the above applies to Mexico City, which was founded purely as a headquarters for power.

The capital was a bureaucratic invention from the start.

In a paternalistic society as ours has always been, being the seat of power brought great prestige to the city. It attracted the richest and the poorest, who all took the Spanish saying at face value: *"El que a buen árbol se arrima, buena sombra le cobija"* ("A good tree gives good shelter").

The prestige factor, while certainly the most important cause of the demographic explosion, was abetted by two horsemen of the Apocalypse: Famine and War. Each time a war or a revolution broke out, the city was overrun by refugees who came seeking shelter, who grew used to doing nothing, and who could not be persuaded for love or money to go back home. The land, for its part, was eroded after years of cultivation with backward methods; agriculture collapsed, and a new solution had to be found. Thus came industrialization. Mexico City's only qualification for being a hub of industry is its proximity to the country's largest market and to the largest center of communications. Industry means job opportunities, and the city swelled some more.

The final factor in Mexico City's growth is the congenital tendency of Mexicans to reproduce senselessly, without rhyme or reason.

Tacubaya, 1978

JOSÉ JOAQUÍN BLANCO

For several years, the city government has launched spectacular high-way projects that benefit motorized individuals. This state of affairs, se-rious enough already, is becoming worse by some even more alarming developments. The constructions favoring the individual transportation of the privileged not only take precedence over public transport for the masses but positively hamper it, making it even slower and more tire-some; they destroy the lifestyles of the neighborhoods they cut through; they tend to ghettoize the poorer enclaves (some of which were not so badly off before, when a mixture of social classes brought with it better services). These areas are thus turning into quasi-underground slums, covered by fast, streamlined bridges carrying the privileged driver across and preventing him from touching or even seeing what lies be-neath as he cruises in a matter of minutes from one upmarket zone to another. The proliferation of bypasses, urban freeways, expressways, turnpikes, and the like has a twofold purpose: to link the affluent parts of the city while insulating them from the indigent parts with the retaining walls of these grand constructions. A textbook case can be found in the neighborhood of Tacubaya.

Surrounding the Tacubaya metro station, let's say within the space of roughly one square kilometer, lie two massive transit networks: one above, on the expressway bridges, and the other below. A mess of tunnels, underpasses, traffic islands, wire-netted crossings, pedestrian bridges, subway entrances, and staircases are crossed, all at one and the same time, by the Viaducto and Periférico expressways, and the highways (though they are still called avenues) of Jalisco, Revolución, Parque Lira, and Observatorio. If there is not a traffic jam, cars are free to whiz through the tangle in a matter of seconds. With the leftovers of these modernizations, a vast warren of mass transit was organized underneath the bridges: every day thousands, possibly millions of people line up here before the dozens of bus stops, hoping to board microbuses or *peseros*, or at least a subway car. These stops are blindly and randomly located alongside bridges and highways, surrounded by hulking stairways and tunnels, dusty footways, and hundreds of grimy vending stalls attracting customers who must dodge the powerful vehicles and conduits of the privileged. This subterranean mass terminal was thrown together in deference to the requirements of the more important individual transportation; its users can expect to waste over half an hour to go from one stop to the next (because public transportation requires frequent transfers, one has to get used to getting on, getting off, and getting across). All this in addition to the time spent lining up, surrounded by an unbreathable congestion of buses and *peseros* (these don't benefit from the fast roads but must squeeze through smaller, more tortuous streets to drop off their human cargo)—a veritable inferno of wasted time, exasperation, heat, dust, et cetera. Drivers take a few seconds to drive over the bridge; pedestrians, on the other hand, take more than an hour to walk under it.

These two transit networks have ruined the Tacubaya neighborhood's way of life. The highways of privilege chopped the area into little pieces; you cannot walk for more than a hundred yards without running into a public-works barrier. Tacubaya became a place to get through, then a mess to get away from. The chaos of mass transit drives anyone who can afford it to move elsewhere. The neighborhood is becoming working class, even *lumpen*, and has ceased to receive the services it enjoyed when it was more socially mixed—less street cleaning, less sanitation, less policing, and so on. Those who resign themselves to remain here do so because they have no choice. They live uncomfortably, in a place that has become unfamiliar, in constant dread of being thrown out to make room for more public works. The social decay of the area is clearly laid out in Avenida Jalisco. It starts at the intersection with Benjamin Franklin, and for three blocks it desperately tries to survive with its old, small businesses; but by the time it reaches Observatorio, it has become a misery street, and so it straggles on up the hill in a bankruptcy of old shops and dilapidated housing until it finally vanishes from view into the Periférico.

Mass transit has changed the neighborhood's economy. . . . Now there are hundreds of street vendors and stalls. Hotels renting rooms by the hour are thriving. Whereas in a "respectable" area you'd be hard put to find a public bathhouse, here there are at least a dozen, flaunting their gallant chimneys like steamboats on the Mississippi: Lupita's (with its mural of colorful musclemen painted in a spontaneous fit of naive artistry it is not only a bathhouse but also a gym and boxing club) and many others with names like Tacubaya, La Morena, Primero de Mayo, Cartagena . . . Taco joints, markets, tacky department stores (El Taconazo, cheap clothing and music warehouses, brimming comics stands and dispensers of porno-tabloid rags, esoterica and religious paraphernalia; metal knickknacks, sunglasses, combs and cosmetics; bags and rucksacks; fruit drinks, fry-ups). Everything comes together at the metro entrances and in a dingy little plaza where an enormous plaque—now here's luxury—informs us of the love with which President (golden letters) GUSTAVO DÍAZ ORDAZ dedicated the square to his faithful people and elected to name it after no less a proud personage than—wow—Charles de Gaulle.

This small square shows no sign of socioeconomic variety; nobody who's not a loser has any business living under the bridge, and there is no security—to protect whom, after all? Let the riffraff bury their own. This attracts a migrant population of junkies, glue sniffers, and alcoholic down-and-outs, especially old ones—fugitives from other areas where the police would pounce more promptly. There's a striking number of noonday drunks, stoners, and druggies, and even more jobless men on the prowl, playing dumb, in case there's anything to scam—at the expense of their fellows in misfortune.

The rationale is obvious. Neighborhoods with mixed populations are troublesome. They need expensive public services and—even worse—they escape political control. It's far more profitable to transform—or rather ratify—Mexico City into a lake of stricken ghettos over which the islands of affluence float lightly, joined by high, efficient, fast bridges.

Charles de Gaulle Square, with its broken-down fairground booths, its crowded street commerce, its beggar-mimes with colored chalk smeared over their faces, is getting tenser as the evening draws on. Anything can set off a scuffle at any moment either there or at another plaza that's even smaller and absurdly shut in, next to the Taconazo. Actually, these "squares" were built not out of love for humanity but out of the need to do something with the left over wedges that remained after completing mighty roadworks.

On the benches around a half-dead tree or on the sidewalk, the lowest of the low are killing time, checking each other out, getting stoned or wasted, talking, arguing, and soon—how else to end the day?—smashing each other's heads in.

Avenida Álvaro Obregón, 1979

JOSÉ JOAQUÍN BLANCO

Once Colonia Roma was aristocratic, but lately it has fallen on hard times. In the 1950s it had already gone euphorically middle class and was starting to become a hub of commerce and activity as wealthier residents sold up and moved out into the latest blue-chip areas. Today, despite the persistence of a handful of antique, emblazoned apartment buildings and mansions, Avenida Álvaro Obregón is a seething track of people and vehicles between hotels, baths, trade academies, gyms, taco holes and luncheonettes, cantinas, Chinese cafés, and all manner of stores: auto parts dealers, dentists, hospitals, billiard halls, furniture warehouses, administrative offices, car parks; derisory dime stores (like the one at no.187, called Che Pa La Bola), car dealerships, beauty salons, and barbershops.

For the nostalgic reporter who fancies himself the reincarnation of Artemio de Valle-Arizpe, the most rewarding spectacle of all is the effect of time on the buildings, which is a chronicle in itself. Decrepitude sets in on the ground floor, as the jewelers, gift shops, and boutiques give way to butchers' shops and grocery stores. At the same time, the ornamental details are falling apart; no one bothers to replace the broken windows in the maids' rooms (now sublet by penniless singles, students, and prostitutes). The buildings are crowned by colossal, luridly colored billboards showing girls in bikinis.

The middle floors usually cling to their soigné, elegant status for a few years longer, but their decline too is beginning to show in the window bays. In contrast to the new high-rise condominiums, where a window is just part of a wall, how full of life the old windows seem, especially when they become downright decadent. I entertained myself for almost two hours scanning all the windows along Álvaro Obregón: though they hang on to their stone balconies, art nouveau wrought-iron grilles, and art deco wooden frames, they've overcome class prejudices and now allow things like gas cylinders, bicycles, or vacant wire birdcages to be exposed to view: buckets, plastic trays, baby's crib (we could never throw it away, but where to store it?), modest home liquor reserves—all on display for passersby. Meanwhile the façades flake, blacken, and crack, still displaying the most whimsical and varied items of heraldry.

Here are three case studies, two of them examples of this living chronicle and the third, a short but protracted novel.

1) The little market of El Parián, its architecture a blend of the Gothic, the Moorish, and the tacky, leads into a narrow roofless passageway flanked by two facing pavilions full of windows. The tenants have pioneered a poetic clothes-drying system: broom handles protruding like flagpoles from the windows, hung with an array of dripping floral dresses like medieval banners, fluttering over the vegetable and tomato stalls lining the patio of the passage.

2) A building bearing the name Edificio Asturias, cleft and sunken, subdivides what were formerly several spacious apartments into tiny digs, and produces unexpected street numbers: 151-A, 151-Lower, 151-Upper, 151-Bis, 151-B, and so on. Ivy has rooted in the deep cracks, the top rooms are caved in and unoccupied (and with traces of improbable renovations), the fine wood-framed windows with missing panes are plugged with cardboard and rubber. But oh how proudly, in the center of the pitted façade, does the shield of Asturias endure!

3) The novel unfolds—soon, in a few days, we'll say that it once did—in the building at the southeast corner of Monterrey and Álvaro Obregón. I remember passing it on my way to school when I was seven years old. In the building still graced by a Tacos Licha sign there was a beauty parlor on the ground floor, with doors onto both streets. This

enterprise also included a stylist training school. The bulk of the clientele consisted of housemaids and other underpaid female workers because the place was a real bargain: you were practiced on by students who were learning from their mistakes. When a maid was assigned to some very gifted trainee, she would have to return to her mistress's kitchen under a towering pompadour built from coarse, hardened layers of curls, some ginger, some flaxen, the rest mahogany. The salon was called Alfonso and Marcos. One day the partners had a fight, and the business was split into two separate sections with their own doorways. One of the doors was soon labeled "ALFONSO and marcos"; in furious riposte, the other door displayed the sign "alfonso and DON MARCOS." For twenty years the pair kept up a duel of notices, boasts, and barbs that was fought out on their respective walls, with the sole aim of disparaging the other and stealing his customers. Using nothing but the names Alfonso and Marcos, plus the conjunction "and" and the crafty insertion of the honorific "don," they wove a living novel that was to last for two decades. And by the size of the signs, the colors, the arrows, the occasional sketch, onlookers could keep abreast of the saga of the two partners. Sometimes they felt like making peace, and the tone of the announcements softened; other times they were so angry that the signs flared up and swelled, in a deadly duel. One day there appeared, hitched to a new salon, "Alfonso, Stylist to the Ladies," while at the Monterrey entrance stagnated a laconic "Marcos." The building is now demolished. Alfonso's section turned into Tacos Licha, now boarded up and on the verge of collapse. The upper floor of the scabby building still has its run of parapets and miniturrets, as well as a blurred niche housing a Virgin of Guadalupe. On the other side of Insurgentes, however, there appeared an intriguing sign for a newfangled and patently prosperous academy-cum-beauty salon which calls itself—with unwonted even-handedness—Alfonso y Marcos. A happy ending.

During the last presidential term, some brainbox from the city government had the bright idea of planting copies of Greek and Roman statues all along Álvaro Obregón. They repaved the central promenade with cobblestones and dotted it with green cast-iron benches bearing the national emblem of Porfirio Díaz (full-frontal eagle wearing a Phrygian cap and all the rest). Now the craze for building expressways might deal the deathblow to this kitschy promenade with its benches, trees, and narrow grassy verges—a favorite resting spot for tramps, lunch-hour clerks, satyrs on the prowl, and toddler-laden mothers escaping the smog, the dust, and the hubbub of whizzing cars. Despite its tackiness, the cobblestoned walk with its Porfirian benches and classical fountains is a good place to score: for after a sidelong glance of lust one can always feign to linger on for a good look at the discus thrower, Saint Sebastian, Mercury, Venus, and Eros, or the pederastic Satyr with Cherub.

The city's growth pushed aristocratic neighborhoods toward zones that were ever further removed from the rabble. The early noble colonias lost their pedigree. They're becoming hotel neighborhoods, fast food districts, random shop boroughs. We could dream about the palmy days when Ramón López Velarde or Antonieta Rivas Mercado strolled down Avenida Jalisco, now Álvaro Obregón. But let's not; this avenue is surely more streetwise now than ever before, more alive, more windowed, more diverse. The buildings graced by coats of arms, balustrades, masonries, and ornaments could not have found, in their majestic past, better tenants than the riotous and déclassé populations of today.

San Juan de Letrán

JOSÉ JOAQUÍN BLANCO

The vivid and venomous street of San Juan de Letrán . . .
Efraín Huerta

Neither the "sad and super-vulgar bourgeois" nor the "airhead chicks with their candies and Yankee movies" nor the "ice-cream youth with garbage filling" of Efraín Huerta's poem are to be spotted nowadays along San Juan de Letrán, and it's a rare day they turn up anywhere in the Centro. They are now ensconced in their ritzy suburbs, surrounded by malls, discos, and exclusive bistros. The Centro, once the heart of the New World, the country, and the city, is fast becoming—after its desertion by the rich and powerful—a churning backwater of hopeless brown trash and bureaucrats trapped in a dusty set of distilled smog and oppressive dry heat (reflected and magnified on the metal bodies of the cars). The masters of power and wealth are fleeing the center: luxury commerce has vanished, and most government offices and financial concerns are backing off in the direction of more reputable addresses; anyone who can, moves away; hotels, travel agencies, and entertainment businesses lead the way. This slow flight from the center will stretch on for some years. It's not that easy—impossible maybe—to relinquish the traditional seat of power, money, and status. Be that as it may, poverty, squalor, and social resentment are already the new masters.

Number 27 is a dirty, decaying building, its doorway cluttered with makeshift signs advertising the trades within: Invisible Patching and Mending, Professional Training in Illustration Art (oil, watercolor, pastel, etc.), Juárez Tailoring, Dr. Salazar—Secret Diseases, First floor No. 3, Dental Surgery—Dr. Calderón, *Tortas* at Back, Become a Comics Illustrator—professional instruction (diploma signed and sealed and work opportunities guaranteed!), Pure Sugarcane Juices "El Cañaveral."

San Juan de Letrán isn't brash enough to stick to its own name: It's called Niño Perdido up to Izazaga; San Juan de Letrán as far as Juárez; then for a fleeting two blocks it adopts the colonial name of Juan Ruiz de Alarcón in order to live up to the lofty premises of the Palace of Postal Services, the Palace of Fine Arts, the Bank of Mexico, the Guardiola Building, the Latinoamericana Tower, the headquarters of Seguros La Nacional, the Sanborns Restaurant known as the House of Tiles, and the Alameda Gardens. After that it frankly drops down a couple of rungs by calling itself Aquiles Serdán, where one finds the Mariscala Cinema, warehouses offering piles of cheap clothing (as well as lipsticks, nail polish, sneakers, T-shirts, dresses, shiny matinée idol pants), the Blanquita theater, and so on up to Reforma, changing its name all the way.

I see a single street, running from the Viaducto expressway to the statue of General San Martín and reaching its apotheosis in a classic stretch: along half a dozen blocks the flâneur will be treated to some twenty dispensaries for "sexual infirmities, psychosomatic medicine, electro-sleep, homosexuality, frigidity, impotence, hypnosis, urinary tract infections, sexual exhaustion, gynecology, nervous afflictions, psychotherapy, prenuptial blood tests, secret diseases," and a host of dentists; business and management schools, training institutes for secretaries, tailors, and beauticians; music and dance schools offering crash courses and rehearsals for the coming-out parties of teenage *quinceañeras;* at the paradigmatic Cine Teresa a screening of *The Tender Lovers*, featuring such gods dished up by the industry to passers-by as Lyn May, Sasha Montenegro, Isela Vega, Jorge Rivero . . .

I imagine that in the past, this street would have specialized in a particular type of trade. Now most of the fancier, larger shops have gone, following their clientele to the residential neighborhoods, to be replaced by an assortment of retail for the mass market. The sidewalk is crowded with the unemployed and those employed but living on starvation wages, forced to jostle amid jabbing elbows, blaring horns, pushing, coughing, and cursing. The cheap stores are an insult in themselves, with their trashy merchandise piled up on tables but trying to ape the perceived fashions of the rich. Cops are everywhere, the main characters in these stores, for every customer knows that the masters of power and wealth regard her as a delinquent. In the would-be swankier places, they hire poor boys and girls of the same physical type as the customers, only better looking, and dress them up in the best of the stock so they can lounge around the entrance all day—vigilant, alluring mannequins—in hopes of persuading the shopper that a few pesos will suffice to render them as elegant and leisured as the models.

Hardware stores, parcel services; specialty shops whose names will be forgotten in coming years as we become used to buying everything under one roof: *churrerías* and *chocolaterías* for donuts and confectionery, *alpargaterías* and *calceterías* for hemp soles and hosiery. Record shops where John Paul II has dislodged Lucha Reyes, Julio Jaramillo, Daniel Santos, Cepillín, "Waltzes for a *Quinceañera's* Coming Out Party," and even salsa sounds. Manolo's Shoeshop exhorts you to "Walk Toward the Bright Mexican Future." Jewelers display crummy trinkets in improvised sheds of about thirteen square feet, their cases temptingly stuffed with shiny pens, lighters, and watches.

The people on the street are on the edge of ruin, trying to convince themselves that they will not plunge into it if they dress up like the models of consumerism: fashion, makeup, hairstyles, sneakers, T-shirts, and suits bought not so long ago and already mangled from being carried on nonleisurely bodies (unlike those of the folks for whom they were designed). They never looked right, in fact, on lives so far removed from the world of display windows.

As evening descends, pickpockets, hustlers, and dealers begin to weave in and out of the crowd, followed by policemen, streetwalkers, and a swanning parade of transvestites. Wretched side streets (Vizcaínas, Meave, Ayuntamiento, Independencia, Delicias, and others) sink into the torpor of sleazy hotels, infra-diners, con artists, and grime; foul cantinas and costly, useless schools-for-losers. This prospect, lengthening after the Izazaga intersection and defining the segment of Niño Perdido that corresponds to Colonia Obrera, shows the wages of commerce all the way down the street: storefronts, cheap products and cheap ads, the vicious manipulation of promises and hopes, all seem by night to pollute the soiled awnings of bars, cantinas, and seedy hostels of despair. . . .

Social bitterness shines even more brilliantly after closing time, when the names of showgirls twinkle out—Susuki, Dayra Solie, Fanny Dix, Olga Swan, Diana Kiss—and the "vivid and venomous street of San Juan de Letrán" fills with anxious faces and hands, held back by deprivation, goaded by the need to consume, slapped back into misery, and poised to catch something—anything will do—before the new day rises.

Ambulantes
Street Vendors I *(1995–2001)*

FRANCIS ALŸS

The streets of downtown Mexico City—and their chaotic jumble of people from all walks of life—provide the setting for most of Francis Alÿs's performance pieces. *Ambulantes* (1995–2001) focuses on the hurdles faced by those whose livelihood depends on their ability to walk the streets: the thousands of street vendors who peddle everything from miraculous ointments to pirated computer programs. They are known as *ambulantes*, a term derived from the Spanish verb ambular, to wander. Like their name implies, they wander the streets, pushing their carts until they find an appropriate spot to set up shop for the day. Most of the vendors are unlicensed, unregistered, and uninclined to pay taxes. They form the backbone of Mexico's "informal economy," and they are one of the most visible signs of the city's life (there are no street vendors in generic cities). This kind of wandering street work provides a means of subsistence for several million Mexicans—an impressive feat, especially in times of recession and rampant unemployment.

Alÿs's *Ambulantes* depicts the variety of ways in which street vendors make a living: there are those who sell food on the streets (they
push carts loaded with candies and vats for steaming *tamales*); others
work as *bricoleurs*, picking and recycling garbage (several photos depict
cartoneros—men who collect discarded paper and cardboard and sell it to
paper mills); there is a plant vendor pushing half a dozen cacti through
the streets, and a balloon vendor whose face and torso are obscured by
her colorful wares.

Cuauhtémoc

JOSÉ JOAQUÍN BLANCO

I

The Cuauhtémoc District, like the rest of Mexico City's district boundaries, was a brain wave of President Luis Écheverría that our city hardly deserved. It was drawn with an arbitrary stroke of a highlighter over a city map, with no regard for history, economics, or demographics. Why separate the Zócalo from the nearby La Merced market, yet lump it together with the distant Zona Rosa?

Districts are bureaucratic fabrications. All they require is a map, a pen, and the whim of a self-important official. They are consequently devoid of any history but that of the caprices of Écheverría's urban planners. I don't see the Cuauhtémoc District as a harmonious entity, but rather as a ragbag of clashing locations.

The most important of these, the Centro, was destroyed during the regime of Miguel Alemán by a bureaucratic folly. They decided to expel from the Centro its most lively, cheerful, and colorful inhabitants: the student population. The university was the first to go, followed by other schools and colleges, all relocated way down south or elsewhere on the outskirts. "You troublesome students, out of the Centro at once! Get ye to your educational concentration campuses!"

Downtown was thus deprived at a stroke of the vitality, beauty, and merriment of tens of thousands of youths complete with girlfriends, buddies, and books. And this had been *all* of the Centro's appeal since the days of Porfirio Díaz: those antique palaces swarming with thousands, then tens of thousands, of students. What laughs, what mischief! And yes, sure, a student demonstration every now and then (more cheerful affairs, at any rate, than the ones which currently invade downtown streets every other day).

The Alameda Gardens were a hotbed of youth and love during the 1940s, as was Santo Domingo Square. Businesses catering to students prospered: cafés, soda fountains, bookshops, cinemas, theaters, hairdressers, beauty salons; discerning billiard halls, bars and restaurants, fashion and sports outlets. What did the Centro receive in exchange? Hundreds of thousands of peddlers, beggars, con men, traffickers, and street vendors. The former "university district" became a mercantile pigsty: three-penny consulting rooms for "secret diseases," crash courses in computing and Internet for illiterates, barbarous cantinas promising excellent poison, with a thrashing thrown in for free.

II

The Zócalo was once green with trees. They were cut down for the sake of expanding the great cement concourse on which servile multitudes were to render quasi-fascistic homage to PRI presidents. Now it provides round-the-clock service as a vast, maudlin, filthy courtyard of wailing, rancor, and antigovernment protest. It reeks of bile and piss. Much bile. More piss. The national latrine.

Other bureaucratic nonsense, such as rent control—which did less for the poor than for shrewd wheeler-dealers who knew all about pocketing corrupt attorneys and judges and getting into the good books of influential party officials (fed up, long-suffering landlords finally bailed out of their old buildings rather than confront our PRI-controlled court system)—consummated the lumpenization of a neighborhood that was, as recently as the 1940s, a coveted place of residence for the middle and even upper-middle classes.

In the 1950s, the middle classes abandoned the center en masse, in the wake of the students, faster than a war or a revolution could have chased them out. Landlords left their buildings to rot. (The owner of a house in the Centro was dubbed, by presidential decree, a "bourgeois exploiter" to be punished by means of "frozen" rents, whereas the owner of entire blocks in the fancy districts of Lomas, Polanco, Pedregal, or Satélite was a progressive capitalist, worthy of special privileges.) Nobody was prepared to invest in rental properties downtown. Controlled rents dealt the final blow to this district as any kind of self-respecting place to live. The great murderers of the Centro have always been, first and foremost, the Mexican presidents.

This beautiful architectural ensemble, of enormous historical and aesthetic importance for the world, was reduced to a warren of warehouses, shabby shops, dingy cantinas, sleazy hotels, and the plague of street vendors. Though it's impossible to get a permit for building a decent condominium, courts readily grant permits for setting up a hundred thug-infested police stations, all extremely violent. The lumpencenter of our urban lumpendecadence. Only a handful of major companies have had the guts to stay on here: thank you, Puerto de Liverpool; thank you, Palacio de Hierro; thank you, Casino Español; thank you, Danubio Restaurant.

The government itself spirited away almost all of its offices. Half a century of the unanimous rallying cry: "Everyone escape from the Centro! Now!" The president rarely makes an appearance in the National Palace; he's always holed up in his bunker at Los Pinos. And after the earthquake, well . . . suffice it to inspect the bombed-out environs of the Alameda Gardens.

The Zócalo was bombed before the earthquake, with admirable premonition, by know-all archaeologists who—urged by President López Portillo—gouged a hole in the gorgeous panorama of palaces around the square to decorate it with a rubble of foundations: the ruins of the Great Temple of the Aztecs. We weren't treated to the restoration of any sacred teocalli, oh no; only the exposure of a crater of wreckage, like a monumental sore. Three cheers for our nation's history of resentment and ruins! Would Paris demolish the Rue de Rivoli to lay bare the pile of garbage that remains of some Celtic temple? Why weren't all those funds used to repair Teotihuacán, since that at least contains more than a rancorous heap of stones?

III

Other sectors of the Cuauhtémoc District, like Colonia Roma, Condesa, Juárez, and Cuauhtémoc, were thrown to the lions of real estate speculation. Worthwhile residential spaces were converted to offices and shops, sloppily, like a creeping plague. Without a proportionate expansion of services (water, power, drainage, roads, parking, security), substandard high-rises shot up on plots that could barely accommodate two or three pleasant houses.

During the day, these areas have become a giant marketplace: a chaos of traffic and profiteering, restaurants girdled by attack dogs and even fiercer parking "valets," an invasion of outsiders trampling over the locals, often driving them out altogether. By night, it's a desert of buildings under lock and key and guarded by private security firms, while the dark, desolate streets are helpless against rowdy lumpenprostitution at knifepoint, shady locales, and holdups by the police.

There are always several ear-splitting car alarms going off simultaneously, down any street, apt to go on shrieking for six hours before either their owners or the police take any notice. Alarms don't protect cars; their sole purpose is to drive the neighbors crazy. (If you plan on living in Condesa, it is advisable to stock up on silicone earplugs. Warning: only imported ones work.)

IV

One image, already around fifteen years old, encapsulates the entire district: Paseo de la Reforma. Ever since the early 1980s this avenue has sported a mixture of arrogant skyscrapers (most in deplorably nouveau-riche taste), empty lots, fallen-down buildings (the Roble cinema, the environs of the monument to Columbus), and whole packs of indigents, like seething tribes of gutter Apaches.

Instant skyscrapers, in execrable taste, pop up amidst the battered remains of their immediate predecessors (the IMSS building, for example, or the environs of the Monument to the Revolution).

The meager greenery along Reforma provides a backdrop for the action of squeegee men, beggars, belly-button-shakers, mimes, and muggers. Rats, excrement, hopelessness, and garbage decorate the entrances to glassy "postmodern" bank towers that look as though they could be plastic . . . or Nintendo. These are nothing but a bunch of oversize, vertical dog droppings with architectural pretensions.

Without stopping for a second, locked inside their expensive bullet-proof vehicles, business tycoons speed in and out of their skyscrapers along Reforma (e.g., the stock exchange), contriving not to set eyes, even for a moment, on what used to be the Mexican answer to the Champs Élysées. Reforma: sump of the Lumpeniforma. Reformatory of the Excretoforma. Cesspit of the Skyscraperforma.

V

(Exordium)

Let's toast then to Diana, patroness of squeegee men and vendors of bug-infested tacos! Diarrheic Diana: mythological lunar diuretic of drunken bums, muggers and muggees, beggars, and the rest of Mexico City's crass court, where the nouveaux lumpen triumph alongside the nouveaux riches.

Diana must be given her alms. It's so she can buy herself a fat roll of toilet paper. Is the borough president keeping an eye on Diana's little gastrointestinal problems? Couldn't he have her stopped up? She's stinking out the whole district.

Give what you like to the loose-boweled Diana, but make it at least a peso: no need to insult the lady. She's not naked because she's hot but because she's broke. She's only pretending to shoot an arrow from her stringless bow, like a traffic-light clown. That's what she is, a big-assed traffic-light clown. A grimy, ragged scrounger in the midst of her putrid fountain of sewage and piss.

"Cough up a peso for Diana, you son-of-a bitch, or I'll bust your fucking windscreen!"

"Who's There?"

The Art of Opening and Closing the Door

JORGE IBARGÜENGOITIA

Many years ago, we lived in a four-apartment house on Avenida Chapultepec. The entrance was virtually impregnable. There were two identical cast-iron gates: the one on the right opened onto a little staircase leading down to the cellar and was labeled Concierge; the one on the left led to a little staircase going up to the front door. This door had a safety glass window, so during the daytime we occupants could make out quite clearly, without being seen, who was ringing the bell. At night, however, when there was more light inside than out, the reverse was true: before being identified, the visitor could see that someone was coming down the hall to open the door unless—this house was pretty well thought out—unless the occupant had taken care to surreptitiously slide the window open, lean out, and assess the bell-ringer by examining the top of his or her head.

The initial hesitation between two identical gates, compounded by the prospect of ascending a staircase to reach a door with four buzzers, added up to a first-rate deterrent. It had to be a very hungry—or a very pushy—beggar who would dare to surmount all these obstacles just to ask for some spare change to buy a taco. Besides, in those days there were no foot-in-the-door salesmen and no polling teams. We lived in bliss.

The hassles were of a different order. If someone, too plain lazy to climb the stairs, went down to the "concierge" to ask for me, that person was almost certainly told: "He's not in," "He moved away years ago," or "I never heard the name." Why? Because the super was convinced that anyone who came looking for someone was here to place a tax lien, make an arrest, or carry out some other evil deed.

To my knowledge, these denials never caused me any great loss, except that of a typewriter. I'd applied for a loan to buy it, and one day the manager came to interview me; since I wasn't home, he asked the super about my finances, who obligingly told him I hadn't a cent to my name.

That's how things stood when a doctor opened his office in the downstairs apartment and put up two signs outside: one read Such-and-Such, Skin Diseases, and the other Such-and-Such, Medical Diathermy. From that day on, every drug company agent with a suitcase of samples invariably rang my bell, too stupid to notice that the two signs bore the same name and assuming there were two doctors, one upstairs and one down. But since the house was so well thought out, I could see them from halfway down the stairs during the day, or from the upstairs window at night, and I never opened the door.

After that, I got lucky and moved to my present abode, which I own, but it does have the disadvantage of a front door that for some reason attracts beggars, maids looking for work, raspberry vendors, people inquiring after my vacuum cleaner, discount salesmen, pollsters, street musicians demanding "a contribution" after making a racket on the corner, and so on.

What amazes me is not the abundance of visitors, but their way of getting to the point. For instance, someone buzzes. It's two thirty in the afternoon. The door opens to reveal a man with a piece of stuffed *chile* hanging out of his mouth. Is this a way to start a conversation? But the caller is undeterred:

"If you don't mind, could you call your maid? I have some lovely dresses for sale."

Another day, the bell rings. I open the door and two youths clutching clipboards and pencils pipe up in unison: "Good afternoon, are you watching television?" "No, I am not. I am opening the door."

Another day, the bell rings. I open the door and there's a young lady carrying two suitcases. "Good afternoon, sir. Could I ask you a few questions about your cultural interests? We'd very much appreciate your opinion about a new program . . ." If I don't slam the door she'll try to sell me a recorded English-language course—at an outrageous price—and if I tell her I speak English already, she'll say then all the more reason to buy them, since I'll be able to understand every word.

And don't tell me I can solve my problem by installing an intercom. It's not true. I would always be asking, "Who is it?" only to get back the invariable "It's me!"

Klaxons and the Man

JORGE IBARGÜENGOITIA

At a gathering one day, the conversation turned to an individual who was not present. A certain charitable woman reprimanded a friend of mine, "How can you say you don't like him, when you don't even know him?" My friend retorted, "What I do know is, he's fitted his car with a horn that plays 'The Marseillaise.' Isn't that bad enough? Even if I don't know him, I thoroughly dislike him and have no desire to ever meet him."

On hearing these words, I felt the shiver that comes with the realization of a new, shattering truth. Buffon said of writers, "Style makes the man," but it seems that among brutes, it's the horn that makes the man. And not just the horn, but the style of using it. The lady who sooner than get out of her car to open the garage door blows the horn for fifteen minutes until the maid comes to the rescue; the guy who double-parks his car (usually a Mustang) and sounds deafening chords while waiting for his date to finish putting on her face; the roadhog who speeds across intersections at full speed, blowing his horn as if to warn *"abran cancha que lleva bala"* ("get out the way cuz this gun's loaded"); or the cretin who believes that insistent hooting will revive the broken-down vehicle blocking his way. . . . These are symptoms not of a bad habit but of the deepest putrefaction of loathsome souls.

To elaborate on the above, which is a mere preamble, let me relate something that happened to me the other day, an experience that still worries me.

This is how it happened. There I was, quietly playing Scrabble with a friend of mine who lives in an apartment building, when suddenly we began to hear a horn, not too loud but repetitive and very annoying, sounding two short blasts followed by fifteen seconds' pause: beep-beep, fifteen seconds, beep-beep. . . . Five minutes went by. We gave up on our game for lack of concentration. At that point we got up and went to look out the fifth-floor window. This is what we saw: down in the parking garage sat a white Datsun, unable to park because another car had taken his spot. I should mention that in this building, each tenant pays ten thousand pesos for forty square feet of reserved parking. The Datsun kept going beep-beep, fifteen seconds, beep-beep.

At the next pause, I shouted at the top of my lungs: "Hey you, shut up!" And at the next break, I added: "Go see the guard, and stop being a . . .!" Here I uttered a word the equivalent of "nuisance," though stronger, but still falling short of the curse words that come to mind in a situation like this. I shall refer to the term I used by the letters P-I-N.

No sooner had I said this, the car went quiet. A magic fix. My friend congratulated me on my performance. We returned to the living room and continued our game of Scrabble.

Twenty minutes went by. When all seemed forgotten, the doorbell rang. I get up, open the door, and I see a young man, gasping for breath after climbing five flights of stairs. "I came—to apologize for having—disturbed you with my honking."

I was touched. Not just the apology, but the puffed state, and that tie he had on. "Don't mention it!" I smiled.

I instantly regretted having said this, because with the apology out of the way and his breath recovered, he went on, "But you should talk like a civilized person. Problems can always be resolved amicably. All you had to say was, 'Please stop sounding your horn,' and I would have stopped. There's no need to swear like a trucker."

"What trucker? I said, 'Shut up.'"

"You said, 'Stop being a P-I-N.' If you said that, you could have said any other dirty word."

"I could, but I didn't. Besides, why shouldn't I call you a P-I-N, if a P-I-N is what you're being?"

Here he began to whine about his trials and tribulations, the way they steal his parking spot night after night, and to top it all he gets showered with insults from a balcony. I refrained from explaining that if I weren't a coward I would have flung a Molotov cocktail instead of curses. The most bizarre thing of all was that after having presented his excuses and lodged his complaint, this man took his leave by saying, "Very nice to meet you," intending to be sarcastic, but clearly seething inside.

So I have to ask myself, where do these people get their thinking from? School? The office? The bosom of the family? No one could be born so wrong-headed. Here's a guy who gets home and finds his parking spot occupied, and all he can think of is to deafen fifty or sixty families with his relentless horn. And then he feels they owe it to him to trek down five floors and ask, "Excuse me, would you mind not blowing your horn?"

On the other hand, if someone gets home, finds his spot taken, blows the horn, and gets yelled at, then he has two choices before him. The sensible option is to go home and drink herbal tea. The other is to rage up to the fifth floor and challenge the culprit with "How dare you yell at me?" And face the consequences.

But to climb all that way with an apology, on the assumption that this entitles you to reciprocal fawning, is something that honestly forces me to the conclusion that no, we just can't talk like civilized people.

The Quivering Arauca

"The sole defect of Mexican children," according to a well-known anthropologist, "is that they're exactly like their parents."

So true. The first thing a Mexican child learns to do after arriving in the world is to whine tirelessly for everything it wants. The second thing he learns is to blow Daddy's car horn, for the same reason. The child honks the horn, and honks it some more, until fifty years later he is still honking, in hopes of achieving a wide range of goals, such as urging a broken-down car to start moving again; making the offending car vanish, occupants and all; alerting drivers approaching on nearby intersections that here comes a rocket piloted by one who would sooner die than give way; reminding kids at breakfast that they will be late for class; or telling a rheumatic, overworked maid that the lady of the house is outside the gate, her car wedged at an angle blocking the traffic, her key in her purse, and no intention of getting out and using it. Et cetera.

The goals I have listed may appear banal and often inexplicable, yet they are, considering the rich diversity of uses for a car horn in this region, among the most rational. Some are even stranger.

Let me cite as an example the gentleman who has fitted his car with a whole array of horns, capable of playing the first few notes of a pop song now defunct, which starts: *"Yo nací en una ribera del Arauca vibrador"* ("I was born on the banks of the quivering Arauca").

Once this rudimentary, but reliably expensive, instrument has become part of the car, the owner proceeds to cruise around town at eight thirty in the morning announcing at every corner that he was born on the banks of the quivering Arauca and, further, by inference, that he is presently engaged in torturing the residents of Coyoacán. What on earth can he mean by this?

The great drawback of car horns lies precisely in their language, which is crude and impersonal, but so piercing that it is impossible to ignore, just like the wail of a baby.

Just as it is easier to start howling than to expound a complex argument, so it is easier to hit the horn than to examine the factors that impel one to do so, and weigh the chances of achieving the intended results.

But however unfathomable the intentions of your average horn artist, the city dweller accustomed to their noise learns to tell the honks apart. He is able to decipher the "message" and also to assess the performer's state of mind, character, sex, and social rank. Oh, and especially his or her mental capacities.

All this is probably more than the ordinary Joe, cruising along in his car and punching distractedly away at the horn, would care to conclude. But the trained ear of the expert listener can itemize: "There's one who can't get through. Over there it's a woman who wants the gate opened for her. That other fellow is furious because they've stolen his parking spot. And there's the moron who honks to tell wife that he's left the office, has made it to the building, and will arrive panting at the apartment in a couple of minutes."

The catch is that these messages lack any interest except for those directly concerned—and probably not even for them—but nevertheless, they are imposed on all persons of healthy hearing within a radius of two or three hundred yards.

Now, since horn artists have no intention of showing their true colors, and since their audience does not listen out of interest but out of sheer inability to block their ears, we thus conclude that the car horn as we know it today is an inadequate, obsolete instrument.

It must be replaced without demur. There are several alternatives. The one that strikes me as the most sensible and expedient consists in replacing the horn with a machine gun. Then, when you find a car blocking the way, instead of honking like a wimp you can pull the trigger and waste the culprit. Needless to say, any such action would be undertaken at your own risk.

Another possibility is to enrich the language of the device. To this end, the repetitive blare of trumpets could be swapped for a series of prerecorded remarks—customized, in the car owner's own voice—to be emitted at an adjustable volume. Among other phrases, I recommend "Excuse me," "Get out of the f____ way," and "You're going to be late . . . you're going to be late . . ."

Then there's what you might call radical customizing. Instead of announcing that you were born by the quivering Arauca—which besides being a boring piece of information applies to far too many other people—the horn could simply boom out your name. This would not only advertise the driver's personality but also, as the PRI slogan has put it so well, would make one "take responsibility for oneself."

7

The Earthquake

The Earthquake

ELENA PONIATOWSKA

It started out like a normal day, says Elia Palacios Cano. My husband woke up before me; he had a business breakfast at eight. Then I got up and went into my daughter's room. I took out her school uniform, laid it on her bed, and went to the kitchen to make a fruit salad. "Wake up, *gorda*, your friend's already out the door!" We lived in an apartment building on Bruselas and Liverpool: Bruselas 8, apartment 5, second floor. Our neighbors from apartment 3 had just left. "Coming, Ma, just putting my shoes on!" I was about to rinse a glass and I felt nauseous. "It's shaking," I said aloud, and then I thought, why am I saying that and watching the lightbulb swing up and down. "It's an earthquake," I said. I yelled out to my daughter, "An earthquake!" "Yes, Ma," she said and came close to me. My son was still asleep, and I carried him in my arms to the door. Enrique, my husband, ran out of the bathroom and grabbed Leslie's hand, then tried to undo the top lock and the lower one. He kept dropping the keys, picking them up, and at last he opened it. The door started banging violently from side to side, so I said, "We can't go out, we'd be thrown down the stairs," and I looked out the window. The building across the street was swaying like you've never seen, crashing into the one next to it, and this enormous crack opened up in our living room wall. "This is a major earthquake." I thought of my mother, who lives in Colonia Obrera in a very old and broken-down house, then I felt myself falling and shouted, "Enrique, the girl!"

Mom, You're Squashing Me, It Hurts

It was so quick. I landed on my left arm and my chin because I had Quique under my right. I didn't want to fall on him, that's why I stuck my chin out. When we stopped falling the child said to me, "Mom, you're squashing me, it hurts." "Get out then, quick," I said, and pulled him out from under me. I tried to sit up, but my left arm was trapped. I felt Quique over and asked him if anything hurt. "It's all dark," he says. "Yes sweetheart, the lights went out, just stay where you are." I looked for my husband, feeling around in the dark and found his head: "Enrique, say something." He didn't answer. I felt his pulse; nothing. I shook him; nothing. He was dead.

Since I couldn't sit or stand, I remained face down on the floor. I realized what was happening; I had to stay very calm and keep a grip on myself. I tried to picture which part of the roof had collapsed, or which wall, but it was too dark. I groped around for my daughter. I called her, "Leslie, Leslie!" and when there was no reply I told myself it was for the best, she'd died an instant death, she hadn't suffered. I touched my husband again, his head was bleeding; I took his pulse again but no, no, no, no, no.

I couldn't be the only one trapped in the building. I had to be alert in case someone came to rescue us, then I told myself again: "I have to keep calm," so I don't use up all the oxygen in this space we were caught in. I wonder what happened to my mother's house. Right now, everyone must be looking for their relatives, and since I haven't phoned them, they'll come looking for me, and when they see the building has collapsed they'll get me out. "At least I hope so," I thought.

Help Me, Help Me

After ten or fifteen minutes I heard someone calling for help: "Help me, help me," they said. I started up as well, "Help me, help me!" it was probably someone else from my building who was trapped, but it was useless. I couldn't help him and he couldn't help me, so I called over, "Calm down, they're going to get us out, don't waste the oxygen." After a while I heard voices, a man and a woman asking, "Is anyone there?" I answered, "Yes, me and my son," but they didn't hear me because my jaw was broken and my voice wasn't very clear.

We were in this very tight space, not more than six feet long, about two feet wide and at most two feet high. I was face down, and my feet were holding back a giant slab from falling down on us. It was a tiny gap we were in. When César, my nephew, rescued us, he had to climb right on top of me to free my arm because there was no room for him to work. That's why I think it was only about two feet wide. I was saying to my nephew what terrible luck it was that we couldn't have all been together and all survived, and he said between the four of us we'd have used up the oxygen in that tiny gap. And after, it was so painful to think, "If only I'd gotten ahold of my daughter as well . . ."

It smelled of gas. The pilot lights had probably gone out on the stove, maybe a living room wall had caved in and the kitchen was standing, so I told Quique to crawl and see if he could get to the kitchen, get some juice or a soda or a piece of fruit from the fridge. I told him to lean out the balcony and yell that we were here, but he didn't want to, and it's just as well, he couldn't have gotten anywhere. The gas smell went away, or maybe I got used to it.

I tried to free my arm. There were some boards nearby and I hit my arm with one of them, trying to break it: "I'll yank hard until it breaks, then I'll cut it off, and tie it up with my nightgown to stop the bleeding." I went at it with the heel of my shoe, with a stone, but it didn't work. I said to myself: "If God wants me to be stuck here like this, he's got a reason, maybe the building's completely collapsed and if I try to get out I'll die." Quique didn't have a scratch on him and I was thinking, "Oh, God, let me out of here alive, let me remain well, because if I go my son will be left here all alone, trapped, and it'll be a horrible end, so I've got to hold on." I lay quietly beside Quique. I felt some towels by my feet. I pulled at them but couldn't reach, but Quique was able to sit up, so I said, "Honey, feel along my legs and when you get to my feet, you'll find them." He gave me the towels, and I tucked one around my husband's body so my son wouldn't touch it; another I gave to Quique so he could lie down, and the last I tried to shove under my legs because there was a pile of rubble there, cutting into me, but I couldn't manage. Quique said he was cold, so I covered him, though I think he was just nervous and not cold. He didn't ask me for food or water or anything, he just asked what happened and I told him there'd been an earthquake. "But they're coming to get us, don't worry, we just have to wait, the two of us together." And he fell asleep. He slept soundly.

I Was Crying Out, "We're Here!"

Hours later I heard the machines close to us, and I heard shouting and drilling. This made me feel better, but I was also worried they might accidentally dislodge the slab that was protecting us. I could hear them, but they could never hear me. I was crying out, "We're here, help us!" That was one thing that kept me awake most of the time, the fear they'd get too close and drill through the slab covering us. In all that darkness you couldn't know if it was day or night. I figured it was nighttime when there was less noise out there. "It must be nighttime; they're not working so much."

After a day and a half I got very thirsty. My face was burning but I didn't feel hungry, more like thirsty and worried that they might hurt us while trying to save us, but I also had a tremendous desire to live, a longing to live, to be out of there. I heard them getting closer all the time, I could smell them, hear them right by us, and I kept calling, "Be careful, we're alive but I can't get out, please be careful!" I thought they'd pull the slab off, rescue my husband and Leslie, my daughter, and then Quique and me. When I heard them right above I took my husband's arm, I touched his hand and told him, "Now they're coming for us, and they're taking you away." I stroked his face and put my arm around him. "We're going to be physically apart, but we'll always be together." I said my farewell to him. That's when the second earthquake began. I heard the people outside saying, "It's shaking, people, keep calm, nobody panic." I pushed the boy face down, covered his head, braced my feet up against the slab, and prayed to God not to let our little place fall in on us. They no longer tried to rescue us. I think I fell asleep, because later I wasn't sure if there had really been an earthquake or if it had been a dream. I didn't know if the rescue teams really came so close or if I'd just imagined it, but yes, I guess they got scared and went away.

Later on, I found out my nephew was the only one who kept on digging.

On Saturday, the day they found us, I was hallucinating. I saw my mother and my sisters in perfect health, and they were telling me not to worry, and I felt better, but then I dreamed I'd been taken out and was back at home, and I said to Quique, "You're going to sleep in your room." "What room, Ma?" "Your room, the TV is on for you." But he knew what was really happening.

"No, Ma, it's not true," he told me.

I dreamed I had a lot of money and bought myself a house with a pool. We even had a maid. There were all these stones around the pool, and they were digging into me: "Fix up these stones please, wax them, polish them, paint them, do something, because I can't stand them any more." I asked Quique what he wanted to eat. "But there isn't any food, Ma!" "Sure there is, ask the maid, she'll fix you whatever you want." "I want spaghetti with cheese." "That's all? Go on then, honey, since you can stand up, there's your food on the table, go for it." "No, Ma, it must be a dream because I can't see anything, I can't eat anyway, I'm not hungry." That was one of my hallucinations, and that's why when Quique got out, the first thing he asked for was spaghetti.

At one point he said to me, "Guess what, Ma, I have a better idea for us to get some food. Why don't you go out and buy some?" He didn't know I couldn't move.

Another time I saw a light and felt someone next to me but I couldn't see who it was. I said, "Please help me, I'm not asking much, only that you please help free my arm. Look, I won't tell on you, I won't say you didn't want to help." But instead of freeing me he only drilled more so I laid the child flat again and brought my feet up, and in this position I told the imaginary person, "Now look, I'm not mad or drunk, I'm stuck, and if you help me get out I won't tell anyone that instead of saving me you let the roof fall on me. I'll never tell, but please help. Don't you have a heart, don't you have sisters? Why don't you show some compassion?"

I figured I was ill and very weak. What was going to happen to Quique?

"Tell me, son, what's your name?"

"Oh, Ma, I'm Quique, of course."

"All right, repeat after me, my name is Enrique Cano Palacios."

"My name is Enrique Cano Palacios."

"I'm three years old."

"I'm three years old."

"My sister's name is Leslie and she's six."

I made him go over it again and again.

"My name is Enrique Cano Palacios. I'm three years old. My sister's name is Leslie. She's six. My dad's name is . . ."

When he knew it by heart, I felt better.

The first thing they saw was my feet. Someone said, "Stop! Stop the machine, there are people alive down there." I recognized the voice, even though I'd been hallucinating the moment before. It was my nephew César. He said, "Stay calm, ma'am, don't worry, we're going to get you out right away, what's your name?" "It's me, son, it's your Aunt Elia." His voice changed, he was all overcome with emotion, and that was when I regained my peace of mind, I became myself again. "Elia, Elia, are you okay? Do you have enough oxygen?" "Really, I'm fine, the boy's fine too. Take it easy and you'll get us out quicker."

He started cutting through the rubble, spraying water so as not to raise the dust. "I'm almost there, I'm getting you out!" My kid saw his cousin. "You're César, the one who was going to give me the puppies! And you're the one who's getting me out of here!" And then for the first time he broke out crying. My nephew dug a hole big enough for Quique to climb through. Then César came in and began trying to free my arm.

I saw my husband's body. Three days had gone by. It was decomposed and smelled bad, it had gone all black. I thought it was a puppet and I said, "César, are we in a theater?" "I don't know where we are, stay with me, relax, so I can free your arm." They lowered some gauze soaked in water. "Don't drink it, just rinse your mouth and spit out the blood." When I stopped spitting blood they gave me some rehydration fluid, and I drank the whole bottle. Later I heard it had taken César three hours to get me out. While we were talking, I asked him what had happened, and what day it was. The hole was so small, he had to lie stretched out on top of me while they handed him the tools because there was no space to work. I asked him if I still had my fingers, if he thought my arm would have to be cut off. He said he didn't think so, but he knew it was a lie and he didn't have the heart to amputate it there and then.

He put me on a stretcher and they pulled me up from outside. "I'm covering your face because it's very dusty."

It was raining. They held an umbrella over me, there were strangers staring, and my family surrounded me. They carried me into an ambulance. Quique had been taken to a first aid station; he was fine. They bathed me and called the doctors, who saw I had a fractured jaw and hooked me up to a drip. Another doctor arrived. He said, "Ma'am, I see you have all your self-possession, so I'll speak frankly. Your arm doesn't look good. We're going to do our best to save it, but you spent almost sixty hours with it crushed, so we have to see how far up we can save it." "I don't have to tell you, Doctor, I'd love to keep my arm but if you tell me there's no choice, and you can save me by cutting it off, then go ahead." They took me to the operating room, where I was out until 2 A.M. on Sunday. When I came to, I felt these cramps. I lifted my arm till I laid eyes on the stump. I took it as done. When I was trapped, with my arm right next to my husband's decomposing flesh, I realized perhaps I was only injured, and cutting it off was one way I could save my life.

A crowd of people came to visit me at the Red Cross, relatives and friends. I didn't want them to start crying and drain me off my last strength.

The Gaps Were Like Tunnels of Hope

I'd never been to the building on Bruselas and Liverpool. Elia had moved there a short time before—says César Piña—and I couldn't believe that was her building. In that mountain of rubble, the gaps were like tunnels of hope. I saw one hole and got inside, hoping to hear something. "Elia, are you there? Answer, please answer, is anyone there?" I heard some noises. "Quiet, everyone, for God's sake, quiet." The first corpse I took out was of a man completely covered in mud, the next was a younger man, almost a boy, blond, with funny hair. I said to the people, "Help me carry him, I can't do it on my own." And nobody took ahold of him, they couldn't bear to touch him, his chest was crushed.

I got back into the hole and crawled around hoping to find Elia and the family. By now the crane had arrived. I climbed down to speak to the operator.

"Lift that slab of masonry up a bit, so that I can climb in deeper."

"No way, the crane might tip over."

"Goddamn it, I have my family under there. If it was your relatives you'd do it, wouldn't you?"

At last he came around. When I shone my flashlight in under the slab, I saw another light-haired man, and got excited thinking maybe it was my uncle. I went closer. It wasn't one corpse but two. They lay stiff, naked in each other's arms, their faces touching, their legs tangled up. They would have to be taken out together. I was wiping tears and sweat off my face: "Don't give up, hold on a little longer." When I lifted them I saw the girl, too, was blonde. The people outside were pointing and whispering:

"Look how he's holding them, look at this, look at that!"

Fucking ghouls, snickering instead of helping.

I dived back in the hole and lost track of time.

They called me to the other end of the building. There was a woman, they said, and asked me if I could I deal with her. She was kneeling, lifeless. I dug out the hardened body and took it in.

This Isn't the Corner

I began flinging everything I found out into the street, I was yelling at the crane to raise a slab here, another one there, I was in a frenzy, ordering the crane operator to move everything. Then, pretty soon, I found the walls of the kids' room: "Here we are, this is it!" I entered the room, no one there. I found a wad of U.S. dollars and flung it out; my own family was shouting at me, telling me not to throw anything out, that it was Elia's stuff. We combed through the space, every bit, and I went into the room I guessed was the children's room, and then on to the living room, and there was nothing. There were family snapshots scattered around the floor and it broke my heart. I stumbled on bundles of clothing. I thought I found them, but no go. I recognized the furniture and the records. Where were they? Maybe in the stairwell. An engineer who was working next to me said, "Now what, César, what should we do now?" "Dig holes so the crane can do the lifting." It must have been around four in the afternoon when someone shouted, "Something's moving!" We saw this foot, and it was moving. "Hold it, there's people here, keep quiet."

"Ma'am, are you okay? Don't worry, we'll get you out, are you all right? What's your name?" "It's me, son, it's your Aunt Elia." I yelled back, "Elia, I'll rescue you, I swear it, I swear I'll get you out of there." And she said, "Take it easy, son, take it easy and you'll get us out all the better." I told one of my cousins to go out and let the rest of them know that Elia was alive and I was getting her out.

We made the hole bigger till I could lower myself in, and Quique recognized me. I was amazed at how unfazed they were. I shone my flashlight, and nearly died. The slab was hovering just two feet above them. It smelled terrible, of gas and rotting bodies. I started cursing. This couldn't have happened to them. I could see my uncle's head, right next to Elia, and it was black.

She asked me to get the boy out first. I looked for Leslie but couldn't see her. I wet their lips with water and showed Quique how to climb out, squatting; he did it just like I told him. When he came out into the afternoon light we felt as though the kid had been born again, that this child was the best thing that ever happened.

I got back to Elia, and I started working to free her arm from under the beam. My uncle was right by us. I asked her not to turn around. We could barely fit. I couldn't reach Elia's arm, I was sweating and sobbing, I was at the end of my rope. They sent us an oxygen tank and bottles of rehydration fluid. Elia slowly sucked the liquid through a plastic tube until her lips were overflowing. I didn't realize she had a broken jaw, and she didn't tell me. It was so hard to work squatting like that, so I said, "Elia, I'm sorry but I'm going to have to climb on top of you." I pricked her arm with a knife: "Can you feel that?" "No." "And here?" "No." I could see only half of her arm. Everything I needed dropped through that hole. It was like a hardware store. I wanted a screwdriver, there it was; I asked for oxygen, there it was. I was working with a hammer and chisel. At one point I heard the doctor say, "César, I can take over now if you want." I must have looked pretty bad for him to offer.

Please, God, Give Me Strength

Elia started talking nonsense, about how she'd already been rescued once, about all the servants she had. We were at it for three hours. People kept asking what was happening. Elia was saying, "No more, get me out, I don't care how you do it, just get me out," and I didn't have the stomach to cut off her arm. "So cut it!" she was saying and I felt awful. She was losing her mind, she thought her husband was a puppet, a marionette belonging to Frederick Van Malle, a theater director who lived in the same building and shared an apartment with Rockdrigo. In the midst of her ramblings, Elia tried to encourage me. She'd say, "Calm

down, I'm fine, you're in worse shape than I am, just take it easy and
you'll get me out quicker." I asked for some baby oil and there it was in
less than two minutes. I dug a hole with a screwdriver, poured oil all
over her arm, pulled as hard as I could. She turned her head away and
the arm was out. It came out a mess: the hand was squashed flat, without a drop of blood, like a piece of cardboard. Elia wanted to touch it. I
pulled her toward the hole. She wanted to know who was out there. I
said a crowd of people and she told me, "Cover my head then, because
I'm not giving any autographs."

8

Maids

Maids I

AUGUSTO MONTERROSO

I love maids because they're unreal, because they leave, because they don't follow orders, because they embody the last vestiges of unstructured labor and they lack insurance and benefits; because they arrive like ghosts of a lost race, they enter other people's homes, they snoop, they pry, they read the abyss of our darkest secrets in coffee grinds, wine glasses, ashtrays, or simply by directing their furtive gazes and eager hands into our closets, under the pillows, picking up bits of torn paper and the echo of our arguments, while they dust and sweep our sadness and the scraps of our hatred when they're home alone all morning singing gleefully; because they're greeted like the annunciation when they show up with a Nescafé or Kellogg's carton full of clothes and brushes and minuscule mirrors still covered with dust from the last unreality they inhabited; because they say yes to everything and it seems they'll always be there to give us a hand; because they end up leaving just like they arrived but with a deeper understanding of human nature, of compassion and solidarity; because they're the last envoys of Evil and because our wives don't know what to do without Evil and they cling to Evil and beg Evil never to abandon this world; because they're the only beings capable of getting back at said wives for the abuse they put us through by simply leaving, taking with them their loud clothes, their things, their bottles of cheap face cream now filled with fancy cream, slightly soiled, the fruit of their unskilled pilferings. I'm leaving, they say, as they vigorously repack their cardboard boxes. But why? Because. (Oh ineffable freedom.) And there they go, malignant angels, in search of new adventures, of a new home, of a new cot, of a new sink, of a new lady who loves them and can't live without them; planning for a new life, refusing to be grateful or acknowledge how well they were treated when they were sick and were tenderly given an aspirin lest the next day they couldn't wash dishes, which is more exhausting than cooking. I love watching them arrive, call, smile, come in, say yes; but no, always on the verge of being employed by a Mary Poppins who will solve all their problems and those of their parents, their older and younger siblings, including the one who raped them once; who will come to their bed at night and teach them to sing do-re-mi, do-re-mi until they fall asleep thinking sweetly about tomorrow's dishes soaking in a foamy detergent, fa-sol-la-ti, and will stroke their hair and get up very quietly, treading softly, and put out the lights just before leaving that room of vaguely unreal proportions.

Maids II

GUADALUPE LOAEZA

There is no starker contrast in a typical Mexican home than that between the main bedroom and the room assigned to the servant, domestic worker, house help, or simply—as she's called by employers with anglophile pretensions—*la maid*. Regardless of the family's neighborhood, social class, or bank balance, the difference between these two bedrooms is appalling (the fancier the house, the stronger the contrast). Let's pretend we're visiting a maid's room in a monster home located in any of our fancy neighborhoods: Lomas, Polanco, San Ángel, or Pedregal.

We climb a spiral staircase—going up, around and around—until we reach the maid's room. There's a smell of ripe fruit, face cream—Teatrical Rosa—and freshly ironed clothes. The room, about nine by nine feet, is painted light blue. There's a leak in the ceiling, and the walls are peeling. There are two fold-up metal cots. One of the beds is made; there's no comforter but there's a pillow embroidered with two doves holding a ribbon with the phrase "My heart is yours" flying over a red heart. The other bed is unmade, covered with sheets and an old blanket. The nightstand between the two beds is piled with stuff: a tape player, nail polish, two plastic curlers, several hairpins, a brush full of

very black and tangled hairs, half a peeled orange, a stick of Mum de-
odorant, a small bottle of Nivea cream, an Avon perfume, a little vase
holding three plastic flowers, and a coin purse. Between the two beds
there's a scrap of carpet (left over from when the living room was redone) thrown over the linoleum floor. There's also an old issue of *Foto-
novelas* with Lucía Méndez on the cover. The walls are decorated with a
photo of the pope, two calendars—one featuring the Virgin of Guadalupe, the other Luis Miguel—and two snapshots—taped to the wall—of
the family's kids. There's also a huge wardrobe on the brink of collapse.
One of its doors is open and we can peek inside: three pink-and-white
checkered uniforms, an extremely old plaid skirt (a present from the
lady of the house), four polyester shirts, six flowery dresses. The lower
shelf holds several pairs of worn out-shoes (presents from the lady of
the house), plastic sandals, and a relatively new pair of patent leather
pumps. To the right there's a K2 television set (property of the cook)
on a low table covered by a lace cloth. The TV is surrounded by half-
empty Orlane, Lancome, and Clinique face creams. The table has three
drawers, all ajar, overflowing with sweaters, pastel-colored underwear,
wrinkled aprons, pantyhose, socks, "I Love NY" T-shirts, and a stack of
slips. On the floor, against the wall, there's a row of empty Coke bottles
and a tray holding a soup plate and scraps of stale tortillas.

Next to the closet (used only to hang the family's freshly pressed
clothes) there's an ironing board holding an imported Phillips steam iron
and three recently ironed blue dress shirts. The laundry hamper is close
by. The lady of the house has no idea that her white linen skirt is thrown
together with her cotton blouses, the girl's Spanish smock and school
uniforms, three kitchen rags, a tortilla wrapping cloth, a pair of wool
trousers, a cashmere sweater (dry clean only), and countless kids' socks.

Next door is the tiny maid's bathroom. There are no tiles. It's
painted bright yellow and the walls are peeling. The shower is behind a
moldy plastic curtain. Lukewarm water—the water heater is broken—
spurts out of six of the showerhead's countless tiny orifices. There's an
old sock draped around one of the faucets to keep it from dripping. The
soap dish holds a sliver of Darling soap and an old scouring pad. The
sink is always clogged. The toilet has no seat and is also clogged. There's
no toilet paper anywhere in sight. Leaning against the wall is a piece
of broken mirror, a bit of Teatrical face cream, a bottle of egg-scented
Vanart shampoo, three toothbrushes, and a capless, flattened tube of
Colgate toothpaste.

Despite all this, the lady of the house often makes comments like, "Just imagine what their life was like back in the boondocks; here they live like queens!

"They're so uncivilized these maids, I've tried to tame them but no way. They break everything, they ruin everything. And when they drop something their only excuse is '*se me chispó*, I messed up!' They're filthy, just look at their rooms. They're always throwing paper into the toilet and then they complain when it gets clogged. Let them deal with it. *I'm* not going to pay for the plumber. I refuse to go into their room, it makes me angry and depressed. It probably looks like a pigsty. How depressing!"

Lucha in Las Lomas

Dressed in a pink-and-white checkered uniform, lace-trimmed apron, Windy's plastic sandals, and sporting a Verónica Castro–inspired hairdo, this exemplary maid tells her employer: "Ma'am, I want to let you know that if you don't gimme a raise by next week there's another place where they'll pay me more." Upon hearing this, the lady of the house feels her jaw dropping, her eyes clouding, and her blood pressure climbing. "But I just gave you a raise last month," she replies, as if begging for mercy. "Ma'am, do you think 1,000 pesos is enough these days? This imflation [*sic*] is terrible, and I can't afford anything. Look, ma'am, I just spent 8,000 pesos on my girl's school supplies and 12,000 on uniforms. But ma'am, if you can't give me a raise, you should start looking for someone else, cuz I need to make more money," she explains as she looks down at her purple nails and dark-skinned hands.

The lady of the house feels blackmailed, abused, mad at herself for being so dependent on these horrible *maids*, as she likes to call them. "Pushy servants, all they do is ask for more and more, they're so annoying and ungrateful. Not in a million years did these Indians ever imagine that they would end up living like civilized people and not like animals in that hick town they come from. Lazy girls, so rude and good for nothing, you give them a hand and they ask for an arm, what else can they possibly want, they have their own room with a TV, three meals a day, hot water, uniforms, and on top of it all they want to be paid like executive secretaries when they can't even answer the phone properly." All this goes through the lady of the house's mind as she politely tells the maid: "But I'm already paying you 40,000 pesos! I'm very pleased with your work, though you do make mistakes here and there. The kids love you. And I really can't give you a raise every month."

The maid stares back, and suddenly she remembers she hates the woman, despises her, can't even stand the sight of her: "Old hag, if I make mistakes here and there then you're one big mistake, that's why your husband always misses dinner and gets home so late. So you're pleased with my work? Then how come I get more abuse every day? It's always: don't even think of eating the steak, I bought you some beans and tortillas, remember the cheese is for my husband and the fruit is for the kids—did you eat all the cookies?—you watch too much TV, I don't like it when you use the phone, bring me my purse, go get me some cigarettes, iron my silk blouse, answer the phone, make me a glass of orange juice, go buy the new issue of *¡Hola!*, don't say *trajistes*, don't swear in front of the kids, bring me some Nutrasweet, all day abusing me like a donkey, the stingy bitch!" All this goes through the maid's mind as she answers: "Ma'am, but my friend's making 60,000 pesos working on Virreyes, and she doesn't have to water the garden or polish the silver. Really, ma'am, I can't get by on what you're paying me. Jacobo just told me that milk, bread, tortillas, and the bus fare are all going up. And clothes! Look, ma'am, I just bought a skirt and a *bleser* [*sic*] and I paid over 23,000 pesos."

When she hears this last bit of information, the lady of the house feels like laughing: "Who does she think she is? When did maids start wearing *blazers*? How depressing! Ponchos replaced by *blazers*," she says to herself in an English accent, "sandals by pumps, coin holders by leather purses. No wonder they can't make ends meet, they spend all their money buying on credit from Avon. I pity them, they want to dress like us—what ever happened to social classes?—they now demand rubber gloves, vacuum cleaner, washer and dryer. When I think of the sorry state they arrived in . . . and now they demand a raise to buy *blazers*." Making use of her perfect command of good manners, the lady of the house explains in a soft voice: "Look, you should try to stop spending so much and start saving. To think of all the old clothes I've given you: imported clothes in perfect condition. You can't complain: you have a day off *and* I let you take a free afternoon a week. Remember I flew you to Disneyland with us, just imagine how much I spent on your ticket."

As she listens to her boss, the maid feels two hot irons burning her cheeks. Fuming, she wrings her sweaty palms—she feels like using them to strangle her boss—inside her apron's pocket. "Well, ma'am, you either gimme a raise or I leave," she says making a face. The lady of the house, now suffering from stomach cramps, makes a face as well. "How much do you want to earn now?" she asks without looking at her. "I need to make 50,000 pesos to give my daughter a good education," she replies. She was only asking for 10,000 more, but then the lady of the house would be forced to give raises to the cook, the gardener, and the driver. And her budget was already strained. "What should I tell her," the lady wondered, while the maid thought "Stingy bitch! Who else would put up with her?" The silence became heavier, more intense, and unbearable.

Chapultepec and the Maids

JOSÉ JOAQUÍN BLANCO

The figures, the stubborn figures tell us so: neither crime, nor clouds of beggars and knickknack vendors, nor the pollution, nor the filthy dumps that formerly celebrated areas have become, are enough to discourage provincial tourists from coming to Mexico City.

This is surely an indictment against the malls and other modern commercial systems, including the Internet, that are available in the provinces. People still come in droves to buy buttons on Correo Mayor; natural unstyled wigs on República de Chile; saints in frames or under bell jars on Donceles, Tacuba, or Guatemala; love tokens in minicoffers under the arches of the Zócalo.

Nor is it much of a compliment to the conservative inclinations of many city halls and state governments—which have banned or severely curtailed their own local Garibaldi-like drunken hangouts and table dancing venues—or to the hick entrepreneurs of vice who allegedly persist in promoting mariachis and dancing girls of an even more ghoulish standard than those in the capital.

But does the traditional list of sightseeing attractions—La Villa,

La Diana, Chapultepec Park, followed by lunch at a downtown restaurant—still apply?

Not La Villa, anyway. It would be hard (but not impossible, calling for only a minor miracle) to transfer it to Perisur or Santa Fé. But what a Villa! Every week the basilica's priestly authorities call in vain for a police squad (made up of cherubs rather than pigs, at least for the day) to "expel the merchants" from the atrium and environs of La Villa, because it's got to the point where more drugs, flesh, porn, and pirated goods are being flogged in the holy hills of Tepeyac than in Tepito itself.

Chapultepec Park is even worse off, though neither the Aztec goddess Coatlicue, nor the Austrian Empress Carlotta in her castle, nor the lions and pretty pandas have (yet) managed to pull off a police raid like the one celebrated yesterday, virtually to the sound of *Te Deums*, by the arch- and other bishops of La Villa.

Chapultepec has been more or less under siege for the last fifteen years, when the major entrances to the park were closed off, or rather walled up; car access was restricted to the local bureaucrats (after showing ID and a shouting match with the guards); pedestrians were subjected to a fumbling inspection of bags, baskets, and knapsacks (to forestall vendors who stealthily introduce their wares buried in a picnic basket, ant-fashion, trip after trip); several areas of the park were wire-fenced like concentration camps to protect them from vandal-visitors (for example: the environs of "Carlotta's staircase," which I climbed for twenty-five years to reach my office at the Historical Studies Department, until we were transferred to the sister republic of Tlalpan in 2000); several million rats, gorged on picnic leftovers, were attacked with the aid of several million traps which only succeeded in trapping friendly squirrels; the glasshouse was converted into a senior citizen hangout, and finally the zoo was reborn as a kind of dreary, pedantic, ecological museum.

And yet, in spite of everything, the park's paths, alleys, and grassy meadows are still there, ready to be invaded every Sunday by flocks of maids.

There's the odd construction worker or bum, looking lost and fearful amid the sea of women, countless maids, freshly bathed and dressed in their Sunday best: new skirts and copious ribbons on their hair.

The maids' invasion of Chapultepec Park has gone virtually unexamined, as has the fate of countless out-of-town tourists who come in search of the bucolic Poets' Alley or the legendary springs where Nezahualcóyotl and Moctezuma once bathed, only to run into an unexpected mob of maids.

But where else are Mexico City's servants to gather on Sundays, before their weekly outing to watch films starring Sylvester Stallone's progeny? Look at the numbers: a population of seventeen million, of whom one quarter—let's say four million people, that is, a million households—can afford to hire help.

There are, therefore, a million maids free on Sundays. It's their only day off, and they have nowhere to go except Chapultepec Park.

Each and every one of them turns up here. Because it's pretty, it's got trees, grass for the kids to run around, you can have three steamed tacos for ten pesos (late twentieth-century pesos), and best of all, there are gazillions of other maids.

What maids find most appealing about Chapultepec is its sheer abundance of fellow maids.

We're talking about a veritable feminist congregation of broom-wielders.

And they have no time for silly, cultural stuff. They turn their noses up at museums, still banging on as they have for decades about the same old national history, same old archaeology, same old avant-garde "modern" nonsense.

They make sure to get off the buses or subway in batches of three, six, and as many as eight maids.

They enter the park in rank and file, all of them intent on out-giggling and out-squealing the rest, decked out in their best clothes and clutching their boom boxes (blasting the latest hits of Thalía, Gloria Trevi, Luis Miguel, Los Temerarios, or Los Tigres del Norte), Queens of the Woods (for a day). They find pleasure and repose in this city park, the only one that can contain them (though of course they overflow it).

The park becomes a giant stadium, complete with playing field and seating areas: Chapultepec for the maids. All it needs is a monument— perhaps on an island in the lake—a monument to the Unknown Maid, to María Isabel or La India María.

Truth to tell, this may be the best and most useful service the park has ever performed. However scandalizing to the provincial tourist on the trail of Carlotta's wardrobe or some secluded garden, however inconvenient for the families who have the nerve to venture into this lush sanctuary for single mothers (and aspirants to that status).

Exiled from this swarming land of women, sidewalk Romeos wait for evening, when the army of maids splinters into less intimidating groups, before attempting any catcalls, winks, or greetings.

They're also waiting for the girls to turn down their boom boxes. What Don Juan can compete with Bronco?

So they post themselves around Chapultepec Park, on street corners, at bus terminals or subway entrances, where, content with their morning's recreation—their compact and demographic regiments now unraveled into more manageable groups or pairs—some girls arrive to discuss with the rediscovered opposite sex filmic possibilities for the final hours of the day.

9

Corruption and Bureacuracy

Trimmins for the Comanche

RICARDO GARIBAY

DUTY OFFICER: Take off your hat, this is the attorney general's office.

CITIZEN: Uh, sorry, yes, sir.

ATTORNEY: If you'll allow me, officer, my client's a little jumpy. If you'd just let me explain . . .

OFFICER: You keep quiet. Let's hear what he has to say.

CITIZEN: It's about my brother, sir, you see they put him away yesterday, in solitary confinement. I'm afraid they beat him up. They wouldn't let me see him, so I asked this gentleman to come with me . . .

OFFICER: Solitary, eh? Beaten up, eh? Did you see it with your own eyes? And who wasn't allowed to see him? That's a very serious accusation you're making.

ATTORNEY: Actually, officer, we just wanted a quick word with the police officers who brought him in.

OFFICER: The patrols come back at six. Who arrested the suspect?

CITIZEN: It was a man who goes by the name of El Patán and another . . .

OFFICER: El Patán? We don't use no nicknames here. What's his real
name?

ATTORNEY: Never mind, officer, thanks for your help. We'll just wait
outside till six.

Fuming, the lawyer scolds and lectures his client, asks if he
brought the money, then orders him to keep his mouth shut when
the cops arrive. They both smoke fitfully, pacing up and down. The
colossal lobby begins to fill up with downcast, desperate people. Around
7 P.M.:

CITIZEN: That's him! The fat guy with the gold chain and platform
shoes, and there's the other one with him.

ATTORNEY: Remember now, not a word. Just slip me the cash when
I say.

They run forward and intercept the two cops. The lawyer explains.
One of the cops wanders off, the other, known as El Patán, follows the
lawyer to a quiet corner.

EL PATÁN: Naaaah, no way man, law's the law. He's fried, he's goin'
straight to a fancy cell in Lecumberri.

CITIZEN: But what's the charge, for heaven's sakes, how . . .

EL PATÁN: He friggin' confessed. We questioned the guy and he
friggin' spilled the beans and it's all down on paper. Robbery and
assault.

CITIZEN: But can't I just see him? I mean, it's been more than twenty-
four hours and I don't even know where he is.

EL PATÁN: In the basement, wheredyathink, nice 'n cozy in the basement, law's the law.

ATTORNEY: We were wondering if you might perhaps consider . . .

EL PATÁN: Thing is, to get 'im outtathere before shifts change, but like
I say it's fucked, gotta check with my pardner and I tell you, you better start thinkin', like, two, at least two grand, plus the trimmins to
keep the Comanche happy, cuz that Comanche he's dead straight
nowadays, know what I mean, real straight, man.

CITIZEN: The Comanche?

ATTORNEY: Hey, officer, what do you say we go see your partner?

EL PATÁN: I'm tellin' ya, my pardner's tuff like nails, he ain't got no heart, but me I feel sorry for this guy. Hold on, be right back.

El Patán leaves.

ATTORNEY: How much do you have there?

CITIZEN: The best I could do was fifteen hundred.

ATTORNEY: That's it?

El Patán returns with partner in tow.

PARTNER: Naah, can't see it, no way, law's the law, he's goin' straight to Lecumberri. Gimme two grand plus some trimmins for the Comanche.

CITIZEN: The Comanche?

PARTNER: I'm givin' you a break cuz my pal here feels sorry for the guy.

EL PATÁN: What 'cha got? Cough it up!

ATTORNEY: Fifteen hundred.

EL PATÁN AND PARTNER: No way José, go pump some more and come back 'fore shifts change. Hell, just the Comanche's trimmins is two grand!

CITIZEN: The Comanche? Why don't we go talk to him then? Who's the Comanche?

EL PATÁN: Watch yer mouth, mister. The Comanche, he's the law.

PARTNER: Watch yer client, lawyer, he's got a big mouth.

ATTORNEY (to Citizen): Shut up!

PARTNER: Here he comes now!

The two trot over to the doorway and stand stiffly to attention, with reverent expressions. A desiccated figure with darting serpent eyes mounts the steps, draped in a chic English overcoat. "My Commander, sir," say the cops. "Good evening, Commander, at your service, Commander." The Commander ignores them. His carriage and demeanor leave behind them a wake of solid, inflexible legality.

EL PATÁN: Holy shit! The Comanche's straight tonight! Gonna be a tough nut, tellin' ya.

PARTNER: Three grand and let's get outta here. Tell the guy, and fleece 'im the fifteen hundred.

In the Same Boat

RICARDO GARIBAY

What Rockefeller said about all of us being "in the same boat" is partly true, partly false, because there's a world of difference between being the captain on the bridge and serving as the stoker in the engine room. Yet my soot-smeared labors are not entirely the captain's fault, and my pathetic destiny as a boiler baster owes something to my character, just as his job strutting around the deck barking orders owes something to his.

This helps explain the following situation. One day when those closeups of the moon were being broadcast on TV, there was I, chatting with a friend in his office about technocracy and bureaucracy. He is warehouse manager for a government ministry, so I said, "Listen, seeing as you're the boss here, don't be mean, get me some paper."

"You've but to ask," he beamed, pressing a bell. A girl came into the office. "Be so kind as to bring me two reams of bond paper, twenty-four pound, letter size."

"Certainly, sir."

My friend, by name Augusto, is a lucid reader of philosophy. He went on: "Do you know that Romain Gary, in his letter to De Gaulle, said exactly what I've been telling you for ages: it's no longer a question of ideological conflict, doctrines at loggerheads, or different ways of conceiving humanity; it all comes down to technicalities, two great technological bands carving up the world into zones of influence and exploitation. Technology and markets."

"Well," I said, doing my utmost to disagree, "but those two big technological bands imply only a tiny amount of people, compared to the rest of the world which includes anyone from a British nuclear physicist to a wild Indian in the Colombian jungle."

"Absolutely," enthused Augusto, "and so what! None but the citizens of the empire will have any right to autonomy, sovereignty, real life; the third world has suddenly expanded to contain everyone who happens to be neither Soviet nor North American."

"What ever happened to my paper?"

He rang the bell. The girl came in. "My dear, what's holding up the paper I requested?"

"Oooh yes, sir, I'm very sorry. I'll tell Porfirio to bring it up now."

We continued our discussion. "The imminently immense third world will forever remain a dispenser of raw materials and a consumer of manufactured products, nothing more; because however spectacular its progress, its distance with respect to the technology of empire will grow ever greater."

"Look here," said Augusto, "the difference between a crack North American scientist and a Tzeltal Indian, for instance, has gone beyond economic or social disparities to an actual species leap, as you'll agree if you reflect that even a European scientist of the first rank hasn't got a clue about the physical and mathematical operations involved in traveling to the moon. Just think, he wouldn't even be able to pilot the rocket."

"Where's my paper?" I reminded him.

This is when bureaucracy, or should I say bureaucratic underdevelopment, came down on us like a ton of bricks. The young lady minced in for the third time, explaining that Porfirio called in sick and the other office boy took the day off, so there was nobody to take the order. It was suggested to her that she get in touch with the warehouse herself. Shortly she reappeared, to say they were on their way, and while we waited for the warehouse employees to arrive, Augusto and I attempted to represent to ourselves the nationwide organization required for a trip to the moon and the complex preparations that must precede and accompany such an endeavor. The warehouse men, five of them, jostled and shoved their way through the door.

"What's this," frowned Augusto, "a union meeting? I only asked for two reams of bond paper, twenty-four pound, letter size."

Off they went and back they staggered twenty minutes later, carrying between them all a gigantic drum of rolled-up paper. "We couldn't find twenty-four pounds of loose paper, so we brought you the whole bale instead, Mr. Augusto."

When Augusto had calmed down enough to repeat the line about two reams of bond paper, twenty-four pound, letter size, and the warehouse men had gone off to tell their supervisor to report personally to the director general for his instructions, we fell to discussing the crisis of philosophy, to which neopositivism denies any kind of validity, and the way neopositivism itself tends to function as mere cheerleader for technology. Twenty minutes went by and it turned out the head supervisor had gone home because he had received the summons just five minutes before his lunch break at half past two, and there was no one else in the warehouse, and Augusto started vociferating, "This is too much. Tell the supervisor I want him in my office now!" and when the supervisor arrived Augusto held him personally accountable for the two reams of bond paper, twenty-four pound, letter size, and after the supervisor withdrew in terror, our musings switched to the extreme scientific rigor of neopositivism, which makes Hegel's grand architecture look like cowboy's comic. The supervisor reappeared, looking worn out.

"The paper's downstairs, sir."

"Good, so bring it up here, to my desk."

"Your desk, sir?"

We heard the puffing and panting of some people laboriously mounting the stairs. We looked through the door. Three men were hefting a box crammed with paper, pencils, penholders, chalk, erasers and blackboards, and a school desk.

AUGUSTO: What's this!

SUPERVISOR: Your order, sir.

AUGUSTO: I ordered two reams of bond paper, twenty-four pound, letter size, you moron! Get that garbage out of my sight!

SUPERVISOR: But as there wasn't any paper like you said, I thought best to . . .

AUGUSTO: Out!

I tried to appease my friend by pitching a few questions to him, of the kind that usually hit his soft spot; but Augusto was so enraged that he started hollering all manner of things I completely agreed with:

"And since you disagreed with me about species leap, now tell me what possible resemblance there is between one of these cretins and a man who steers a rocket two hundred thousand miles in the air! Multiply one of this lot by sixty million and that's where you'll find me, and that's where you're at as well!"

"Never mind," I said, "I'll just have to buy the paper, and at least the nation has been spared one disgraceful fraud."

On our way out, however, we found the supervisor and his carriers hovering by the door, looking moody.

Augusto: What now?

Supervisor: Well, sir, it's just we don't like the way we've been treated, see, I mean, like what you said, because that's no way to treat decent folks, me being a responsible manager, I come in at eight and you don't get in before ten. I don't mean no disrespect, sir, I'm just trying to be responsible and, and these are hard-working boys, sir . . . Your paper's inside your car and the order's been carried out just like you wanted. If not, anyways, the boys they're set on filing a complaint with the union . . .

We rushed toward the car. The doors stood open, lashed with string, and inside lay the huge bale that had been brought first, on seat covers that were torn from one end to the other. I felt something coming on that I love: a fit of helpless laughter.

The University

JONATHAN HERNÁNDEZ

The National University of Mexico (UNAM) is the largest university in the world, with more than 250,000 students and almost 30,000 professors.[1] Between April 1999 and February 2000, the university students went on strike, bringing all academic and research activities to a halt. The strike awakened painful memories of 1968, when a similar shutdown led to a series of protests that culminated with the Tlatelolco massacre, the bloodiest moment in the seventy years of PRI rule. This time around, however, the strike led not to tragedy but to a comedy of the absurd: student leaders and government officials proved equally inept at productive dialogue. The deadlock ended when President Ernesto Zedillo ordered a special police task force to enter the campus and reclaim it from the striking students.

In 1995, four years before the strike, the artist Jonathan Hernández created a photographic series that exposed the nightmarish structure of UNAM's bureaucracy. The work, *Credencial sordomudos (Deaf-mute ID)*, details the labyrinthine process the artist had to follow in order to replace his student ID card.

The artist pretended to be a deaf-mute student, and he showed university officials a sign describing his problem and asking them to "please write down on a sheet of paper the next step." The resulting work consists of almost three dozen photographs documenting the different offices Hernández visited before finally receiving his ID card. The Polaroid snapshots are accompanied by sheets of paper on which university employees wrote the steps to be followed. These telegraphic messages reveal the bureaucratic labyrinth found in the university: "Go to your departmental library and ask for a confirmation that no books are owed. Take that sheet to the central library and get it stamped, then come back here," reads one. "We can do it after 12:00. It is 11:00," reads another.

From the vantage point of the 1999 strike at the university, Hernández's piece can be seen as an uncanny premonition of the disaster to come: how can a university function when it takes three dozen steps—lines, forms, stamps—to merely get a replacement ID? *Credencial sordomudos* can be seen as a timely critique of UNAM's greatest problem—the excessive bureaucratization that undermines its teaching mission. The piece also references a somber moment in Mexican history: during the Tlatelolco massacre, many students caught in the plaza-turned-mousetrap destroyed their university ID cards to avoid being identified by soldiers.

Notes

1. In 1999 UNAM counted 269,516 students and 29,795 academics. See "Población escolar" and "Personal académico," *Agenda estadística* (Mexico City: UNAM, 1999).

Jonathan Hernández, Credencial sordomudos
*(1995). Series of Polaroid photographs. Courtesy of
La Colección Jumex, Mexico City*

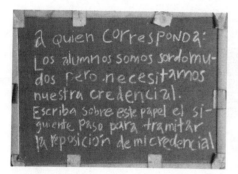

"To Whom It May Concern: We students are
deaf-mute, but we need our ID card. Write on
this paper the next step to process the replacement of my ID card."

11 ENE. 1995

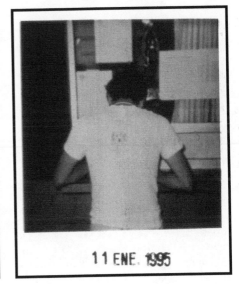

11 ENE. 1995

IR A LA BIBLIOTECA DE LA ESCUELA POR
UNA CONSTANCIA DE NO ADEUDO DE XXXXXX
LIBROS.ESA HOJA LLEVARLA A LA BIBLIOTE-
CA DE C.U. POR OTRO SELLO. REGRESAR
AQUI NUEVAMENTE.

UNIVERSIDAD NACIONAL AUTONOMA DE MEXICO

"GO TO THE SCHOOL'S LIBRARY FOR A CER-
TIFICATE STATING THAT NO XXXXX BOOKS
ARE DUE? THAT SHEET YOU MUST TAKE TO
THE C.U. LIBRARY FOR ANOTHER STAMP.
COME BACK HERE AGAIN."

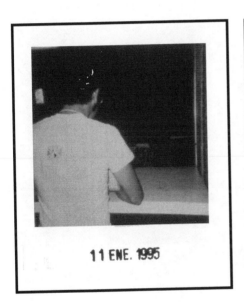

11 ENE. 1995

11 ENE. 1995

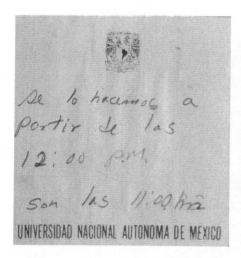

"We do that after 12:00 P.M. It is 11:00 A.M."

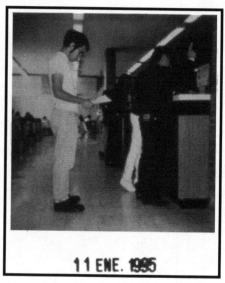

UNIVERSIDAD NACIONAL AUTONOMA DE MEXICO

"Check your info. Thanks"

11 ENE. 1995

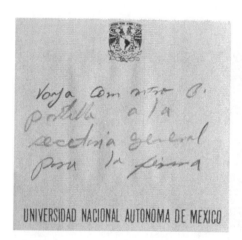

"Go see prof. G. Portillo at the general secretariat"

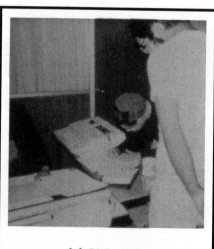

VE HACER TUS TRAMITES A BIBLIO-
TECA CENTRAL TIENE 72 HRS.
DE TRAMITE.

UNIVERSIDAD NACIONAL AUTONOMA DE MEXICO

12 ENE. 1995

"GO MAKE YOUR REQUEST AT THE CENTRAL
LIBRARY. THE REQUEST TAKES 72 HRS."

12 ENE. 1995

12 ENE. 1995

UNIVERSIDAD NACIONAL AUTONOMA DE MEXICO

"Pay at the mall/School services"

13 ENE. 1995

13 ENE. 1995

13 ENE. 1995

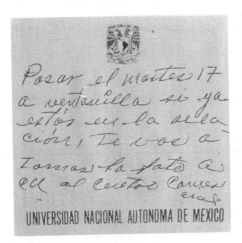

UNIVERSIDAD NACIONAL AUTONOMA DE MEXICO

17 ENE. 1995

"On Tuesday the 17th go to the teller if your name appears on the list. Go to CU to take your picture at the mall."

17 ENE. 1995

IR A LA ZONA COMERCIAL DE C.U.
A TOMARSE LA FOTO, PAGAR EN LA CAJA
DE C.U.

UNIVERSIDAD NACIONAL AUTONOMA DE MEXICO

"GO TO THE MALL AT C.U. TO TAKE YOUR
PICTURE. PAY THE CASHIER AT C.U."

18 ENE. 1995

18 ENE. 1995

"Thanks."

Te falta ir a la caja (2° piso) a pagar $41=
por resello de credencial .... y luego...
ir a servicios escolares con tu comprobante
a pedirle a la amable señorita (si es que está)
que te selle tu credencial. Ahora sí

GRACIAS

Ya eres alumno de la UNAM

"You still need to go to the cashier (2nd floor) and pay for the restamping of the card . . . and then . . . go to school services with your receipt and ask the helpful lady (if she's there) to stamp your ID card. All set. Thanks. Now you're a UNAM student."

10

The Margins

Garbage

ALMA GUILLERMOPRIETO

This is not a healthy place.

Garbage has become an obsession for the inhabitants of Mexico City, spawning any number of fantastic stories, all of them true. There is, for example, the story of the open-air garbage dumps that spontaneously ignited one day in July, spreading fire and toxic fumes over acres of refuse stacked twenty yards high. There is the story of the cacique who controlled more than half the city's seventeen thousand-odd *pepenadores,* or garbage pickers, demanded sexual favors from the garbage pickers' daughters, and also took all his workers off to Acapulco on vacation once a year. There is the story of a sixty-square-mile garbage dump that the city government decided to turn into a park, complete with picnic tables—tables that have since been sinking gently into the settling layers of trash and loam.

Then, there are the rats. One of the most memorable stories dates from the beginning of the decade, when an evening paper announced above the fold that a "giant mutant rat" had been discovered floating dead in a sewage canal. The article said that the rat was the size of a Volkswagen, and in the accompanying photo one could verify the caption's claim that the beast had "the face of a bear, the hands of a man, and the tail of a rat." Two days later, a morning paper explained that the corpse belonged to a lion owned by a three-flea traveling circus. The old thing had finally died, but before throwing the corpse into the sewage canal the owners had decided to skin it, in case the pelt proved salable. Purists among those who collect accounts of Mexican trash dismiss this story on the ground that it turned out to be false, but the point is not that the mutant rat was a figment but that in the general state of decay and disrepair of one of the world's most overburdened cities many of us who read the story assumed at the time that it was true. The fact is that once started on the subject most city residents can come up with giant-rat stories of their own, and few are more convincingly told than the one offered by Iván Restrepo, a genial scholar of garbage who directs a government-financed institute for ecological research called the Centro de Ecodesarrollo. Five years ago, in Chapultepec, the city's most popular public park, Restrepo and his center mounted an exhibit on the subject of garbage. A tent, designed by an artist, had a long, dark entrance, filled with giant illustrations of microbes and garbage-related pests, from which the public emerged into "the world of garbage." One of the exhibits, Restrepo said, was "the most gigantic rat we could find."

Restrepo was telling his story in one of Mexico City's best restaurants, and he interrupted himself briefly to order roast kid, guacamole, and a mille-feuille of poblano chilies and cream. "It was huge!" he went on, gesturing enthusiastically. The rat, one gathered, must have been about the size of a large cat. "It weighed almost eight pounds. But we had a problem. We began to realize that the rat was dying on us. It wasn't used to the nice, healthy pet food, or whatever it was, that we were feeding it. So we went out and collected fresh garbage for it every evening. Kept it happy. And that was important, because thousands and thousands of people came to see the garbage exhibit, and the rat was the absolute star of the show."

If *capitalinos*—the residents of Mexico City—flock to an exhibit on garbage featuring large vermin, it is because the subject is never very far from their minds. The problem of waste disposal may be only one of the critical aspects of the city's ongoing public-services emergency, but it is certainly among the most pressing. One of the world's three largest urban conglomerates, the city never had a proper service infrastructure to begin with and has been growing too much too fast for too many years. Figures from the 1990 national census show that although the Federal District, or capital proper, has a relatively stable population of

8.2 million, the surrounding sprawl in the neighboring state (also called Mexico) brings the total urban population to 16 million. This is triple the 1965 estimated total, and the rate is not slowing. By the year 2000, if current trends persist, the urban area will be home to 20 million souls, all clamoring for services that are already strained to the breaking point in some areas and nonexistent in others.

Not only are services dangerously insufficient but there is almost no way to expand them. Water is now piped in from as far as fifty-five miles away. Ringed by mountains, the urban area is also gasping for fresh air. At least fourteen tons of waste, including lead, carbon monoxide, and what is known euphemistically as the products of "open-air fecalization," now floats in what the city breathes every day. Visibility has improved markedly since late last year, when the government passed a law restricting circulation of a fifth of the city's 2.5 million vehicles each weekday, but, because public transport is also in an awful state, car owners are now buying spare vehicles to use on the day the irregular cars aren't allowed out. The poor, who can't afford any car at all, can spend as much as four hours a day traveling between the outlying shantytowns and their urban workplaces: the metro system, which has seventy miles of track and provides more than four million rides a day, serves only a small part of the Federal District, which covers some 579 square miles, and the same is true of the crowded, aging buses that spew their fumes along the city's uncharming streets. Twelve million more rides are provided by a network of *colectivos*—privately operated minivans and small buses—which clog traffic and gouge working-class salaries. And the deep-drainage system—nine miles of cavernous tunnels and thousands of miles of pipes, hailed as an engineering marvel when it was inaugurated, barely fifteen years ago—is now hopelessly overloaded, as anyone knows who saw the sewers backing up during each of this summer's downpours.

Bad as the city's public-service difficulties are, most of them appear to have fairly straightforward solutions: build more subways, install more phones. Not trash. The question is not how to put more of anything in but how to reduce the sheer bulk of what exists. The poor, who constitute the vast majority of Mexico's population, have lately produced almost as much waste as the rich; eager initiates into the world of junk consumerism, they find some consolation for their fate in the first world's plastic-encased gewgaws. And although the city has so far heroically managed to keep more or less abreast of the growing tonnage of waste, cleanup-service problems merely have their beginning in the dumps. Here Mexico's first and third worlds meet and fester. Rats are the least of it. There is pollution and, above all, the tangle of human misery and political intrigue represented by a peculiar sector of Mexico's body politic—the thousands of pepenadores and their leaders, who stand in the way of neat solutions.

Contemplating the lovely city of Tenochtitlán, rising from the now vanished waters of Lake Texcoco, the conquistadores marveled not only at the personal cleanliness of the inhabitants but at the immaculate streets that fanned out in an orderly grid from the great plaza, now occupied by the National Palace and the cathedral. The Aztec people could hardly conceive of waste: they used cornhusks to wrap food in and inedible seeds to manufacture percussion instruments. All organic waste went into the compost-filled rafts with which the Aztecs compensated for their lack of agricultural land. Each street was swept clean every morning, and the day's cargo of excrement was deposited in a special raft tied at the street's end.

By contrast, colonial Mexico was a filthy place, but the long-term accumulation of waste did not really become a problem until after the 1910 revolution, which yanked the Indian population out of self-sufficient subsistence economics and into the world of buying, selling, and discarding. In the 1940s, when the economy finally stabilized after the long devastation of civil war, consumerism made its first inroads. Waste multiplied. Each month, thousands of peasants abandoned their land and came to the capital looking for a better life. By the 1960s, urban prosperity had proved to be a mirage, but the situation in the countryside was infinitely worse, and the mass urban migration continued. The newcomers settled in shacks along the roads leading into the city, stole their electricity from the highway power lines, and made do without running water, drainage, or garbage-collection systems. The communities grew at such a rate that one of them, Ciudad Nezahualcóyotl, is the country's fourth-largest city. Thoroughly integrated by now into the consumer economy, its million-plus inhabitants carry their groceries home in plastic bags, use their spare change to buy hair spray, splurge at United States–based fast-food chains on soda pop served in plastic-foam cups, and pour milk for their children from plastic-coated cardboard cartons. The intractable accumulation of mixed waste—rotting, toxic, and nonbiodegradable—generated by this fraction of the

third world's urban poor can be contemplated at the Bordo de Xochiaca municipal dump, on the southern edge of what was once Lake Texcoco, and a few blocks away from Nezahualcóyotl's city hall. Not many
who pass by it linger; the stench causes motorists to accelerate way past
the speed limit, and in their haste they may fail to notice what is most
striking about this vast expanse of putrefaction. Scarecrow-like figures
can be seen moving slowly over the dusty mounds, poking methodically.
The garbage is inhabited.

   The best view of Bordo de Xochiaca is from the driver's seat of
a tractor that is used all day long to flatten out the incoming loads.
From this vantage paint one can look north across the clay-colored lake-
bed to the volcano-ringed horizon. In the opposite direction, the garbage dunes recede for half a mile to Ciudad Nezahualcóyotl. A few
people work the edges of the dump, and a few others live in plastic-
and-cardboard shanties there, but most of the dump's activity takes place
in a clearing in the center—where people try to sift through a newly deposited truckload of garbage before the tractor runs over it—and in an
expanse just to the west of this clearing, where Celestino Fernández
Reyes, the dump boss, weighs and purchases the scavengers' daily take of
glass, rags, tin, cardboard, wood, plastic containers, animal bones, and
other recyclable materials. Behind the scales and Celestino's headquarters, a row of shacks marks the beginning of the living quarters—scores
of lopsided houses, some of them quite large, that are built of and on rubbish, along reeking alleys and paths with names like Virgin of Guadalupe
Lane.

   It proved a little difficult to get into Bordo. At a sentry gate set
between two small hills of garbage, a stocky man in dark glasses, jeans,
and cowboy boots waved in a procession of trucks and quite a few mule-
drawn carts—the latter belonging to the Nezahualcóyotl municipal service and decorated with the red-white-and-green logo of the nation's
ruling party, the Partido Revolucionario Institucional, or PRI. The sentry said there was no access to the public. As I argued with him, loaded
trucks continued to file by, and the drivers of trucks not belonging to
Nezahualcóyotl's municipal fleet stopped to press the sentry's hand,
which then flew to a pocket in his quilted vest. During the seconds required for these transactions, children climbed up on the trucks' back
wheels and then onto the loads of refuse, and as each truck moved past
the gate the children scrabbled frantically through the load, throwing
things overboard; they would return to collect them as soon as the truck

reached the dumping site, which is invisible from the gate, being hidden by hills of piled-up trash. Eventually, the sentry agreed to let me in for a brief visit.

After a week of rain, the pickers were working ankle-deep in a thick slush; it was tinted blue or bright red in patches, and these exhaled a mist of choking chemical fumes. Oblivious of the smell, a cluster of children crouched in a blue puddle, poring over a small pile of plastic comic-book figures—the Joker, Superman, and the like. The children did not want to talk to a stranger (indeed, they avoided even looking at me), but after I made a couple of tries the tallest boy answered a question, saying that he and his friends wanted the toys not to play with but to sell. Nevertheless, as they salvaged the few dolls that had no arms or legs missing they deployed them in a brief, soundless mock battle before tossing them into a scavenging sack.

One of Celestino's overseers waved each arriving truck to a spot on the edge of the clearing, where a family or a team of friends was waiting, each member equipped with only a long-handled pitchfork, and no boots, masks, or other protective gear. The team began sifting through the waste even before the truck's shower of refuse ended, expertly plucking out the salvageable bits with their bare hands. The fork was designed to help the pickers separate the mounds of trash on the ground, but an elderly man in faded blue overalls said that since the tractor had been brought in there was hardly any time for the garbage to pile up, so a lot of salable material was left unsalvaged. (The tractor was somebody's idea of a landfill operation, but since the garbage wasn't covered with anything after being flattened out it seemed to serve no practical purpose.)

The garbage pickers proved to be a closemouthed lot, especially when I asked their names or put questions about Celestino, but the man in overalls was willing to explain the various stages of trash-picking. "You have to know what to select," he said, working with precision and delicacy as he talked. "For example, this pair of trousers is good, because the buttons and zipper can be removed and sold. If they were made of natural fiber, like cotton, you could sell the cloth as rag. There are a lot of tennis shoes in this pile, but they're not good enough to sell to the secondhand-clothes dealers." He was picking through a revolting pile of what seemed to be the refuse of a very large family, but by the time the things he had chosen to keep reached his sack they looked almost clean. He waved toward a point in the rubbish heap which I found indistinguishable from its surroundings. "That's my spot," he said. "When I'm through for the day, I take my sack over there and sort it. It's not enough just to pick the garbage. We have to put work into it afterward to make it salable."

A truck unloaded a pile of refuse from what someone said was an open-air market—a cascade of burst tomatoes, crushed bananas, empty egg crates, clear plastic bags, and wadded-up vegetable peelings. None of it was rotting yet, but, according to a group of women and children investigating the pile, there was nothing of any use other than a score of orange halves that had had most of their pulp pressed out of them, and that one woman picked up and immediately began eating.

I struck up a conversation with another member of the team, a woman with long gray braids who was wearing a clean checked apron over a faded dress. She told me that in general market waste was virtually worthless, except for an occasional pile of butcher-shop bones, which gelatin and bouillon-cube manufacturers would buy. Other pickers were saving the organic waste for pigs they kept along the edges of the dump, but she said she didn't own any. While quite a few of the garbage pickers looked filthy, her clothes, I noticed, were not only clean but crisply ironed. "I used to wash clothes for a living," she explained. "But now my arms can't take being in the water so long." The sun was directly overhead, and hitting hard, so the smells around us—acetone, vegetable rot, used disposable diapers—ripened and concentrated in the heat. Several of the workers had stopped for a noonday snack at a lopsided tent made of bits of plastic and wood, but the woman told me she would not buy the potato chips or lemonade available there. "The younger people make more money, but I can only clear about five or six thousand pesos a day," she said. Six thousand pesos is about two dollars. "I get here at ten or so, and work as long as my arms and legs can stand it. Then I eat when I get home." Soon, she said, she would carry her sacks, one at a time, to the weighing area and collect her pay from Don Celestino. Then she would try to make the hour-long walk back to her squatters' community before the afternoon rains started.

Others told me they lived near the weighing area, in shacks made of salvaged cardboard, plastic, and tin. Mexico's continuing economic crisis is constantly expelling residents from Ciudad Nezahualcóyotl, where they can no longer afford to pay rent, mortgage, or utilities. Many are emigrating to the edge of the urban sprawl, where they must begin life over again, as they did two decades ago in Ciudad Nezahualcóyotl—in bare fields, with no lights or other services. Some of the poorest, or frail-est, of these exiles appeared to be ending up in Bordo. I walked away from the picking fields in the general direction of the dump's headquar-ters with a woman carrying a sack of glass jars which was almost as tall as she was. She lived a few blocks away, she said, but she couldn't afford the payments on her plot of land now that her husband was out of a job. Soon, if Don Celestino would permit it, she would move to the dump with her family. There was no electricity here, and the nearest public water faucet was a half hour's walk away, but at least it was free, and she wouldn't have to pay for transportation to get to work. "He's a very nice man," she said of the dump boss. "He doesn't charge anything for let-ting you live here. All you have to do is ask permission to come in, and promise to sell your material exclusively to him."

Though it is estimated that some seventeen thousand people work in Mexico City's garbage dumps, no one has tallied the number that work in Bordo de Xochiaca and the other dumps in neighboring Mexico State—dumps that are for all practical purposes part of the same urban area, and are often used by capitalinos. Like the cigarette peddlers, the street-corner fire-eaters and cartwheel turners, the windshield washers and parking-space finders, the pot menders, the sidewalk violinists and portrait painters, the curtain-rod fixers, and the outright beggars who swarm through the city, the pepenadores are a result of Mexico's con-stant failure to find a social space for its very poorest. But, unlike mil-lions of their fellows who also have to forage for each day's bread, they are a geographically stable population, tied to the arrival of a loaded truck. Their stability makes them easy to organize—a fact that the PRI, which has now been in power for sixty-one years, could not fail to no-tice. Throughout those years, the PRI has demonstrated a scavenger's genius for wasting nothing and no one, and a truly pre-Hispanic voca-tion for building pyramidal social organizations. Not long after Mexico City started producing serious amounts of garbage, the scavengers who flocked to it became small but extremely useful cogs in the PRI's politi-cal machine. Men like Celestino Fernández Reyes, who as a member of the PRI's Confederation of Popular Organizations became Bordo's overseer, make sure that the relationship between the party and the scavengers is a smooth, productive one.

"Do you think I'm here for the pleasure of it?" Don Celestino asked me. "This is a terrible way to earn a living! Pickers can make good money—up to 240,000 pesos a week. A lot of them have saved enough to move out of here and set up a little business on their own. Me, I have the thankless part. I have to fight with the buyers, keep prices up, go offering the pickers' wares from factory to factory. Plus, I'm a sick man, a diabetic, and this is not a healthy place. I would never have chosen to come here—I was doing fine buying glass from the dump—but the party asked me to come and establish some order. 'Celestino, we need you here,' they said. So I came." Don Celestino is rumored to be a wealthy man, but his office is a one-room, tin-roofed brick house in the heart of the dump, furnished with a cot, two rusting metal chairs, and a makeshift desk. A small, trim man with extraordinarily liquid dark eyes, he dresses neatly but unostentatiously in a white guayabera and sporty blue slacks, and, until he relaxes, he moves and talks with meticulous humility. Our interview took place somewhat earlier than I had hoped. While I was wandering through the dump's residential area, trying to estimate the total population, and, to my surprise, discovering further paths and alleyways at every turn, a horse pulled up just behind me with a loud snort. Riding it bareback was a very beautiful youth with long hair and cold eyes. He demanded my business. I answered that I was looking for Don Celestino, and he said firmly that he would escort me to him.

In his dilapidated office, Don Celestino gradually lost his air of subservient courtesy as he explained the garbage market. He made it clear that the pepenadores were utterly dependent on him. "It's not that they can't transport their salvage to the factories," he said. "A lot of the buyers have warehouses right across the highway from here. But who's going to pay any kind of price for a dozen empty bottles?" In his own eyes, he was the community's benefactor. "I brought a doctor in here to look after the pickers full time. She charges for the visit, but who do you think pays for the medicines? Me!" He didn't smoke, he didn't have the face of a heavy drinker, and he kept a close watch on prices and profits. "Times are hard!" he exclaimed. "It used to be that factory owners came after me looking for things to buy, but ever since Salinas de Gortari"—the nation's president—"came up with his free-trade policies we've been getting undercut by United States waste products. There's trains and trains of them coming in! And, you know, American products are always better. The gringos are selling clean, nicely tied-up cardboard, and they're selling it cheap. Who would want ours? Now buyers are complaining that it's dirty, that often half the weight is moisture. I bought cardboard at three hundred pesos a stack the other day, and I couldn't get rid of it for a hundred and fifty. I tell you, I don't know how I let the party talk me into this."

In the past, the PRI provided similar encouragement and support to Rafael Gutiérrez Moreno, a former garbage-truck driver who, in 1965, took over from his father as leader of the Mexico City garbage pickers. Gutiérrez Moreno turned his constituency into a rapid-response force at the service of his political sponsors. In the late 1970s, he also served briefly as an alternate member of the Chamber of Deputies, but after one term he chose to return to the political sidelines. Whenever a show of support was needed for the capital's appointed mayor, or for the president, or for a foreign head of state, Gutiérrez Moreno, known to his followers as El Líder, saw to it that his people were there, waving green-white-and-red paper flags or, it has been rumored, wielding billy clubs and metal pipes as part of the notorious *Halcones* (Falcons), who operated against strikers and student demonstrators in the early 1970s. In exchange, the authorities looked the other way as he tightened his hold on the pickers. In 1983, city officials ordered Gutiérrez Moreno to close down his fiefdom, the vast dump of Santa Cruz Meyehualco. A fire that had raged there for five days in 1981, and reports that toxic chemicals were leaching through the trash into the city's water supply contributed to the decision. Gutiérrez Moreno negotiated room for half his followers at the city's second-largest dump, in the western part of the city, and moved the rest to land he had acquired east of Santa Cruz, in the district of Santa Catarina. El Líder, who was reported to distribute as much as ten million pesos a day in bribes around the city bureaucracy, built himself an extravagantly appointed house on the Santa Catarina grounds; he also built housing there for the workers which was significantly better than the garbage hovels at the old dump. He paid for drinks and decorations for yearly fiestas, and it was he who took everyone off once a year for a beach holiday. All that, however, did nothing to diminish his reputation as a singularly heartless exploiter of the garbage pickers' penury. He punished them if they left the dump grounds, by cutting back on their allotment of garbage or by beating them, and—again, according to published rumor—assassinated those who questioned his leadership. In pursuit of his declared goal of fathering 180 children, he took his pick of the community's teen-age girls, including his nieces. (Forty-five offspring have been legally recognized so far.)

Héctor Castillo, who wears a ponytail and plays drums with a pretty good rock band, is a social scientist, and he has spent a considerable amount of time trying to figure out how garbage communities and their caciques come into being. He began his research on the man he describes as "the most powerful of all the country's urban caciques" a decade ago, by sneaking past watchmen into Gutiérrez Moreno's dump several times, and he has since worked and drunk with the pepenadores often. At the heart of the problem, as he sees it, is Mexico's finely wrought system of intermediation between the ruling party, the government, and the citizenry. "Mexico's system is patrimonial, and that means that it operates through concessions, from top to bottom," Castillo says. "The garbage-collection concession is granted to the Federal District's Sanitation Department. From that point on, a number of subsidiary choices have to be made: whose trucks are going to collect the wealthiest garbage—the residential-zone garbage, with its mattresses and wine bottles and discarded clothes—and who is going to drive those trucks, because, of course these things are scavenged by the truck crew long before they reach the dumps. At each step in the process where there is money to be made, a concession is granted, and at the end of the line are the garbage caciques, who tie the whole system together securely, and declare that the garbage is in its place, that the city is clean, and that its politicians are even cleaner."

This is probably a fair description of a system that is now dying: for most of the century, the PRI has ruled Mexico through the web of patronage and concessions that Castillo describes. His account, though, leaves out the layer of commitment to social change underlying the regime's all-embracing populist rhetoric. For all its inefficiencies and other faults, the patrimonial system worked well enough to pull a largely rural and illiterate population into the twentieth century, insuring levels of education, health care, public services, and social mobility which comparable societies (Peru, Brazil, and Colombia, say) never achieved. For decades, Mexicans appeared to take equal pleasure in mocking the state—for its corruption, its verbosity, its ruthlessness, its endlessly scheming system of privilege—and in boasting of it to outsiders who failed to appreciate the subtleties of its achievements. The wily old PRI might have endured even longer in its pristine corporatist form except for three devastating blows. One was the economic bonfire provoked by José López Portillo, who, as president from 1976 to 1982, promised to "administer the prosperity" generated by Mexico's newfound oil wealth. With the glee of a nouveau tycoon leaping into a pool full of naked women, López Portillo plunged the whole country into a reckless and corrupt spending binge, which came to a disastrous halt only with the collapse of the international price of oil, in 1981. By the following year, Mexico's $83 billion foreign debt was draining the government budget, and even the money to pay for things that Mexicans had come to consider their right—things ranging from adequate schools to cheap public transportation—was scarce. Then came the 1985 earthquake, in whose aftermath the government appeared merely corrupt and inept, while tens of thousands of citizen volunteers rescued the concept of an engaged society from the rubble. And then there were the 1988 elections, in which, largely as a result of the previous two crises, the PRI lost enormous numbers of votes to a new left-wing coalition. Many members of the foreign press who traveled through the country think that the PRI may actually have lost the election, but government officials angrily dismiss the charge as "nonsense." Still, the PRI certainly lost Mexico City, and even Ciudad Nezahualcóyotl and the area around it, where Gutiérrez Moreno had his power base.

The combined result of these crises has been to open the doors for a new elite, whose head and symbol is President Carlos Salinas de Gortari. He and his youthful band of highly trained economists and statisticians take pride in representing everything that the old-style *priístas* do not—they scorn the pork-barrel theory of politics, disdain bribe-taking as lower class, play squash regularly, and sound reverent only when pronouncing the word *modernidad*—but they remain, for better or worse, members and leaders of the party that brought them to power. The tensions between the old-time corporatists and the new neoliberal technocrats may ultimately split the party. For the moment, the two sides remain united, because neither can rule the country without the other. The newcomers need to keep the country running on a day-to-day basis while they implement a devastatingly painful program of structural economic reform. The old guard, for its part, senses that its methods may be bankrupt, but it must somehow start delivering results again if the party is to avoid any more losses like its crushing electoral defeat in the capital's "circle of misery." As a result of such convergent renovating impulses, officials were desperately maneuvering to get rid of the lord of Mexico City's garbage pickers even before his death, in 1987, at the age of forty-eight.

Rafael Gutiérrez Moreno was shot to death in his own bedroom late one night, and his wife was sentenced to twenty-five years in prison for the crime. Gutiérrez Moreno had beaten her brutally ever since their marriage, ten years before, and had raped her sisters and nieces. She had many motives for attacking her husband, but so did any number of his subjects, and when the murder finally took place the only wonder was that someone had not done in El Líder long before. Héctor Castillo points out, however, that a community capable of fighting back could hardly have let itself become so abject in the first place. "Most of the garbage pickers have never known a different way of life," he says. "There are people here who are third generation. The pickers are born and grow up in the garbage fields. They have almost no schooling, and they know that their position in society is extremely weak." After Gutiérrez Moreno's death, the pickers proved incapable of choosing themselves a new leader—a situation that set off a battle for his political inheritance.

A colleague of Héctor Castillo's, Rosalinda Losada, has been following the succession struggle. She is a friendly, energetic woman who once spent some time picking garbage as part of the research for her graduate thesis, and she has struck up something of a friendship with El Líder's principal rival, the rather more genial Pablo Téllez. "When Gutiérrez Moreno had to move from his original power base to Santa Catarina, he sent nearly half of the other pepenadores to a dump at the opposite end of Mexico City, Santa Fé, then dominated exclusively by Téllez," she explained. "As his stand-in there Gutiérrez Moreno delegated someone known as El Dientón." (The name translates roughly as Bigtooth.) Téllez cannot have allowed El Dientón into his site willingly, since the partition effectively cut his own take in half, but he was almost certainly persuaded to do so by Gutiérrez Moreno's allies in the local government. "When Gutiérrez Moreno was killed, everyone thought El Dientón would replace him," Losada continued. "But then one of Gutiérrez Moreno's former wives appeared, out of the blue, to claim his inheritance. This wife—named Guillermina de la Torre—didn't even live in the dumps, and no one knew very much about her, but she seemed to have the support of a lot of local officials. Now the Gutiérrez Moreno pepenadores are divided into Guillermina's followers, at Santa Catarina, and El Dientón's, at a place called Prados de la Montaña, in the northwest of the city, built in the winter of 1986 to replace Santa Fé, which was overflowing by then."

Officials in the new city administration who are trying to keep Mexico's garbage problem under control tend to get huffy in the face of insistent questions about garbage picking, for they have plenty of critical issues to worry about besides scavengers and the leaders who control them. There is the ecological problem represented by the old, unplanned dumps, which may still be polluting the groundwater and air in their vicinity. There is the logistical problem of transporting garbage across the enormous, chronically congested capital city. And there is the question of the increasing volumes of garbage generated by what Professor Restrepo defines as "this poor, underdeveloped society's penchant for consuming like a first-class industrial power, with everything wrapped in more and more layers of plastic." The director of Urban Services, José Cuenca Dardón, has his own list of hurdles: "We are behind in every aspect of sanitation, including the concept of what the service should be and the legislation surrounding the problem. If you add to this the social problem of people whose livelihood for generations has consisted of garbage picking, the issue becomes doubly complex. And we have to try to solve it with our municipalities' extremely weak financial base, historically backward infrastructure, and very poor citizen awareness." Politically, Cuenca represents the PRI's transitional stage; he is not upper class or foreign educated, and he deals comfortably with the city's caciques, but he is a legendary compulsive worker, who can speak about garbage with unremitting intensity for hours at a stretch, reeling off figures and achievements that include the total number of kilometers of roadways swept clean every night, the percentage of garbage processed by the city today versus the percentage a decade ago, the total number of trips saved by a new system of transfer points. "We have learned," he says, eyes shining. "Now we know how many sweepable surfaces every main thoroughfare presents, and how many man-hours are needed to sweep two- and four-lane roads."

Cuenca packed me off on a tour of the city's garbage infrastructure, beginning with a visit to the new transfer points, where small garbage trucks unload into trailers six times as large, and including a new landfill, whose main virtue, the engineer in charge of it said proudly, "is that it is garbage-pickerless." But the garbage itself *was* being picked through, at every stage of its collection and dumping, by Urban Services employees sensible enough not to let anything go to waste. Along the noisy thoroughfares, I saw orange-clad street-sweepers busy setting aside cans and bottles. A garbage truck pulled into a transfer point with a six-seat sofa tied neatly across its bow. The point's supervisor beamed. "We have very good-quality garbage here," he said. "It comes from first-class neighborhoods." Spontaneous recycling was taking place throughout the city. Then what was being left for the real pickers?

"Practically nothing," said Luis Rojas, Bigtooth's second-in-command, at my last stop on the official garbage tour. "The truck drivers are stealing us blind, no matter that it was El Líder who got them out of the dumps and onto the trucks in the first place. Now they want to forget where they're from, and we're at war." At the gate of the new Prados de la Montaña dump, I and a traveling escort of Urban Services officials had been met, in what is known here as the best *oficialista* style, by a lineup that included plant managers, chief engineers, Rojas, and Pablo Téllez, the man who had been Rafael Gutiérrez Moreno's fellow-cacique and life-long rival. Téllez turned out to be a bouncy, loquacious man, who clammed up only when he was questioned about the practical aspects of his business—how much he pays and how he weighs the pickers' merchandise. (Some time ago, Rosalinda Losada revealed in an article the unsurprising fact that the scales he uses are fixed.) He shook hands amiably and chatted about the nice new dump facilities. Standing next to him, and looking steadfastly in the opposite direction, was Luis Rojas. He wore a torn pink-and-green polo shirt, with a heavy gold chain around his neck and a few diamond rings on his fingers. He was uncomfortable talking in the presence of Téllez, with whom he was apparently not on speaking terms, but he did loosen up enough to describe the truck drivers' unfair scavenging advantage and Bigtooth's betrayal by El Líder's former wife. And as we left he made a little goodbye speech, saying that he had been pleased to see us, particularly since this visit represented yet another instance of cooperation between city officials and the pickers. "Because if that cooperation ceased to exist," he went on, "there's no way you could have got past the entry gate." The city's top sanitation technicians, who just moments ago had been so full of talk about sweepable surfaces and pickerless landfills, now nodded and smiled gently. A barrel-chested thug was proclaiming that they were at his mercy, and they stood there and took it, because he was right.

The true extent of the garbage lobby's power, which enables it to pervert official goals, was only too evident at our earlier stop, which represents Urban Services' most ambitious attempt at change: the vast new landfill is supposed to take over in five or six years as the city's only dump site. Although scavenging there is strictly forbidden, no alternative arrangement exists for making the site economically viable through an industrialized recycling operation. "We didn't really have time to put one in," a site engineer explained apologetically. "In reality, we decided to open this site very quickly to give ourselves some kind of negotiating leverage with Rafael Gutiérrez Moreno, who was getting a little out of hand. Once he saw this site, and understood that we were planning to do without him, he became more manageable."

"The fact is that there are two or three things you can't mess with in Mexico City," a city official remarked to me reflectively. Young, Harvard educated, and as clean cut a representative of the PRI's new whiz kids as can be found, he nevertheless seemed to have taken a crash course in pragmatics. "You can't touch the metro, the deep-drainage system, or garbage. Because, for better or worse, those things work, and the proof is that in this city which is built on a lake, we've never suffered a major flood. But can you imagine what would happen if the sewer-system workers went on strike? It's the same thing with garbage. All things considered—that this is a third world city in the middle of a financial crisis, that there are sixteen million people throwing tons of trash away every day—this is a clean city. But what would happen the day the garbage pickers shut down the dumps on us? Or if the truck drivers, most of whom have family ties to the pickers, went on strike? And you can't just solve the problem by removing the leaders; you have to find a way to replace them, or you'll have people killing each other just to get their own little garbage concession. We have to change things slowly, with the people we have."

Sometime in the not too distant future, if the Mexican economy improves, if desperate communities of scavengers cease to rise on the fringes of Mexico's cities, if the PRI relaxes its hold on power, the pepenadores and their rulers will vanish as one of the most shameful blemishes of this society. In the meantime, Mexico City's garbage *líderes* have played old-time PRI politics in masterly fashion, not only to ward off the unemployment that poses a threat when any significant modernization of the waste-disposal system is undertaken but also to obtain benefits for their constituencies which the garbage pickers at Ciudad Nezahualcóyotl's Bordo dump—or at dumps in Bogotá or Santiago de Chile, for that matter—cannot yet dream of. A city official who was privy to all the talks between Urban Services and Gutiérrez Moreno and Téllez once told me that Téllez built his power base in city politics by playing good guy to the intractable Gutiérrez Moreno. While El Líder's people protested the move from the old Santa Fé dump nearby to the new Prados by setting fire to government property, Téllez decided to make a deal. Out of that negotiation came what is now the pride of the Urban Services Department: a *colonia*, or residential neighborhood, for some five hundred pickers and their families, just across the street from the dump. It has a kindergarten, a grade school, a market, and houses with electricity and running water, all of which are shared by Téllez's people and Bigtooth's people.

As we wandered through the immaculate stands of the colonia's new market, admiring the produce and taking in the smell of freshly cooked tortillas at a stand operated by two former pickers, an Urban Services dump-site manager was obviously filled with pride. He had been involved in the move to the new housing compound from the beginning, he said, and he still couldn't get over the fact that at first the pickers had refused to move in, preferring to sleep in their old hovels and use the new houses as storage rooms. "Then they moved in and started scavenging the houses," he went on. "They unscrewed everything that was removable and sold it. They used the toilets to wash clothes in. We decided to bring in a team of social workers, and they helped the women adjust. They taught them things like home management, personal hygiene, and how plumbing works. One day, we noticed that the families had actually begun to settle in, and several of them had even bought real furniture to set up housekeeping with." The grade school and kindergarten are now at least partly occupied, though Luis Rojas is ambivalent about the dump's new restrictions on child labor. "I suppose my children will do something different," he said, when I asked if he thought there would be a fourth generation of pepenadores in his family. "Because, thanks to the gentlemen you see here"—he pointed to the Urban Services officials—"our children under the age of ten are no longer allowed to come in to work with us."

The brand-new colonia is the Mexican system at its old-time patrimonial best and also at its most typically inefficient: the investment to build it was not small, but when the dump reaches the scheduled end of its useful life, in two or three years, the housing complex will probably become obsolete. This seemed a quibble, though, on a recent sunny morning when I stood with María de la Luz López in the living room of her two-bedroom house and watched her point proudly to her kitchen, her bathroom, and her dining room, with its matched furniture and hard, dry cement floor. Her two small children were watching television peacefully, and a washing machine was giving off a comforting hum. She was born in a garbage dump twenty-one years ago, she said, and what she remembered most about the nineteen years she spent there was the older women's horror whenever rats climbed through the rubbish into the huts to bite the babies' cheeks and fingers. Now she hoped that her own children might study through ninth grade, and she was happy to stay home and take care of them, because her husband earned enough at the dump for all of them to get by on. "This house is very solid," she said when I asked what she thought its chief merit was. "It doesn't collapse." She waved goodbye to me from the doorway, next to riotously blooming geraniums that an Urban Services social worker had shown her how to plant, and I remembered a rather long lunch with the sociologist Héctor Castillo when he had said that the obsessive question for him was whom to blame for all the garbage pickers' misery. In the bright light of Mrs. López's home, an even more disturbing question arose: whom to thank for her new surroundings? Among the ghosts rising up to take a bow stood El Líder.

SEMEFO

The Morgue

CUAUHTÉMOC MEDINA

Organs trade

One day in the spring of 2000 the corpse of a young punk arrived at the morgue in Mexico City, another casualty in the endless war of drug trafficking and gangsterism that pervades the slums of the biggest megalopolis in the Western Hemisphere. Peacefully resting on the stainless steel examination table of the mortuary, the man's slender body told a story of deprivation and defiance. This heroin addict—heroin has recently displaced other substances as the Mexican underworld's drug of choice—had tattoos covering most of his body and carried a wide array of piercings. Despite their fashionable dissemination in mainstream society, these forms of "ornamental disfigurement" amount to an "honorable degradation" that conveys the person's resentment of the social or metaphysical order.[1]

We all know that—despite popular beliefs—death is not egalitarian. Social taxonomies are reinscribed not only in the cause of death but also in the fate of our remains, the quality of our funerary rites and

monuments, and the amount of public attention generated by our disappearance. So despite the fact that the punk's body had been officially
identified and claimed by his family, it risked suffering the ultimate ex-
clusion: being disposed of in a common grave or, worse, ending up as a
specimen in a medical school's amphitheater to be stripped of its carnal
properties. Not only had the dead man been denied education, social
security, a satisfactory job, or any semblance of a future, but his remains
were condemned to bureaucratic oblivion because his mother could not
afford to buy him even a modest coffin for burial or cremation. This, of
course, made the man's passage through a postmortem examination
even more absurd. In a country where over 90 percent of crimes are
never solved due to the inefficiency and corruption of the judiciary
system, most—including this young man's murder—go unpunished.[2]
Why conduct an autopsy if it will not lead to prosecuting his killers and
is not needed for legal identification?

The man's inert beauty and his terrible case caught the attention
of Teresa Margolles, leader of SEMEFO, an artist's collective that took
as its name the acronym for Servicio Médico Forense [Forensic Medical Service], as Mexico City's morgue is known.[3] For over a decade,
SEMEFO has devoted its art to exploring the aesthetics of death—or
more precisely, what its members called "the 'life' of the corpse," the
transformations undergone by the body after death.[4] Without hesitation, Margolles came up with a daunting proposal. She was ready to
offer the mother a casket to bury her son in exchange for a section of
his corpse, which she would then exhibit as a "ready-made." Margolles
hinted that she would like to acquire the man's tongue or penis, because
both had piercings and, therefore, metaphorically "spoke" about his defiance of the social norms. Those body parts would convey his claims of
marginal and global contemporaneity, his subcultural identity.

It would certainly be easy to suggest that both tongue and penis are
exchangeable sexual organs, and that in bargaining for them Margolles
implicitly pointed to the symbolic castration implied in the killing and
silencing of the young man. But her offer did not seem to offend the
man's relatives and friends, who, forced by circumstance and their belief that they were in some way commemorating the deceased, agreed to
exchange his tongue for a metal coffin. This, to be honest, was a pretty
good deal for Margolles: she already owned not one but two caskets,
which she had previously purchased in order to discreetly retrieve from

the morgue a series of body casts for a previous sculpture, *Catafalco* (1997).[5] Ironically, the casket made two trips in and out of the morgue: first, to smuggle "works of art" in a blatant infringement of the law, and later, as party to an ethically uncomfortable bartering that yielded a body part to be shown as contemporary art. After being forensically preserved, *Tongue* was displayed in three different exhibition sites in 2001. It was first exhibited at La Panadería, an artist-run space in Mexico City, before being shipped to ACE Gallery in Los Angeles and making it across the border in an overnight courier service. Finally, it was included, as one of the main works, in the poorly curated and "official" historical overview of contemporary Mexican sculpture at the Palace of Fine Arts in downtown Mexico City.[6]

The symbolic route traveled by this tongue was certainly bizarre: from the deprived margins of the megalopolis, to a fancy gallery in the United States, to one of the most pretentious government buildings on the continent (an affected French-style neo-baroque opera house that was the fantasy object of the Mexican aristocracy of the 1900s). To make things even more extraordinary, since the 1920s the Palace of Fine Arts has been the funeral parlor of choice for artists and intellectuals (Diego Rivera, Frida Kahlo, Octavio Paz, and Cantinflas, among others). The Mexican State pays homage to its national icons in this site. All this adds up to much more than a perverse example of Duchamp's legacy; here is a situation where contemporary art becomes a social anomaly, traversing class, cultural, national, and institutional divides. So if this particular "artwork" by no means tried to challenge the objective conditions of injustice implied in its making, it might provide us with a useful vantage point to discuss contemporary art in Mexico at the end of the millennium.

From Necrophilia to Necropolitics

From its origins in 1990 to the time of its first solo show in 1994, SEMEFO was above all a death-metal rock band and an underground performance group that staged gruesome actions featuring pools of mud, blood stains, and dead animals. Those actions (partly inspired by the Viennese Actionists and the Catalonian theater group *La Fura dels Baus*) were rough explorations of the relations among impurity,

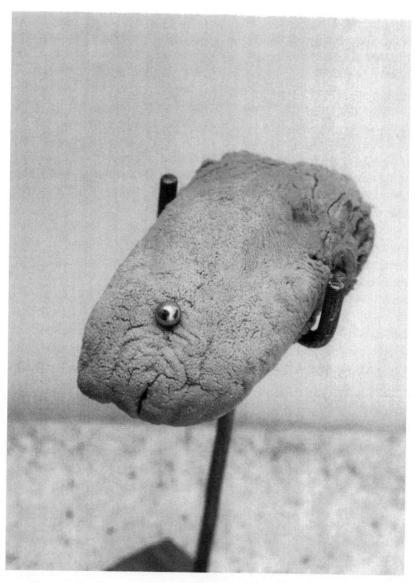

Teresa Margolles, *Lengua* (Tongue, 2000). Human tongue with piercing. Courtesy Galería Enrique Guerrero, Mexico City.

desire, and abjection that were not entirely foreign to a romantic pursuit of transcendence.[7] Much like Victor Frankenstein, the members of SEMEFO were convinced that they could extricate the essence of life by observing the decomposition of corpses. They assumed that there was a fundamental continuity between inert matter and living flesh, and participated in the underground worldview which sees violence, eroticism, and vitality as interchangeable natural forces.[8] Soon, SEMEFO moved from small performance circles into the art world. In 1994, the group had its first solo show in a museum (and what a museum—Mexico City's Carrillo Gil!) for which they created provocative sculptures of dead horses.[9] In a certain way, SEMEFO imploded the stereotype of Mexico's purported kinship with death by taking it to an extreme interpretation. At the same time, the group used the metaphor of "the life of the corpse" to establish a bizarre dialogue with contemporary art.

In the mid 1990s, SEMEFO began appropriating conceptual strategies, applying them to human remains, almost as if the group sought to revise art history from a necrophilic perspective. In 1996, for instance, the group used blood to make imprints of corpses on sheets taken from ambulance stretchers (*Dermis*, 1995), as if mimicking Yves Klein's blue period *Anthropometries* (1960–61).[10] Influenced by process art, they made installations with bodily fluids and exhibited containers taken from the morgue that evoked human remains as if they carried their aura. They also employed indexical methods, like making casts from corpses, or displaying "found" clothes taken from the bodies of children killed by cars.[11] As if questioning the legitimacy of traditional painting, in 1997 they collected tattoos on human skin from the arms of several subjects and later hung them on the walls of Mexico City's Art and Idea Gallery.

Teresa Margolles infused this multilayered practice with references to the many authors who have explored the meaning of death through modernity, including Georges Bataille, Philippe Ariès, Antonin Artaud, and William Burroughs.[12] But aside from the group's theoretical, literary, or thematic underpinnings, it is clear that SEMEFO, like most of its contemporaries, is concerned with the genealogy of contemporary art in the metropolis. Despite their gory inclinations, they have systematically dissected the corpse of conceptualism and minimalism, adjusting such traditions to the third world's dark social setting. Despite the progressive exodus of most of the group's founding members, in the late

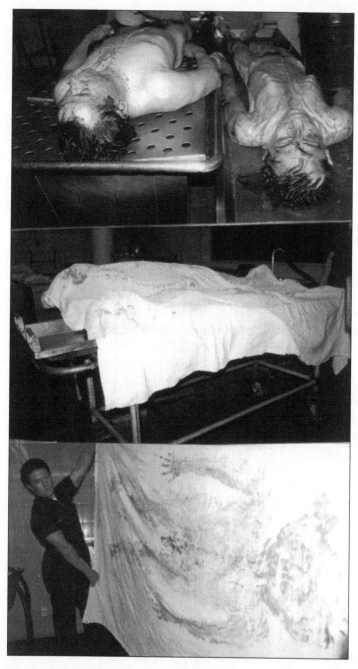

Teresa Margolles, *Dermis* (1995). Imprints of corpses on hospital sheets.
Courtesy Galería Enrique Guerrero, Mexico City.

1990s Margolles continued making works with human remains, turning the morgue into her atelier. She befriended forensic workers and assimilated not only their techniques but also their devotion for a job deemed unfathomable by most people. The morgue became a scenario for her photographs, a self-replenishing warehouse of props and raw matter for performances, ready-mades and installations, and, in a wider sense, a laboratory for political interventions in the social realm.

At this point, Margolles's work entered another phase. The decadent undertones of SEMEFO's early aesthetic faded away as her work became more rigorous and gained a political significance that the group had outspokenly avoided.[13] Her transition to the political was also forced by wider historical circumstances. Beyond its gothic undertones, the morgue is a space that falls in between Michel Foucault's "heterotopias of deviation" (prisons, rest homes, psychiatric hospitals) and the cemetery as archival representation of the modern city.[14] In Margolles's work the morgue became an institution that combined a space of seclusion, a scientific laboratory, and a gruesome archive. Being the destination of all those who supposedly should not have died (those who perished in violent circumstances or whose disease was abnormal enough to merit scientific elucidation), the dissection room provides a dramatic sample of any society.

Although normally hidden from the eyes of the wider public, in the turbulent context of Mexico, the morgue became a showcase for the brutality of the social crisis of the late 1990s. As the PRI's seven-decade-long regime came to an end, there was a dramatic upsurge in criminality, corruption, and violence that disrupted the fiction of Mexico's development and broke down the patriarchal halo enveloping governmental authorities. As writer and historian Federico Navarrete has explained, mass killings and political assassinations turned the morgue into one of the main spaces of representation of this nation: "It is not an exaggeration to state that in Mexico the morgue has come to be at the center of the public arena. . . . Through television, we became witnesses of the beginnings of a civil war in 1994, with its respective massacres and executions, and a few months later we saw presidential candidate Luis Donaldo Colosio's skull pierced by a bullet; in 1996 and 1997, we beheld the bodies of the legions massacred at Aguas Blancas and Acteal, and in 1997 we watched the decomposing remains of drug lord Amado Carrillo's alleged body for several days."[15] In that context, SEMEFO's necrophilia took on a political relevance of its own. In the late 1990s, Margolles created ritual actions that went beyond simply defying social decorum, and started to address the accumulation of bodies in forensic laboratories directly resulting from social and political violence. Therefore, the pursuit of shock was replaced by the invention of conceptual forms of mourning, which were not only subtler but in fact more attuned to contemplative reflection than to the transgressive mood of urban subcultures.[16]

In August 1999, Margolles traveled to Colombia for an artists-in-residence program. In Cali, she organized *Andén*, a collective ritual performance for which she collected and buried objects in a cement sidewalk as tokens for people who disappeared in Colombia's civil war.[17] Months later, Margolles produced *Bathing the Baby*, a videotaped performance in which she tenderly bathed a fetus, which had been donated by a friend who suffered a miscarriage and could not afford the cost of burial. Margolles later buried the fetus in a white cement block that was displayed in a gallery (*Burial*, 1999), making the child's grave read like a visual pun on minimalist sculpture. Eventually the cement block began to crack from inside, defying the hygienic and industrial looks of minimalism.[18] She also presented a performance—in Colombia and Mexico—in which she distributed plastic cards with photographs of people murdered in the drug trade. The cards were symbolically offered as tools to cocaine addicts so they could "cut" their lines of cocaine while consuming the violence generated by their habit. In all of these works, Margolles infiltrated images or residues of corpses as a sociological strategy that emphasized the life and death circle involved in the current Latin American crisis. In the most surreptitious of these actions, Margolles smuggled human fat (taken from a Mexican morgue) into Cuba to create an installation at the Seventh Havana Biennial in November 2000. She clandestinely smeared the fat over the walls of several public buildings in Havana to metonymically comment on the political and economic Cuban disaster.[19]

Periodicity in the Periphery

In light of these actions, the silent brutality of *Tongue* appears not as a raw opportunistic provocation but as the culmination of a process of conceptual refinement. At a time when the right to represent others is

Teresa Margolles, *Burial* (1999). Fetus buried in concrete block. Installation view, South London Gallery. Courtesy Galería Enrique Guerrero, Mexico City.

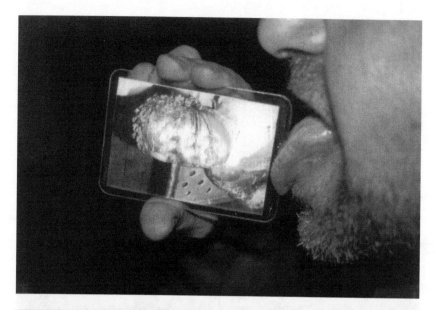

Above and right: Teresa Margolles, *Tarjetas para picar cocaina* (Cards for cutting cocaine, 1997). Cards with photographs of murdered drug traffickers. Courtesy Galería Enrique Guerrero, Mexico City.

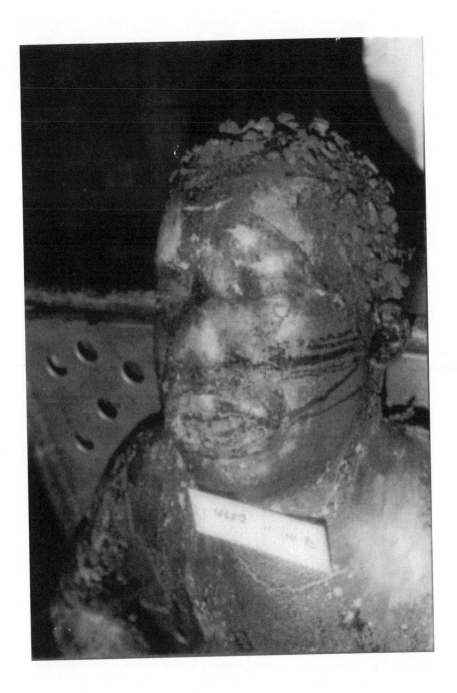

under fire—from the pilfering of archaeological artifacts by museums to the circulation of photographs in the public realm—Margolles's work defies the provisional ethics of artistic practice. But it remains true that her work provokes little or no scandal in Mexico, a fact that only the naive would blame on some kind of cultural relativism, say, the "differences of attitude in Mexican culture regarding the sanctity of remains."[20] On the one hand, Margolles's terrible images are not so hard to stomach in a society used to an overdose of true crime stories and extremely graphic police magazines.[21] Beyond that, it would also be a mistake to see their underground origins and their low profile in the art market as indicative of SEMEFO's purportedly "marginal" position in the local art world.[22] It is quite the contrary. Along its history, SEMEFO has had remarkable acceptance among Mexico City's art institutions, audiences, curators, and critics, who have granted the group exhibitions in state museums, and even helped to establish it as part of official and unofficial Mexican art envoys to other countries. It would not be an exaggeration to claim that Teresa Margolles is, by her own merit, part of the emergent local canon. Contrary to hypocritical reviewers pretending to be morally intimidated by her "objets d'art" for exploiting brutal economic disparities, *Tongue* ought to be taken as a barometer of the situation of contemporary art in Mexico.[23]

In fact, the three phases through which SEMEFO and Margolles's work moved in the last ten years could be abstracted as a provisory schema for the stages of contemporary art in Mexico during the 1990s. Breaking almost completely with the dominant conservative trends of local art since the 1950s, Mexican artists embarked in a remarkable, although difficult, transformation of their aesthetic attitudes.[24] Unlike other countries in the periphery, Mexico started out with an institutionally developed local art world equipped with uneven but nonetheless powerful museums, a local circuit of art critics with a strong presence in the media, a monolithic national art historical narrative actively supported by international and local exhibition programs, and a terribly conservative artistic educational system that discouraged experimentation and innovation. Under pressure from these forces, Mexican artists, critics, and curators in the early 1990s—unlike their counterparts in Cuba, Venezuela, or Brazil—were not eager to get involved in the first postcolonial/postmodern wave of global art. Instead, they were interested in provoking local debates around the critique (or satire) of the state-controlled national narratives, exploring methodologies that would challenge the legitimacy of traditional media, and establishing alternative art centers aimed at their own self-education through experimental art making, curating, and writing.[25] As in the case of SEMEFO, a good deal of these exercises resulted in establishing a critical dialogue with the mainstream history of minimal and conceptual art. This was a process of artistic education that compensated for Mexico's anachronistic art schools—still attached to traditional practices—and soon led local participants to creatively mobilize the social and cultural paradoxes governing a city situated on the front line of the recent expansion of global capitalism.

In the 1990s many artists abandoned the tired modesty that characterized Mexican art in earlier decades to address—poetically and sometimes cynically—the social and cultural contradictions that surrounded them. They turned their original "expressive" and "lyrical" concerns into tools for political and aesthetic investigation. This transformation was in part sparked by the forces of globalization—for if the pressures for artistic change in the early 1990s came from dialogues with a globalized world, the social and political crisis that authoritarian modernization and economic integration produced in Mexico between 1994 and 1995 also radicalized artistic practices. Mexico's entrance into the global economy and its agitated "transition to democracy" were dominated by clashes between global market forces and local Indian communities, the widening of social differences between new tycoons and impoverished masses, and cultural contradictions deriving from the crumbling nationalist, modernizing ideology of the postrevolutionary regime. Its artists represented the country's crisis with boldness.

Perhaps this helps explain the belated appearance of Mexican contemporary art in the global arena. For new art in Mexico could be, at the same time, locally marginal and globally integrated: it critiqued Mexico's modernization, broke with the local pre-1980s canon, and thus could never embody the local elite's celebration of Mexico's modernity.[26] But because of its relative institutionalization, the local art scene did not conform to the multiculturalist expectations of the early 1990s, which assumed that the periphery was to produce a hybrid brand of postmodern culture resulting from the adjustment of vernacular and "non-Western traditions" to mainstream practices. By the year 2000, those same local political interventions, infused with conceptual dexterity but retaining an amateurish look, had gained global currency and managed to create poetical and political tensions within postconceptual practices.

Seen in this framework, SEMEFO is not a marginal phenomenon, but one that is paradigmatic of the overall move from amateurish dissidence to postconceptual self-reflectivity that characterized Mexico's aesthetic politicization in the 1990s. If not necessarily in the same order, most of the artists of SEMEFO's generation moved through these same phases.

Redefining Transgression

Under close inspection, the most disturbing element in Teresa Margolles's forensic art is not the horrific nature of the images and objects she creates but the institutional conditions which make them possible. Works like *Tongue* evoke the negligent conditions that govern the handling of human remains in Mexican forensic practices and, by extension, the institutional crisis of the judiciary system. From one of its earliest pieces—produced for a 1991 salon for young artists—consisting of a coffin that looked as if it had just been unearthed, to more recent works made with human entrails (for instance, a sofa upholstered with human viscera), SEMEFO has transgressed more than sanitary rules. For an artist like Margolles to scavenge through the morgue, taking photographs, collecting samples, making imprints or plaster casts of corpses, there needs to be an extremely permissive administration. Her art owes its existence to Mexico's laxity. Her works are both a candid exposure of the corrupt Mexican state and a product of her complicity with that same system.[27]

The fact that for several years Mexican cultural institutions have actively promoted her art demonstrates that Margolles has managed to slip through a legal and political loophole. It would be impossible to question her methods without also denouncing the idiosyncratic standards of the morgue and of the cultural apparatus. In that sense, the importance of Margolles's work resides less in its transgressive character than in its exposure of a crumbling rule of law. Margolles's art occupies a space of tolerance that is marked by negligence and institutional complicity.

This symbolic gap, of course, is not Margolles's exclusive territory. In November 2000 another artist, Francis Alÿs, bought a 9 mm Beretta on the black market. He loaded the handgun and carried it in his right hand for all to see during a stroll through Mexico City's downtown. Following at a convenient distance, Rafael Ortega videotaped this act—by far the most dangerous action the Belgian-born artist has performed to date. Alÿs walked completely unnoticed for almost twelve minutes before a police car finally pulled over and arrested him. It would seem that the fact that somebody is carrying a weapon in broad daylight is not enough reason to disturb the life of the metropolis: a man flaunting a lethal weapon can walk for blocks in a densely populated area without being noticed. Alÿs later reenacted the whole scene for the camera, aided by the same policemen who had arrested him, in order to create a comparison between the initial action and its conceptual reenactment for documentation purposes. It seems to me that this work, *Reenactments* (2000), would have been impossible to produce in almost any other place in the world. Had Alÿs staged this piece in Los Angeles or New York, he would have been arrested and probably shot to death. Only in Mexico would the public allow a man to walk busy streets with a gun for more than ten minutes; only in Mexico could an artist make simple arrangements with police commanders for his own release; only in Mexico would a suspect receive help from his own captors.[28] The whole action and its documentation attests to the laxness of the security forces in Mexico City, and proves how easy it is for artists to take advantage of their historical situation.

In many ways, the zone of tolerance mapped by these works describes the territory in which Mexican contemporary art operates. The radicalism found in these pieces was made possible by the complete lack of interest shown by government and private institutions. And their radical departure from the general trends of local culture was made possible by the disdain professed by most established writers and intellectuals toward experimental art—a rejection that freed contemporary art from making compromises with the officially sanctioned ideology of national culture. Now, as the publication of this anthology demonstrates, historical neglect is coming to an end. But we cannot foresee how contemporary art practices in Mexico City will change once they are fully accepted globally and locally.

Notes

1. In his study of tattooing in Polynesia, anthropologist Alfred Gell argued that it was mistaken to draw a hard and fast divide between the original Polynesian values involved in skin ornamentation and those of westerners who

choose body mutilation as a means to challenge "civilized" tastes with their apparent "barbarization." In Polynesia tattooing imposed a barrier between humans and gods, reinforcing a "social skin" separating social and cosmological ranks. This symbolic function is not unlike the self-marginalization of those sailors, criminals, prostitutes, and gangs that assert their marginality through tattooing. These analogies are reinforced in the current epidemics of tattooing. Gell concludes: "Thus it does not seem wholly wrong to detect a degree of kinship between the assertive and at the same time paranoid excesses of tattooing in devolved Polynesian politics, and the oppositional element in subcultural tattooing which expresses in class terms a resentment which Polynesians directed not towards the dominant class, but towards the gods, the final arbiters of the human condition." Gell, *Wrapping in Images*, 8–20, 244–62, 296–315.

2. Statistics in this respect are obscure and contradictory. According to the newspaper *La Jornada*, 1.4 million crimes are reported every year. The police arrest suspects in 13 percent of them, but only 10 percent of those accused are sentenced by the courts. See Alberto Najar, "Inseguridad pública, de Zedillo a Fox: La terrible herencia y las primeras incongruencias," *La Jornada*, August 13, 2000. According to a well-publicized report in 2000, more than 95 percent of crimes remain unpunished in Mexico. Guillermo Velasco Arzac et al., Propuesta para el Plan de Gobierno Federal 2000–2006. La Seguridad Publica y El Sistema de Justicia Penal en México," (Mexico City, México Unido conrta la Delincuencia A.C., 2000), n.p.

3. In addition to Margolles, the group included Arturo Angulo and Carlos López. Earlier SEMEFO members included Juan Manuel Pernás, Juan Luis García Zavaleta, Victor Basurto, Antonio Macedo, Aníbal Peñuelas, and Mónica Salcido. Margolles has been the only member to participate as an individual in exhibitions and art events.

4. See the interview with SEMEFO in Dulce María de Alvarado Chaparro, "Performance en México," 321.

5. In fact, she had recently decided to donate the caskets to a nursing home.

6. See the exhibition catalogue *Escultura Mexicana: de la Academia a la instalación* (Mexico City: Conaculta-INBA-Landucci Editores, 2000). Margolles's *Tongue* is reproduced on page 375.

7. A 1993 interview by Renato González Mello includes descriptions of SEMEFO's actions. See Alvarado, "Performance en México," 327–33.

8. I am alluding to an interpretation of Sade and Frankenstein in a work that SEMEFO used frequently as a reference source for its early works: Ariès, *Hour of Our Death*.

9. The exhibition, *Lavatio Corporis*, opened at the Carrillo Gil Museum in Mexico City in May 1994. Inspired by José Clemente Orozco's *Teules IV* (1947),

in which a dead horse lying on a pile of rubble represents the conquest of Mexico, SEMEFO produced a series of "sculptures" consisting of dead horses attached to metal structures, animals cut in slices and preserved in acrylic blocks, and even a carousel made of unborn horse fetuses. (See the catalog *Lavatio Corporis* [Mexico City: National Institute of Fine Arts, 1994].) The museum also produced *SEMEFO* (1994), a sixteen-minute video about the group directed by Elías Levin. I would like to thank Museo Carrillo Gil for granting access to its library and to materials related to this exhibition.

10. Those works were exhibited in two independent spaces that were major forces in the alternative art scene: La Panadería in Mexico and El Ojo Atómico in Madrid, Spain, some of whose members (such as Tomás Ruiz-Rivas and Santiago Sierra) migrated to Mexico City in the late 1990s.

11. Included in *Así está la cosa*, the Latin American contemporary art survey curated by Kurt Hollander in 1997 for Mexico City's Centro Cultural Arte Contemporáneo.

12. For a long time Margolles made her living selling books to students and professors outside the National University's School of Humanities. Through her work, she acquired a remarkable erudition in contemporary philosophy, radical literature, and cultural studies.

13. In their early interviews, the members of SEMEFO adamantly denied that their work had any political motivations. They argued that political interpretations of their work were symptoms of the audience's denial of its taste for morbid scenes. See interview by Renato Gonzalez Mello in Alvarado Chaparro, "Performance en México," 331.

14. Michel Foucault, "Different Spaces," in *Aesthetics, Method, and Epistemology*, ed. James D. Faubion, vol. 2 of *Essential Works of Foucault, 1954–1984* (New York: New Press, 1998), 175–85.

15. Navarrete, "Semefo," 24.

16. This aspect of SEMEFO's practice was studied by Elia Espinosa in "Las aboliciones de Semefo."

17. Margolles organized this performance as part of the artist-in-residence program funded by Colombia's Cultural Ministry and the Mexican National Fund for Culture and the Arts.

18. For a discussion of other works in Mexico that used the social and aesthetic conditions of the third world to challenge minimalist aesthetics, see Cuauhtémoc Medina, "Recent Political Forms: Radical Pursuits in Mexico: Santiago Sierra, Francis Alÿs, Minerva Cuevas," *TRANS>arts.cultures.media* 8 (2000): 146–63.

19. The performance was part of Extramuros, an independent exhibition of Mexican artists curated by Taiyana Pimientel during the first week of the Havana Biennial. Margolles was almost arrested by Cuban police who found her performance suspicious, but was immediately freed when the police found

she was a foreigner (and no doubt because her action was too opaque for the police to understand).

20. Doug Harvey, "Yuck! Tongue and Blood at ACE Gallery Plus Adrian Piper at MOCA," *Los Angeles Weekly*, September 1, 2000.

21. On *Alarma!*, the most famous of these tabloids, see Cuauhtémoc Medina, "Alarma! Crimen y circulación," *Poliester* 2, no. 6 (Summer 1993): 18–27.

22. I disagree entirely with Federico Navarrete when he argues: "Proof of its marginal character is the fact that, after almost ten years of work, SEMEFO has only sold a single work, as their materials and subject matter impede the merchandising of their work." Navarrete, "SEMEFO."

23. "I'm not particularly shocked by the aestheticization of leftover body parts. But the queasy politics of the negotiation that brings a poor Mexican child's pickled organ into a rich, white, home-decoration showroom is . . . difficult." Harvey, "Yuck!"

24. A critical history of the moments of aesthetic radicalism in the period, from Alfredo Jodorowsky's "panic" aesthetics to the slightly overrated 1970s "grupos" collectives, remains to be written.

25. On this point, see Osvaldo Sánchez, "El cuerpo de la nación. El neomexicanismo: la pulsión homosexual y la desnacionalización," *Curare* 17 (May–June 2001): 137–46. Also Cuauhtémoc Medina, "Irony, Barbary, Sacrilege," in *Distant Relations: Chicano, Irish, Mexican Art and Critical Writing*, ed. Trisha Ziff (Santa Monica: Smart Art Press, 1995), 89–101.

26. In my view, this is the thread connecting Mexico City's various artist-run spaces of the early 1990s: Temístocles (1991–94), La Panadería (1994 to date), and Curare (1991 to date).

27. Responding to an e-mail query on May 25, 2001, Margolles argued that her practice is protected by a Mexican law allowing organ donations from a corpse on the condition that no sale is involved.

28. Gun ownership is technically forbidden in Mexico, except for 22 mm guns, which can be purchased with special permits. In normal circumstances Alÿs should have been imprisoned for carrying a Beretta . . . unless he bribed the policemen who caught him! The trade in illegal weapons has surged in Mexico in recent years.

Bibliography

Alvarado Chaparro, Dulce María de. "Performance en México (historia y desarrollo)." Licenciatura thesis, Escuela Nacional de Artes Plásticas, Universidad Nacional Autónoma de México, 2000.

Alvarado Tezozómoc, Fernando. *Crónica mexicáyotl.* Mexico City: Universidad Nacional Autónoma de México, 1998.

Ariès, Phillipe. *The Hour of Our Death.* Translated by Helen Weaver. New York: Oxford University Press, 1991.

Arlt, Roberto. *Los lanzallamas.* Buenos Aires: Compañía General Fabril Editora, 1968.

Balbuena, Bernardo de. *Grandeza mexicana.* Mexico City: Editorial Porrúa, 1980.

Berman, Marshall. *All That Is Solid Melts into Air.* New York: Penguin Books, 1982.

Calvino, Italo. *Invisible Cities.* Translated by William Weaver. New York: Harcourt, 1974.

Carballo, Emmanuel, and Martínez, José Luis, eds. *Páginas sobre la Ciudad de México: 1469–1987.* Mexico City: Consejo de la Crónica de la Ciudad de México, 1988.

Cervantes de Salazar, Francisco. *México en 1554: tres diálogos latinos.* Mexico City: Universidad Nacional Autónoma de México, 1939. Translated as *Life in the Imperial and Loyal City of Mexico in New Spain, and the Royal and Pontifical University of Mexico: as Described in the Dialogues for the Study of the Latin Language* by Minnie Lee Barrett Shepard et al. Austin: University of Texas Press, 1954.

Corona, Ignacio, and Jörgensen, Beth E., eds. *The Contemporsry Mexican Chronicle: Theoretical Perspectives on the Liminal Genre.* Albany: State University of New York Press, 2002.

Cortés, Hernán. *Cartas de relación.* Edited by Mario Hernández. Madrid:

Historia 16, 1985. Translated as *Letters from Mexico* by Anthony Padgen. New Haven: Yale University Press, 1986.

Cuéllar Vázquez, Angélica. *La noche es de ustedes, el amanecer es nuestro: Asamblea de Barrios y Superbarrio Gómez en la Ciudad de México.* Mexico City: Universidad Nacional Autónoma de México, 1993.

Díaz del Castillo, Bernal. *Historia verdadera de la conquista de la Nueva España,* ed. Joaquín Ramírez Cabañas. Mexico City: Editorial Porrúa, 1964.

————. *The Discovery and Conquest of México, 1517–1521.* Translated by A. P. Maudslay. New York: Farrar, Straus, and Cudahy, 1956.

Espinosa, Elia. "Las aboliciones de Semefo," *La Abolición del Arte. XXI Coloquio Internacional de Historia del Arte.* Edited by Alberto Dallal. Mexico City: Instituto de Investigaciones Estéticas, Universidad Nacional Autónoma de México, 1998.

Florescano, Enrique. "Mitos mesoamericanos: hacia un enfoque histórico." *Vuelta* 207 (February 1994): 25–35.

García Canclini, Néstor. *La ciudad de los viajeros: travesías e imaginarios urbanos.* Mexico City: Grijalbo, 1996.

————. *Cultura y comunicación en la Ciudad de México.* Vol. 1, *Modernidad y multiculturalidad en la Ciudad de México a fin de siglo.* Mexico City: Grijalbo, 1998.

————. *Cultura y comunicación en la Ciudad de México.* Vol. 2, *La ciudad y los ciudadanos imaginados por los medios.* Mexico City: Grijalbo, 1998.

Garibay K., Ángel María. *Poesía indígena de la altiplanicie.* Mexico City: Universidad Nacional Autónoma de México, 1962.

Gell, Alfred. *Wrapping in Images: Tattooing in Polynesia.* Oxford: Clarendon Press, 1993.

Groys, Boris. "U-Bahn als U-Topie." *Kursbuch* 112 (June 1993): 1–9.

Gruzinski, Serge. *Histoire de Mexico.* Paris: Fayard, 1996.

Gutiérrez Nájera, Manuel. *Poesías completas.* Mexico City: Editorial Porrúa, 1953.

Hubp, José Lugo. *La superficie de la tierra.* Mexico City: Secretaría de Educación Pública, Fondo de Cultura Económica, 1988.

Kandell, Jonathan. *La capital: The Biography of Mexico City.* New York: Random House, 1988.

Koolhaas, Rem. *S, M, L, XL.* New York: Monacelli Press, 1995.

Lezama Lima, José. "La curiosidad barroca." In *El reino de la imagen.* Caracas: Biblioteca Ayacucho, 1981.

Martínez, José Luis. *Nezahualcóyotl, vida y obra.* Mexico City: Fondo de Cultura Económica, 2000.

Monsiváis, Carlos. *Los rituales del caos.* Mexico City: Era, 1995.

Moravia, Alberto and Elkann, Alain. *Life of Moravia*. Translated by William Weaver. South Royalton, Vt.: Steerforth Italia, 2000.

Navarrete, Federico "SEMEFO," Poliester 8, no. 2 (Spring 2000): 24–31.

Novo, Salvador. *Nueva grandeza mexicana*. Mexico City: Ediciones Era, 1967.

Piglia, Ricardo. *La ciudad ausente*. Buenos Aires: Editorial Sudamericana, 1992.

Poniatowska, Elena. *La noche de Tlatelolco*. Mexico City: Ediciones Era, 1971. Translated by Helen R. Lane as *Massacre in Mexico*. New York: Viking, 1975.

Razo, Vicente. *The Official Museo Salinas Guide*. Santa Monica: Smart Art Press, 2002.

Sassen, Saskia, *The Global City*. Princeton: Princeton University Press, 2001.

Scherpe, Klaus R. *Die Unwirklichkeit der Städte: Grossstadtdarstellungen zwischen Moderne und Postmoderne*. Reinbek bei Hamburg: Rowohlt Taschenbuch Verlag, 1988.

Tovar de Teresa, Guillermo. *The City of Palaces: Chronicle of a Lost Heritage*. Mexico City: Vuelta, 1990. Translation of *La ciudad de los palacios: crónica de un patrimonio perdido*. Mexico City: Vuelta, 1990.

Vittorini, Elio. *Le Città del mondo*. Turin: Einaudi, 1969.

Contributors

RUBÉN GALLO has written articles about contemporary Mexican art and literature. His *New Tendencies in Mexican Art: The 1990s* will be published in 2004 by Palgrave. He teaches cultural studies and Latin American literature at Princeton University.

FRANCIS ALŸS, a Belgian artist, has lived in Mexico City since the 1980s. He has worked extensively with Mexican *rotulistas* (commercial sign painters) who produce multiple copies of his original, small-format paintings depicting surreal or absurd situations. He has had solo shows at Berlin's KunstWerke (2002), London's Lisson Gallery (2001), and New York's Jack Tilton Gallery (1997), and his work has been shown at the Venice Biennale (2001) and the Istanbul Biennial (1999).

JOSÉ JOAQUÍN BLANCO teaches literature at Mexico City's National Autonomous University. He has written extensively about Mexico City in his nonfiction books, which include *Función de medianoche* (Ediciones Era, 1981), *Cuando todas las chamacas se pusieron medias nylon* (Enjambre, 1987), *Los mexicanos se pintan solos* (Pórtico de la Ciudad de México, 1990), *Un chavo bien helado* (Ediciones Era, 1990), *Se visten novias* (Cal y Arena, 1992), and *Álbum de pesadillas mexicanas* (Ediciones Era, 2002).

GONZALO CELORIO, teaches literature at Mexico City's National Autonomous University and has published the novels *Amor propio* (Tusquets, 1992) and *Y retiemble en sus centros la tierra* (Tusquets, 1999). His nonfiction works include *El surrealismo y lo real maravilloso americano* (Secretaría de Educación Pública, 1976), *La épica sordina* (Cal y arena, 1990), *México, ciudad de papel* (Tusquets, 1997), and *Ensayo de contraconquista* (Tusquets, 2001). His book *El viaje sedentario* (Tusquets, 1994) received the Prix des deux Océans at Biarritz's International Festival.

JOSÉ DE LA COLINA edits the weekly *Suplemento cultural de Novedades*, one of Mexico City's most prestigious literary reviews. He was a regular contributor to *Vuelta*, the journal edited by Octavio Paz. His publications include the collections of short stories *Cuentos para vencer a la muerte* (Los presentes, 1955), *La lucha con la pantera* (Universidad Veracruzana, 1959), *Ven caballo gris y otras narraciones* (Universidad Veracruzana, 1959), and *Tren de historias* (Aldus, 1998); a book of film criticism, *Miradas al cine* (Secretaría de Educación Pública, 1972); a collection of interviews with Luis Buñuel, *Luis Buñuel: prohibido asomarse al interior* (Centro Nacional de las Artes, 1996); and a volume of literary essays, *Libertades imaginarias: la literatura como juego* (Aldus, 2001).

GERARDO DENIZ is the author of numerous books of essays, poems, and short stories, including *Adrede* (Joaquín Mortiz, 1970), *Gatuperio* (Fondo de Cultura Económica, 1978), *Enroque* (Fondo de Cultura Económica, 1986), *Picos pardos* (Vuelta, 1987), *Grosso modo* (Fondo de Cultura Económica, 1988), *Mundonuevos* (El Tucán de Virginia, 1991), *Alebrijes* (El Equilibrista, 1992), *Una ventana inmensa: antología poética* (Vuelta, 1993), *Ton y son* (Conaculta, 1996), *Anticuerpos* (Ediciones sin nombre, 1998), and *Fosa escéptica* (Ave del paraíso, 2002). *Poemas/poems*, a selection of his poetry translated by Mónica de la Torre, was published in 2000 by Lost Road Publishers.

LORNA SCOTT FOX is a critic, translator, and journalist who lived in Mexico City from 1987 to 1997. She is a regular contributor to the Spanish daily *El país* and the *London Review of Books*, and her essays have appeared in *Flash Art*, the *Guardian*, *Artes de México*, *Milenio*, and *ViceVersa*. She has lived in Seville, Spain, since 1997.

RICARDO GARIBAY wrote about popular culture in Mexico, from boxing to beach-going families. His complete works were published in 2002 by Editorial Océano, including *Diálogos mexicanos* (1975), *Acapulco* (1978), and *Las glorias del gran púas* (1978), his celebrated text about the boxer Rubén Olivares.

JULIETA GARCÍA GONZÁLEZ has worked as an editor for various cultural publications, including the journals *Origina* and *Etcétera*, and the Web site reforma.com. She is a frequent contributor to *El Ángel*, the weekly literary review published by *Reforma*, and her essays and articles have appeared in *Letras libres*, *Cambio*, *Reforma*, *El huevo*, *unomásuno*, *Milenio diario*, and *La Jornada*. Currently she serves on the editorial board of *Travesías*, a cultural journal.

ALMA GUILLERMOPRIETO is a frequent contributor to both the *New York Review of Books* and the *New Yorker*. Her book *Samba*, an account of the year she spent with the impoverished carnival-makers of Brazil, was nominated for a 1990 National Book Critics Circle award. *The Heart That Bleeds* and *Looking for History* are collections of her essays from the *New Yorker* and the *New York Review of Books*. In 1995 she was awarded a MacArthur Fellowship, and in 2001 she was elected an honorary foreign member of the American Academy of Arts and Sciences.

JONATHAN HERNÁNDEZ is a conceptual artist whose work explores the absurd that characterizes life in Mexico City. He studied at Mexico City's Escuela Nacional de Artes Plásticas, and has had solo exhibitions at Madrid's ARCO art fair, Berlin's Galerie im Parkhaus, and Galería Kurimanzutto, Mexico City. His work has been included in the group exhibitions *Mutations: la video mexicaine actuelle* (Toulouse), *Superficial* (Centro de la imagen, Mexico), *Metropolis mexica* (Musé de Picardie), and *An Exhibition about the Exchange Rates of Bodies and Values* (P.S.1, New York).

JORGE IBARGÜENGOITIA was a regular contributor to *Excélsior* in the 1970s, and he also wrote regularly for *Plural* and *Vuelta*. He published *La ley de Herodes* (Joaquín Mortíz, 1967), a collection of autobiographical short stories, and almost a dozen plays, including *El atentado* (Joaquín Mortíz, 1978), which was awarded the Casa de las Américas Prize in 1963. He died—along with Marta Traba, Ángel Rama, and Manuel Scorza—in a plane crash near Bogotá, Colombia, in 1983.

VICENTE LEÑERO has published essays, novels, and plays. His nonfiction works include *Los albañiles* (Seix Barral, 1964), *Estudio Q* (Joaquín Mortíz, 1965), *Redil de ovejas* (Joaquín Mortíz, 1973), *Los periodistas* (Joaquín Mortíz, 1978), and *El evangelio de Lucas Gavilán* (Seix Barral, 1979). His plays include *Pueblo rechazado* (Joaquín Mortíz, 1979), *El juicio* (Joaquín Mortíz, 1972), *La mudanza* (Editores Mexicanos Unidos, 1985), *Martirio de Morelos* (Seix Barral, 1981), and *Nadie sabe nada* (Departamento del Distrito Federal, 1994). He has been awarded numerous literary prizes, including Seix Barral's Biblioteca Breve Prize and Mexico's Xavier Villaurrutia Prize.

GUADALUPE LOAEZA has published numerous mock-ethnographic studies of Mexico's upper classes. Her books include *Las reinas de Polanco* (Cal y arena, 1989), *Las niñas bien* (Cal y arena, 1995), *Manual de la gente bien* (Plaza y Janés, 1995), *Compro, luego existo* (Alianza, 1992), and *Primero las damas* (Plaza y Janés, 1997).

FABRIZIO MEJÍA MADRID has published *Erótica Nacional* (Cal y arena, 1992), a novel, and two books of essays about Mexico City: *Pequeños actos de desobediencia civil* (Cal y arena, 1996) and *Entre las sábanas* (Cal y Arena, 1995). In 1994 he was awarded the Mont Blanc prize for cultural criticism. He was a regular contributor to the weekly *La Jornada Semanal,* and he now writes a weekly column for the journal *Proceso.* He also writes regularly for *Letras Libres, Gatopardo, Milenio,* and the Mexico City newspaper *Reforma.* He was part of the delegation of Mexican writers selected to attend Hannover's EXPO 2000, and in 2001 he took part in the Second Meeting of Spanish and Latin American Writers in Colombia. His text on Hotel de México was included in *ABCDF,* the visual dictionary of Mexico City.

CUAUHTÉMOC MEDINA is an art critic, curator, and historian. His publications include "A Ghostly Museum for a Vampirelike Figure/Un Museo Fantasmal para un Personaje Vampiresco," in *The Official Museo Salinas Guide,* edited by Vicente Razo (Smart Art Press, 2002); "Abuso mutuo/Mutual abuse," in *Mexico City: An Exhibition about the Exchange Rates of Bodies and Values,* edited by Klaus Biesenbach (P.S.1-Kunstwerke, 2002); and *Graciela Iturbide 55* (Phaidon Press, 2001). He writes regularly on contemporary art for *Reforma,* the Mexico City daily.

CARLOS MONSIVÁIS is Mexico's foremost cultural critic. He has written extensively about popular culture, nightlife, and pop music, as well as on literature and the history of Mexican film. His cultural analyses include *Amor perdido* (Ediciones Era, 1982), *Entrada libre* (Ediciones Era, 1987), and *Los rituals del caos* (Ediciones Era, 1995). He has also published a critical study of Salvador Novo titled *Salvador Novo: lo marginal en el centro* (Ediciones Era, 2000), and has written extensively on the Zapatista rebellion in Chiapas. *Mexican Postcards,* an anthology of his work, was published in English by Verso in 1997.

AUGUSTO MONTERROSO wrote short stories that were incisive and full of wit (including "The Dinosaur," the shortest story in literary history, consisting of only one line). His books include the novel *Lo demás es silencio: la vida y obra de Eduardo Torres* (Joaquín Mortíz, 1978); *Obras completas (y otros cuentos)* (Imprenta Universitaria, 1959); *La oveja negra y demás fábulas* (Joaquín Mortiz, 1969); *Movimiento perpetuo* (Joaquín Mortíz, 1972), a tribute to flies; and *La letra e: fragmentos de un diario* (Ediciones Era, 1987). With Bárbara Jacobs, he edited *Antología del cuento triste* (Santillana, 1997), an anthology of sad stories. Many of his stories have been translated into English, including *The Black Sheep and Other Fables* (Doubleday, 1971),

Complete Works and Other Stories (University of Texas Press, 1995). He was awarded the Xavier Villaurrutia Prize in 1975 and the Juan Rulfo Prize in 1996.

ELENA PONIATOWSKA has written extensively about the most important historical events of twentieth-century Mexico. Her works include *La noche de Tlatelolco* (Ediciones Era, 1971), a collection of testimonials of the 1968 student massacre, and *Nada, nadie: las voces del temblor* (Ediciones Era, 1988), an account of the devastation caused by the 1985 earthquake. She has also published *La flor de lis* (Ediciones Era, 1988), an autobiographical novel, and *Tinisima* (Ediciones Era, 1996), a fictionalized account of Tina Modotti's life.

DANIELA ROSSELL is an artist. Playing with the conventions of ethnographic photography, she has documented the lifestyles of Mexico's millionaire women in their habitats. *Rich and Famous*, a collection of her photographs, was published in 2002 by Turner. She has had solo exhibitions at Greene Naftali Gallery, New York; Galería OMR, Mexico City; and Kevin Burke Fine Arts, Miami. In 2002 her work was included in *Mexico City: An Exhibition about the Exchange Rates of Bodies and Values*, at the P.S.1 Contemporary Art Center, New York.

GUILLERMO SHERIDAN was a frequent contributor to *Vuelta*, the literary magazine edited by Octavio Paz, and he now writes for *Letras libres*. His works include the novel *El dedo de oro* (Alfaguara, 1996), a biography of the poet Ramón López Velarde titled *Un corazón adicto* (Fondo de Cultura Económica, 1989), and several collections of essays, including *Frontera norte y otros extremos* (Consejo Nacional de Recursos para la Atención de la Juventud, 1988), *Lugar a dudas* (Tusquets, 2000), and *Allá en el campus grande* (Tusquets, 2000). He also wrote the script for Nicolás Echeverría's film *Cabeza de Vaca* (1992).

JUAN VILLORO has taught literature at National Autonomous University of Mexico and Yale University. He edited the literary weekly of the Mexico City daily *La Jornada*. His *La casa pierde* (Alfaguara, 1999), a book of short stories, received the Villaurrutia Prize, and *Efectos personales* (Era, 2000), a collection of essays, won the Mazatlán Prize. His novels include *El disparo de argón* (Alfaguara, 1991) and *Materia dispuesta* (Alfaguara, 1997). Since 2001 he has lived in Barcelona, where he teaches at Universidad Pompeu I Fabra and writes for *El país*.

Index of Mexico City Streets

General Index

THE AMERICAS

Jorge Amado
Tent of Miracles

Jorge Amado
Tieta

Gioconda Belli
The Inhabited Woman

Alfredo Bryce Echenique
A World for Julius: A Novel

Rubén Gallo, editor
The Mexico City Reader

José Luis González
Ballad of Another Time: A Novel

W. H. Hudson
The Purple Land

Muna Lee
A Pan-American Life: Selected Poetry and Prose of Muna Lee
Edited and with biography by Jonathan Cohen

J. A. Marzán
The Bonjour Gene: A Novel

Horacio Quiroga
The Decapitated Chicken and Other Stories

Edgardo Rodríguez Juliá
San Juan: Ciudad Sonada

Moacyr Scliar
The Centaur in the Garden

Jacobo Timerman
Prisoner without a Name, Cell without a Number

Davd Unger
Life in the Damn Tropics: A Novel